Robinson Rojas Sandford is a well-
known Chilean political journalist,
who managed to get out of Chile on
a safe-conduct several months after
the coup.

THE MURDER OF ALLENDE

And the End of the Chilean Way to Socialism

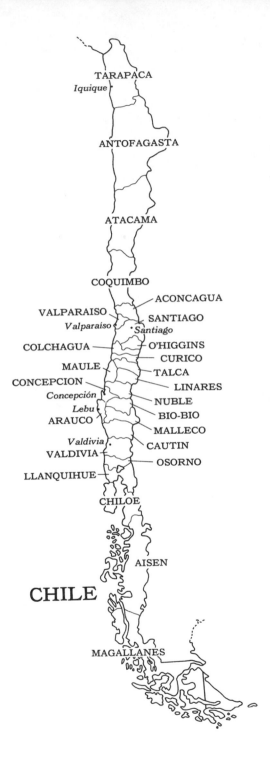

TARAPACA
Iquique

ANTOFAGASTA

ATACAMA

COQUIMBO

ACONCAGUA
VALPARAISO
SANTIAGO
Valparaíso · *Santiago*
COLCHAGUA O'HIGGINS
CURICO
MAULE TALCA
CONCEPCION LINARES
Concepción NUBLE
Lebu BIO-BIO
ARAUCO MALLECO
Valdivia CAUTIN
VALDIVIA OSORNO
LLANQUIHUE

CHILOE

AISEN

CHILE

MAGALLANES

THE MURDER OF
Allende AND THE END

OF THE CHILEAN WAY TO SOCIALISM

Robinson Rojas Sandford

TRANSLATED FROM THE SPANISH
BY Andrée Conrad

HARPER & ROW, PUBLISHERS

NEW YORK, EVANSTON, SAN FRANCISCO, LONDON

1817

Portions of this work originally appeared in *Penthouse*.

This work was first published in Spanish under the title *Estos mataron a Allende*. The present translation is a somewhat revised and abridged version.

Maps by Gary Tong.

THE MURDER OF ALLENDE. English translation copyright © 1975, 1976 by Harper & Row, Publishers, Inc. All rights reserved. Printed in the United States of America. No part of this book may be used or reproduced in any manner whatsoever without written permission except in the case of brief quotations embodied in critical articles and reviews. For information address Harper & Row, Publishers, Inc., 10 East 53rd Street, New York, N.Y. 10022. Published simultaneously in Canada by Fitzhenry & Whiteside Limited, Toronto.

FIRST EDITION

Designed by Sidney Feinberg

Library of Congress Cataloging in Publication Data

Rojas, Róbinson.
    The murder of Allende and the end of the Chilean way to socialism.
    Translation of Estos mataron a Allende.
    Includes bibliographical references and index.
    1. Chile—History—Coup d'état, 1973.
2. Allende Gossens, Salvador, 1908–1973. I. Title.
F3100.R6413   1976   983'.064   74–20413
ISBN 0–06–013748–7

76 77 78 79 10 9 8 7 6 5 4 3 2 1

Contents

A Necessary Explanation

This book is an accusation. As such, it is written in the manner of an extensive police report. It recounts the story of an assassination: the assassination of one particular man, of thousands of other men and women, and of the ideas of these men and women. Here is the story behind the assassination of Dr. Salvador Allende Gossens, the constitutional President of Chile. The main actors in this drama are his murderers: their habits, their ideologies, their meetings, their plans, their conspiracies.

This is not a book that analyzes what happened. It is a book that tells what happened and how it happened. And because I am writing as a journalist, a Chilean, a leftist, and a personal participant in the events in Chile from 1970 to 1973, the reader will also find an Allende very different from the image created by the funeral eulogies, the statues, the posters, the world-wide homages. Here is an Allende stripped of the mask of perfection, of "everything he did, he did well," that so many people have been at such pains to present. Here the heroic picture of Allende changes to one of a vacillating, contradictory man attempting to defend "the Chilean way to socialism" but making the political mistakes that opened the door to the forces of fascist repression in Chile, aided and abetted by U.S. interests, both commercial and governmental.

This is not to say that Salvador Allende was not a hero. No one doubts that. No Chilean is unaware that Allende went down fighting, without any hope of survival unless he surrendered. And he did not surrender. Heroes die like that, and that is how he died. And that is how many thousands of his fellow Chileans also died, hopelessly defending a democracy crushed by the tanks, armored cars, fighter planes, and machine guns of the rebel soldiers. Allende once said: "Let them know this, let them hear this very clearly, let it make a deep impression on them: I will defend this Chilean revolution and I will defend the Popular government. The people have given me this mandate; I have no alternative. Only by riddling me with bullets will they be able to end our will to accomplish the people's program."

So they riddled him with bullets.

A few hours before his death, as the rebel attack was under way, he broadcast a speech to his countrymen: "Thus the first page of this story has been written. My people and the people of the Americas will write the rest."

This is the Allende you will find in this book. And you will read how the common people, the victims of the coup, were denied the opportunity to organize for their own protection. In sum, while this book is a denunciation of Allende's assassins, the generals and admirals in Santiago, Chile, and in Washington, it is also a denunciation of the tragic and vacillating conduct of those who called themselves leaders of the people, but left their people defenseless against the fascist-imperialist attack.

As this book was being written, on Galleries 3 and 5 of Santiago's Public Jail and in its Penitentiary there were 700 prisoners of various ranks: petty officers, officers, and soldiers of the Chilean armed forces and military police who had refused to join the attack against their own people. Their small number, only 700 out of a force of 100,000, is testimony enough of Allende's suicidal policy of preventing the workers from organizing.

The Chilean people paid for this mistake with more than 15,000 dead, more than 30,000 prisoners, more than 100,000 brutally tortured, more than 200,000 dismissed for political reasons, and more than 30,000 students expelled from the university by the military. As Carlos Altamirano, the secretary general of the Chilean Socialist party, summarized the events on January 3, 1974, in Havana:

> The upper bourgeoisie and imperialism have drowned bourgeois democracy in blood. Allende and the Unidad Popular had planned "the Chilean way

to socialism" as a democratic, pluralistic process to be achieved according to the Constitution and with respect for all political ideologies and parties. This concept was overthrown militarily on September 11.

The "peaceful and democratic Chilean bourgeoisie" resorted to armed counterrevolutionary violence to demolish this process of peaceful structural transformation. By doing this, it betrayed everything it had claimed to support: an unconditional adherence to the values of Christian life, democratic government, individual freedoms, and the rule of law.

The Chilean military unleashed their reign of terror against the Chilean people in order to protect the interests of the great North American consortia (Anaconda, Kennecott, ITT, *et al.*), as well as the strategic interests of the military-industrial complex in Washington. They have tried to cover up their real motives for the coup by fabricating false reports of plotting among the working classes. One such, Plan Zeta, was offered as a rationale for the coup.

But Plan Zeta was concocted in such a hurry and so stupidly that even the head of the junta, General Pinochet, felt compelled to declare his doubts to the press on September 17, 1973: "It is very possible that in reality this self-coup was a fake. There are so many rumors going around. There are so many people determined to create doubts or unrest in the population." (*La Tercera,* September 18, 1973.)

The very same day General Oscar Bonilla, Minister of the Interior, asserted that "we soldiers had to react . . . it was them or us . . . we rose up to prevent Plan Zeta from being carried out."

When the "document" of the purported Plan Zeta was later displayed by the rebels, it was rather surprising to read that the Chilean working classes "had assembled an irregular army of 100,000 men," "had infiltrated whole regiments," had arms enough to supply "several divisions" for a "self-coup" that would take place on September 19. On September 11, it was abundantly clear that there had been no such preparation, that the workers' forces were meager, incoherent, and disorganized, and that the "infiltration" in the armed forces was less than one percent. There was no such thing as Plan Zeta.

There was nothing more than the plan prepared at great length and with great care by the U.S. Pentagon and the rebel generals. Nothing more than the meticulous preparation of President Allende's murder by a group of his own generals. Nothing more than the infinitely detailed preparations for the bloody repression of an entire population, not unlike the bloodiest years of the Nazi occupation in Europe. These are the deeds you will find documented in this book.

ROBINSON ROJAS SANDFORD

THE MURDER OF ALLENDE

And the End of the Chilean Way to Socialism

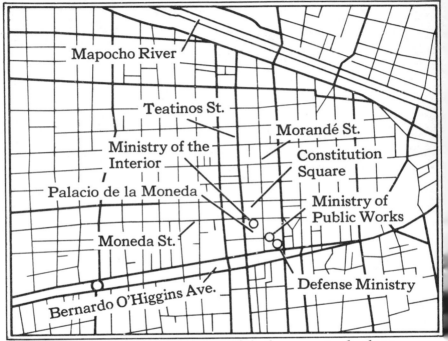

Mapocho River

Teatinos St.

Morandé St.

Ministry of the Interior

Constitution Square

Palacio de la Moneda

Ministry of Public Works

Moneda St.

Defense Ministry

Bernardo O'Higgins Ave.

The area of Santiago in which the coup took place

1 The Artful Staging of a "Suicide"

A disciplined, organized, and aware people is, along with an honest and loyal armed forces and military police, the best defense of the Popular government and of the future of the country.

SALVADOR ALLENDE, speech May 1, 1971, in Plaza Bulnes, Santiago, Chile

And they have the power, they can smash us, but the social processes cannot be held back either by crime or by force. History is ours, and the People will make it.

SALVADOR ALLENDE, speech September 11, 1973, at 9:15 A.M., in the Palacio de La Moneda, Santiago, Chile, taped as the attack by the rebel generals was under way and broadcast by Radio Magallanes

Six or seven minutes past 2 P.M. on September 11, 1973, an infiltration patrol of the San Bernardo Infantry School commanded by Captain Roberto Garrido burst into the second floor of the Chilean Presidential Palace, Santiago's Palacio de La Moneda. Charging up the main staircase and covering themselves with spurts from their FAL machine guns, the patrol advanced to the entrance of the Salón Rojo, the state reception hall. Inside, through dense smoke coming from fires elsewhere in the building and from the explosion of tear gas bombs, grenades, and shells from Sherman tank cannons, the patrol captain saw a band of civilians braced to defend themselves with submachine guns. In a reflex action, Captain Garrido loosed a short burst from his weapon. One of his three bullets struck a civilian in the stomach. A soldier in Garrido's patrol imitated his commander, wounding the same man in the abdomen. As the man writhed on the floor in agony,

Garrido suddenly realized who he was: Salvador Allende. "We shit on the President!" he shouted. There was more machine-gun fire from Garrido's patrol. Allende was riddled with bullets. As he slumped back dead, a second group of civilian defenders broke into the Salón Rojo from a side door. Their gunfire drove back Garrido and his patrol, who fled down the main staircase to the safety of the first floor, which the rebel troops had occupied.

Some of the civilians returned to the Salón Rojo to see what could be done. Among them was Dr. Enrique Paris, a psychiatrist and President Allende's personal doctor. He leaned over the body, which showed the points of impact of at least six shots in the abdomen and lower stomach region. After taking Allende's pulse, he signaled that the President was dead. Someone, out of nowhere, appeared with a Chilean flag, and Enrique Paris covered the body with it.

The furious battle between the first and second floors continued. Dr. Paris's group left the half-destroyed Salón Rojo, whose roof was now in flames. In groups of four and five people, the defenders continued fighting, most of them unaware that President Allende was dead.

Less than an hour later, around quarter to three in the afternoon, the civilian defenders were overcome by troops from the Infantry School, the Tacna Regiment, and the 2nd Armored Regiment. Thirty-two people had survived of the original group of forty-two men and women who had been defending La Moneda for five hours. The entire second floor of the building was now occupied by the invading troops.

The commander of the attack on La Moneda, Brigadier General Javier Palacios Ruhman, followed by Captain Garrido and his patrol, marched into the Salón Rojo, leaned over Allende's body, and pulled away the bloody Chilean flag. Turning to Garrido, General Palacios ordered: "We must seal off this room. Don't let anybody else in. No one is to see the President's body. Put me through to headquarters, to General Pinochet in person."

"Attention Post One! Attention Post One! Combat Unit Alpha One here. General Palacios requests to speak to General Pinochet."

Palacios took the radio microphone and reported in a dry, precise voice: "General Palacios to General Pinochet. Mission accomplished. Moneda taken. President dead."

"How is the body?" the Army's commander in chief asked.

"Destroyed."

"Don't let anyone see it. Wait for instructions."

It was then a few minutes before 3 P.M. on September 11, 1973. At 6 A.M. that morning, the high command of the Chilean armed forces had mobilized some 100,000 men and launched an all-out attack against the economic, political, social, and administrative centers in the country. No less than 3,000 leaders of laborers, farmers, office workers, and political parties were murdered on September 11. Between the eleventh and the fifteenth, 5,500 more were to be killed combating the rebel military forces, and some 6,300 persons would be imprisoned and shot or murdered in some other way between the twelfth and the thirtieth of September. In the first eighteen days, there were approximately 15,000 civilian casualties. Of these, slightly less than 6,000 were in Santiago: 800 murdered on the eleventh, 2,900 killed later in combat, and 2,200 shot or murdered after being taken prisoner with or without "summary trial in time of war."

These tragic statistics are the result of the second part of the coup plan, Operation Beta One, which the rebel generals had intended principally to affect Santiago. It involved the military occupation of the city's two main industrial concentrations: Los Cerrillos, in the southeast, and Vicuña Mackenna, in the central eastern area. In conjunction with these occupations, commando units composed of military personnel and civilian fascists were to engage in "pincer operations." Between 6 and 8 A.M. on the eleventh, these units would arrest about 6,000 persons throughout the country. Prisoners were to be taken to military headquarters, subjected to brief, pointed interrogations, and executed immediately afterward. The military described this as "cleaning up the motors of Marxism"; these people were leaders of towns, unions, farm worker settlements, political parties, and leftist cultural organizations. The list of their names had been in preparation since November 1972. Its compilation was a joint effort of Chilean Army, Navy, and Air Force intelligence. The Chilean military had close affiliations with the intelligence departments of the U.S. Southern Command in the Canal Zone and with members of the Brazilian Embassy in Santiago.

The rebel generals believed Beta One could be completed during the afternoon of the eleventh, but the people's resistance in Vicuña Mackenna and Los Cerrillos surprised them, continuing through the night of the eleventh. Around noon on the twelfth, the workers' scanty munitions gave out, and mass murders in the Santiago labor housing sectors, including La Legua and Lo Hermida, finally stopped most of the resistance.

It was only then that the generals felt confident about announcing the achievement of the first part of the coup, Operation Alpha One.[1]* This was the "suicide" of Salvador Allende Gossens.

During Alpha One, La Moneda was to be taken in order to capture the President himself. Estimated time for its completion was 120 minutes after the onset of the attack on La Moneda (9 A.M., September 11, 1973). The rebels' intelligence estimates did not envision resistance from the handful of civilians inside the palace. They expected Allende to surrender at once when faced with infantry, armored cars, tanks, and the threat of aerial bombardment. After transferring him to 2nd Armored barracks, the rebel generals probably thought that as a result of various humiliations they planned for him Allende would commit suicide if momentarily left without a guard. This would be announced to the country around one o'clock that afternoon.

Instead, it took five hours to capture La Moneda and subdue forty-two civilians armed with submachine guns and one bazooka. This small group held off a siege of eight Sherman tanks (each equipped with a 75-mm. cannon and a .50-caliber machine gun), two recoilless

*Notes, documenting or elaborating on statements made in the text, begin on page 221.

75-mm. cannons mounted on Jeeps, and two hundred infantrymen from two Santiago regiments, and the bombardment of a pair of Hawker Hunter fighter jets, equipped with eighteen rockets apiece (of which eighteen were released, striking their target between 11:56 A.M. and 12:15 P.M.). The jets also strafed the rooftops and the second floor of La Moneda.

It was not until 2:50 P.M. that the rebel high command could announce to the country that "the Palacio de La Moneda has been taken by the armed forces." Owing to the unexpected resistance in La Moneda, the original scenario of Allende's "clean suicide" collapsed. It took the conspiring generals four hours (from 3 to 7 P.M.) to improvise a new script. This entailed "discovering" Allende's "suicide" inside La Moneda and finding an "eyewitness." Their drama was so shoddily concocted that superficial inspection would reveal its many contradictions and obvious lies. The members of the rebel high command were painfully aware of this, and for more than twenty hours they stalled, reluctant to inform the Chilean people of the President's death. Finally, the news was leaked abroad and the Chileans learned from foreign correspondents that their President had "committed suicide."

THE REBEL FORCES

The purpose of this bloodbath has been exposed to the world by subsequent events in Chile. By altering the entire political and economic system of Chile, the rebel generals intended to restore and protect the interests of the North American multinational companies and about twenty Chilean oligopolies in industry, commerce, and finance. To ensure their continuing control, the generals undertook to liquidate the Chilean workers' capacity to fight back and make demands, by subjecting them to a regime of brutal dictatorship, in which factories, offices, farms, streets, and private houses were to take on all the characteristics of military barracks.

These repressive forces had been in the making for more than twenty years. In 1952, Gabriel González Videla, the President of Chile and head of the Radical party, signed a Mutual Aid Pact with the United States. Since that time, the Chilean military had been trained and financed by the U.S. armed services.[2] On September 10, 1973, these Chilean troops and their officers were mobilized to attack the constitutionally elected Chilean government. Their combined strength consisted of:

Army: Just over 30,000 men, organized in six divisions, one of which is cavalry. There are six cavalry regiments, two armored regiments, and two of mobile artillery geared for use in mountainous territory. Ten of the sixteen infantry regiments are motorized. There are five artillery regiments. Out of the total number of regiments, eight are stationed in Santiago, the capital. Training is permanently advised by the U.S. military missions, whose teaching duties range from the Academy of War (for officers in the General Staff) to the Junior Officers' Training School in Santiago. Here all the teaching plans, discussion groups, and courses in "general culture" in the Army regiments (and Air Force, Navy, and military police units) are prepared with the advice of U.S. experts.

Air Force: Just under 9,000 men. It includes bombardier, air attack, antiaircraft, combat helicopter, and ground support units. It depends on the U.S. Air Force to such an extent that its commander in chief prior to the present one (Gustavo Leigh Guzmán, a member of the military junta), César Ruiz Danyau, was known to his aides as "the Yankee," because he was in constant contact with the U.S. Air Force mission in Chile.

Navy: Slightly over 15,000 men. In addition to a combat fleet, the Navy has Marines, naval aviation, and naval engineer units. Its officers are the heirs of British Navy tradition, and its commanders consider themselves the military aristocracy of Chile. In planning the military coup against Allende, they proposed the massive Operation Pincers plan to assassinate popular leaders.

Military Police: Slightly more than 30,000 men. Its organization is militarized, possessing automatic weapons and a company of antiriot tanks equipped with one .30-caliber machine gun each. Here, too, training is overseen by Americans. A major scandal erupted in 1969 when the complete text of the antiriot training primer employed by the motorized section of the military police was published by a leftist magazine, *Causa ML.* Classified "secret" for civilians, this primer had been produced by the U.S. Pentagon.

The entire Chilean armed forces total approximately 85,000 men; these were supplemented on the day of the coup by more than 10,000 civilians (ex-soldiers, reserve officers, and so on), who belonged to armed fascist groups such as Fatherland and Liberty (Patria y Libertad), the ex-Cadet Commandos, and the Rolando Matus Commandos, and supplied with arms by the Marines and the Air Force. These 10,000 civilians played a supporting role during the military coup as "independent units," receiving orders directly from the coup's Central Command.

One would like to believe that not all units of the armed forces participated in the uprising, but the facts show that internal dissent was minimal. For instance, in Santiago, only a very few of the commanders of the Junior Officers' Training School, the Railwaymen Regiment of Puente Alto, and the Military Police School opposed the coup. They were murdered by their own unit companions.

THE BACKGROUND OF THE CONSPIRACY

The conspiracy to overthrow the constitutional government of Chile started in October–November 1972, when American intelligence agencies probably concluded that, despite Allende's devotion to the Constitution, the workers and peasants were now on the verge of going beyond constitutional means to attain their increasingly revolutionary objectives.[3]

About a third of the Army generals, the majority of the Air Force generals, almost the whole of the Navy high command, and the majority of the military police's commanders began to make plans. There is convincing authority for the premise that the U.S. Southern

Command in the Canal Zone, as well as various elements within the Department of Defense in Washington, were carefully apprized of these plans. Two stages were envisioned: first, a "softening" of public opinion, through activities of the Christian Democratic and National parties, and of controversial fascist groups such as Fatherland and Liberty, ex-Cadet Commandos and Rolando Matus Commandos, and employers' guilds such as the Society for Industrial Development (Sociedad de Fomento Fabril, grouping the industrial oligarchy), the National Agriculture Society (grouping the agricultural oligarchy), and the National Confederation of Production and Commerce (grouping the industrial, commercial, and financial oligarchy); second, "attacking the prey," when the prey (the Allende government) was already cornered and breathless and without much popular support.

This scheme included a "wait-and-see" period to evaluate the outcome of the March 4, 1973, elections for the seats of 150 Deputies in the Lower House of the Chilean Parliament and 25 Senate seats (out of a total of 50) in the Upper House. At that time, the fate of Salvador Allende, once he had been ousted, had not been determined. Until June 1973, the prevailing idea had been to send Allende into exile. In addition, a minority of the generals, especially those in the Army, believed that they could convince Allende to head a "national unification" civilian-military government, excluding the leftist political parties from official participation. This they referred to as a "soft coup."

But in the March 1973 elections, Allende's Unidad Popular ticket carried almost 44 percent[4] of the vote. Pressure from laborers', peasants', and office workers' unions began to create the climate for the formation of grass-roots power structures that just might find a way to supplant the economic, political, and social power of the North American multinationals and the national oligopolists. The attitude of the most reactionary generals, as well as that of the Pentagon Latin-American desk, hardened. They began to pressure those generals who still clung to the idea of a "national unification" civilian-military government headed by Allende. On the other hand, Allende himself, impelled by the growing revolutionary tide of his grass-roots constituency, made it clear to Generals Prats and Pinochet that he would not lend himself to heading a thinly veiled military dictatorship.

In July 1973 the high command of the Chilean Navy upset the balance of military opinion with one daring, macabre stroke. A team of professional assassins, led by a member of Navy intelligence, murdered Allende's naval aide, Commodore Arturo Araya Peters, in his own home on the night of July 26, 1973. They accomplished this in concert with the ex-Cadet Commandos.* The assassination had been plotted with the rebel group in the military police, who controlled military police intelligence.

The members of the Navy high command taking part in the conspiracy believed two objectives had been accomplished by this assassination:

1. It prevented Araya Peters, a personal friend of Allende and a member of the "constitutionalist" faction in the armed forces, from being promoted to rear admiral. This would have made him a member of the General Staff of the Chilean armed forces. According to military regulations, in September 1973, when Araya Peters finished his two-year assignment as naval aide to the President, he would be returned to active duty and, also by regulation, would be promoted to the second-highest rank within his section of the armed forces. This would give President Allende an important man in the heart of the Navy General Staff—that is, in the heart of the conspiracy to overthrow the constitutional government, where he just might discover it prematurely. In July 1973 the rebel generals had not yet set a date for the coup. Their consensus was that around the end of 1973 or the

---

*In August of 1973, Roberto Thieme, second-in-command of Fatherland and Liberty, was detained by the civil police and confessed that his men, as well as those of the ex-Cadet Commandos' organization, were trained by Federico Willoughby MacDonald, who is currently the press secretary for the military junta. Prior to the coup, Willoughby worked as a public relations man for the Ford Motor Company. It is believed that Thieme also revealed associations between himself and Willoughby and the CIA.

beginning of 1974 would be the most propitious time, since by then they expected the economic situation to be intolerable, exacerbated by a national work stoppage that was scheduled to begin in August.

2. With the complicity of military police intelligence, the rebel admirals hoped to hatch a plot to blame the Socialist party for the naval aide's death, thus inducing the rest of the senior officers of the armed forces and military police to react favorably to the idea of the conspiracy. The Socialists were the principal party in the government's Unidad Popular coalition (Salvador Allende belonged to it), and his bodyguard, the GAP (Grupo de Amigos Personales, or Group of Personal Friends), was drawn from it.

The commando assassins hired by members of Navy intelligence did a very clean job. Several days after the murder, military police investigators arrested an "alleged assassin." He was an employee of the lowest rank in a branch of the Production Development Corporation (Corporación de Fomento de la Producción), who (surprise, surprise), after being beaten in the first basement of the Defense Ministry under the vigilant eyes of naval prosecutor Aldo Montagna, had confessed that he was a "Socialist" and had agreed to be one of the assassins "by contract with one of the GAPs." He now "repented doing it," for which reason "he had surrendered himself," drunk, to the night guard of the Santiago Intendencia, the location of the First Prefecture of Military Police, which was under the direct command of General César Mendoza Durán, afterward a member of the junta.*

In the second week of August, the tidy little plot began to fall apart. A group of detectives from the Homicide Squad of the Chilean civilian police, whose director, Alfredo Joignant, was a member of the Chilean Socialist party, began to gather up the threads leading to the identity of the commando assassins. President Allende received a police report on the case, in which two facts were established:

1. The man arrested as the "alleged assassin" had been forced to

---

* *Puro Chile* published an interview with the suspect in which he denounced Aldo Montagna.

sign a declaration he had not even read. The text of the confession was known to a legislator of the extreme right (Gustavo Alessandri) and had been read by him in part over the National Agriculture Society's radio station (the property of some large landholders) two hours before the "alleged assassin" had been arrested.

2. The identification of the actual members of the assassination team—seven persons—had revealed at least two with connections to a senior naval officer. A concurrent investigation of the military police intelligence captain who had persuaded the "alleged assassin" to sign the confession revealed that he had met, two weeks prior to July 26, with another senior naval officer.

With this evidence, part of which he made public (omitting the "senior officers in the armed forces"), the President met on the morning of August 8, 1973, with the commander in chief of the Army, Division General Carlos Prats González; the commander in chief of the Air Force, Air General César Ruiz Danyau; the commander in chief of the Navy, Admiral Raúl Montero; and the director general of the military police, General José Sepúlveda Galindo.[5]

The political situation was extremely serious. On July 27 a new nationwide strike of truck owners began: it was directed by León Vilarín, a man directly connected to the coup plot through Eduardo Frei and Onofre Jarpa (see Chapter 5). On August 7 discussions had terminated between Allende and the national directorate of the Democratic Christian party (controlled by the group of Eduardo Frei, whose liaison with the military opponents of Allende was General Oscar Bonilla, the present junta's ex-Minister of Defense). These DCP/Allende discussions had been requested by the Archbishop of Santiago, Raúl Cardinal Silva Henríquez, for the general purpose of "reaching a political pact of nonaggression to stop the civil war that would be unleashed by a military attempt at a coup d'état." Naturally, Frei was not interested in having these discussions succeed.

The same day on which the discussions began, July 30, General Oscar Bonilla met with Eduardo Frei and Senator Juan de Dios Carmona (Defense Minister during the Frei regime) and reportedly urged them to sabotage attempts at political conciliation and to make their fundamental goal "an agreement from Parliament to declare Allende's government illegal."

The morning of August 8 was full of political storm clouds. On the one hand, an industrial stoppage intended to wreck the Chilean economy had begun. On the other hand, the workers' organizations were pressuring Allende to let them "solve the industrial stoppage with our own hands."

Allende's information about the military conspiracy appears to have been fragmentary, most of it contrived by Army and military police counterintelligence. They had painted their own picture of the conspiracy's extent, and accordingly Allende believed that it was restricted to "a small nucleus" in the Navy, headed by the commander in chief of the First Naval District (Valparaíso, Chile's main port, an hour and a half from the capital by freeway) and Vice-Admiral José Toribio Merino (later a member of the military junta), plus another isolated "little nucleus" in the Air Force, which had "the sympathy" of General César Ruiz Danyau. Allende believed that he could solve the huge political crisis he was faced with by a sudden turnabout against the civilian as well as the military conspirators. His plan was to incorporate *all* the branches of the armed forces and military police into his Cabinet of Ministers in order to take the steam out of the workers' organizations' attempts to undermine the oligopolists. He would take a strong public stand backed by the four commanders in chief.

On the morning of August 8, Allende read the four military leaders the civilian police report on the assassination of his naval aide, Commodore Arturo Araya Peters. He then explained that "if the people discover the truth about this, half a million people will die in Chile," that the workers and peasants "would assault the Navy and military police barracks to crush the conspirators and Araya Peters's murderers." He described the police report as a time bomb, and suggested that it would be preferable to solve the problem of the Navy and military police "conspiracy" in a "confidential, institutional way."

Allende added that the civilian police report had a second part, which he chose not to reveal for the time being, in which "the connection between Araya Peters's assassins and foreign military forces" was proved.

Thus, Allende went on, it would be best for "the military institutions of Chile to show their loyalty to and support of constitutionality and the law" by joining a Cabinet of "national unity," "to appease the passions," to find a solution to the work stoppage now as it was beginning, not when it became serious "like the one in October 1972." This would give the Executive Office time to promulgate several laws that the Christian Democrats and the National parties were asking for on behalf of the Society for Industrial Development and the National Agriculture Society.

The commanders in chief accepted. The Navy chief was named Treasury Minister; the Air Force chief became Minister of Public Works; the Army chief, Defense Minister; and the head of military police, Minister of Housing. On the morning of August 13, Salvador Allende dramatically announced to the country the composition of his new Cabinet, characterizing it as one aimed at "national security" and "the last chance to avoid a confrontation between Chileans."

What Allende had done, in fact, was virtually to write the first part of his own death sentence. The consensus among the conspirators in the high command was that Allende was "dangerously close to the truth" and that given time to pursue the investigation, he might uncover the complete Pentagon–Navy–Air Force–Army–military police connection, of which he could make considerable political use in exile. According to sources within the military hierarchy, it was Vice-Admiral José Toribio Merino who first voiced the opinion in the ensuing days that Allende must be killed or made to commit suicide, that there was no other choice.

Still, the final decision to murder Allende was not reached until Tuesday night, August 21, at a meeting which the subchief of the Army, General Augusto Pinochet Ugarte, did not attend. Pinochet probably never knew that Allende was to be assassinated, and most likely found out only on the afternoon of September 11, when the President's death was already a *fait accompli* and the spectacle of the suicide was being arranged. As of August 20, apparently only Vice-Admiral José Toribio Merino, then head of the First Naval District, General César Mendoza Durán, of the military police, and General Gustavo Leigh Guzmán, commander in chief of the Air Force, were agreed that Allende's suicide was essential to the success of their coup.

Their final decision must have been made in response to a major blunder committed by General César Ruiz Danyau. Driven by personal ambition and believing that "the situation was ripe," Danyau arranged the air garrisoning of Santiago from two bases, one for ground support and the other for chase and bombardment, in preparation for a planned "military pronouncement" on Monday, August 20, which, he believed, would draw the rest of the armed forces to his side. To trigger the coup, he resigned his new appointment as Minister of Public Works on Friday, August 17. This meant that Allende would have to ask for his resignation as commander in chief of the Air Force. According to Ruiz Danyau's plan, the Air Force would then rise up and cause Allende's downfall. This would be followed by the nomination of himself, Ruiz Danyau, as head of a military junta.

Allende, partly aware of Ruiz Danyau's ploy, delayed accepting his resignation until the next day. He called a meeting in the Palacio de La Moneda of the Navy chief, Admiral Raúl Montero; the Army chief, Carlos Prats; and the second-ranking general of the Air Force, Gustavo Leigh Guzmán (the latter, unknown to Allende, was one of the heads of the conspiracy). Allende played them a tape recording of a conversation between a retired Air Force colonel and two or three other people.[6] The colonel could be heard saying that "the group" had already begun to "operate various units" to convince the senior officers of the three branches of the armed forces "to abandon Allende" and "join the crusade against Marxism." The tape continued that "the Americans are aware of our activities and approve of them," and said once, "My general Ruiz Danyau is with us to the death."

At that point Allende pointed out to Leigh Guzmán that "this plot" was "treason to our country," since generals "of the republic of Chile" were actively conspiring with a foreign power. Then he ordered Leigh Guzmán to take over command of the Air Force, to approve the forced retirement of Ruiz Danyau, and to persuade those air units that might support Ruiz not to. Leigh Guzmán accepted Allende's orders after the President threatened to "let Chile know about this infamy."

The next day, Sunday, August 19, without consulting Ruiz Danyau, Leigh Guzmán informed Vice-Admiral Toribio Merino, César Mendoza of the military police, and Augusto Pinochet of the Army of what had transpired and told them that Ruiz Danyau had to be dumped. They agreed.

On Monday the officers of the air bases at El Bosque and Los Cerrillos in Santiago mobilized their men and requested support from the Navy Yard in Valparaíso, the Tacna and Buin regiments, the Junior Officers' School, and the 2nd Armored Regiment, quartered in Santiago. At least Ruiz Danyau had chosen the day well: Allende traveled by helicopter to Chillán (some 500 kilometers south of Santiago) to take part in a ceremony commemorating the birth date of General Bernardo O'Higgins, the Father of the Country. Nevertheless, the rest of the conspiring generals, heeding Leigh Guzmán's advice, had decided to abort the "untimely coup" and let the ax fall on the neck of their erstwhile accomplice.

From the Defense Ministry, the Joint Chiefs of Staff took steps to persuade the Air Force officers to demobilize. By noon, everyone was agreed that they had to "wait," and that, in the meantime, General Ruiz Danyau would go into retirement. Leigh Guzmán would become commander in chief of the Air Force, and another Air Force general, Héctor Magliochetti, would be named Minister of Public Works. (Magliochetti is presently assistant to General Pinochet.)

This series of events appeared to be a resounding political victory for Allende. Joan Garcés, a Spanish citizen and Allende's economic adviser, testified to the General Assembly of the U.N. on October 9, 1973: "That night, on his return to Santiago, President Allende was informed that General Pinochet, sub-commander in chief, had been asked to join the coup, but, in his own words, he answered: I am a general respectful of the Constitution and I will be loyal to the government to the end.' "

It is worth noting that until the morning of September 11, when General Pinochet was at Peñalolén in the Andean foothills of Santiago, directing the military invasion of the city and the attack on La Moneda, Salvador Allende considered him a "loyal general" and would call him up to ask, "What's going on, Augusto?"

But Allende's "political victory" was a Pyrrhic one, achieved at the cost of letting his enemies know that he had solid information about the conspiracy. Allende had written the second and final part of his own death sentence. The leaders of the conspiracy were then aware that he knew far too much. Allende in exile, having documents within reach and arousing the sympathy of most of the governments and peoples of the world, would be a more than formidable enemy.

From Tuesday, August 21, Leigh, Mendoza, and Merino began to sketch out the final details of their plan. They were advised by a team of men from SIM (Servicio de Inteligencia Militar), the Army, Navy intelligence, and U.S. Army intelligence. To complement the "basic ideas" of the plan, information about Allende's personality was hastily gathered from those military officers who were said to know him best. They depended chiefly on the opinion of Brigadier General Manuel Torres de la Cruz, commander of the 5th Army Division in the extreme south of the country, and fourth-ranking in seniority among the Army's generals. Torres de la Cruz was the leader of the extreme fascist faction in the Army and since October 1972 had been the prime mover behind the conspiracy against the government. Yet he was considered by Salvador Allende and his "military matters adviser," Senator Alberto Jérez, of the Christian Left, to be "the only Allendist general in the Army" and a "loyal friend."[7]

General Torres de la Cruz's reports caricatured Allende as an "individual who drinks to excess, who is easily swayed, vain, cowardly, the easy prey of discouragement in difficult moments" (this assessment was based on attacks against Allende which appeared in the Santiago right-wing newspapers).

Taking into consideration the views of General Torres de la Cruz, as well as those of military police General José Sepúlveda Galindo and Allende's Army aide, the conspirators, also advised by the U.S. Army intelligence group in the Chilean Defense Ministry, calculated that once Allende was trapped on the day of the coup, either in his private residence on Tomás Moro Street in the eastern part of the capital, or in the Palacio de La Moneda, there were but two probabilities. Some of my informants had access, briefly, to documents which set forth what these probabilities were. According to the transcript they made:

Probability One: The objective, intimidated by the deployment of armored cars and infantry, and under the threat of aerial bombardment, will commit suicide before the battle begins. This is highly probable, keeping in mind that the objective has on innumerable occasions, even in front of senior Army officers, expressed his admiration for José Manuel Balmaceda, a president who committed suicide in 1891 after his troops were defeated by insurgent armed forces.

Probability Two: The objective, realizing his defenselessness and knowing perfectly well that the civilians are incapable of defending themselves against a joint attack of the country's entire armed forces, will surrender. This may happen before or after an aerial bombardment intended to "soften" but not demolish his residence or the palace.

If Probability One takes effect, the military press will assume charge of announcing it immediately and will at the same time begin Press Phase Two involving the disaccreditation of the suicide's character, focusing on an image of a drunkard, libertine, and hedonist (contact will be made with a group encharged to fabricate evidence).

If Probability Two occurs, the objective will be segregated at once from accompanying civilian or military personnel. He will be conveyed under guard to the Military School. Once isolated, he will be taken under maximum security to 2nd Armored HQ. There he will be treated in a degrading manner by selected military personnel of low rank. They will subject him to humiliations (disrobed, in ridiculous poses; objective will be forced to commit humiliating acts, which will be openly photographed) based on information we have about him. Their traumatic effect should result in suicide. Preparations should include allowing objective to see material previously gathered to discredit him publicly. If this inducement is successful, the military press should immediately begin Operation Public Knowledge on the terms cited above.

If objective resists the team's efforts to create a traumatic effect, and if positive results are not achieved 60 to 90 minutes after the surrender, objective will be immobilized and killed as if by suicide. This will be followed by military press activities as described above.

In both procedures, it will be announced that objective was treated with respect for his rank by his captors, and for that reason his clothing was not examined before leaving him alone in the regimental officers' quarters, thereby facilitating objective's concealment of a 7.65-caliber pistol in his clothing. Objective committed suicide while alone in the room awaiting the arrival of the commanders in chief to witness the signing of his resignation, which he had agreed to do, as well as to say a few words to the people so that at no time would they resist the military institutions' activities. Objective had also agreed to leave for Cuba in an aircraft put at his disposal by the FACH [Chilean Air Force].

STAGING THE "SUICIDE"

General Pinochet, the military leader of the insurrection, had known about Allende's death for less than thirty minutes when, toward 3 P.M. on September 11, General Javier Palacios Ruhman informed him that all resistance from La Moneda had ceased. Earlier, Palacios had dispatched an Army Jeep with a pouch marked "classified" (the American word used by the Chilean Army to mean secret information) from the La Moneda area to headquarters at Peñalolén to report details of the assassination to Pinochet. Palacios had discreetly not informed Pinochet over their portable radio-telephone transmitter-receiver set (walkie-talkie). Pinochet and his General Staff must have known that the news of Allende's killing would make the workers' opposition much fiercer; his death had to be made to look like suicide at any cost.

They postponed discussing the suicide details until they actually had possession of the President's body. But, at the same time, they released an "unofficial bulletin" for foreign publication claiming that Allende had committed suicide. To do this, they employed the unscrambled radio-telephone system they had been using all day, knowing perfectly well that Chilean and Argentine ham operators were tuned in, along with all the U.S. news agencies in Santiago.

Around 2:40 P.M. instructions from Pinochet were transmitted in Morse code from Peñalolén to Post 5 inside the Defense Ministry (150 yards away from the besieged Palacio de La Moneda), ordering Post 5 to transmit the news, as if it were secret information, among the various command posts of the military insurrection. Post 5 carried out the order at 2:45 P.M., using the unscrambled radio-telephone system. A leftist ham operator monitoring the military's messages was able to record the transmittal:

"Attention! This is Post Five, Patricio's post [Vice-Admiral Patricio Carvajal Prado]. This is to inform you that Infantry School personnel are now inside La Moneda. The following will be transmitted in English, in case we are being monitored: *They say President Allende committed suicide. Do you read me?*"

To use English to keep a message secret was ridiculous, because English is taught from grade school in Chile. However, as Vice-Admiral Carvajal knew, for the purposes of the North American correspondents listening on their monitors in Santiago and in Mendoza, Argentina, it wasn't at all ridiculous. It facilitated what the rebel generals wanted most: to have the news teletype machines all over the world saturating the foreign public with "Allende's suicide."

But this was the easy part of the script. The hard part began barely fifteen minutes later when Pinochet ordered the palace area cordoned off.

They must have debated for half an hour about a possible means of suicide. Finally it was agreed that the head would be destroyed with bullets from a submachine gun resting under the chin. The body would be dressed again to prevent witnesses from seeing the other wounds. The body had to be moved to another, more appropriate location, since the Salón Rojo was half destroyed. They chose the Salón Independencia, the President's private place to rest and receive visitors. There, SIM men, under the command of General Javier Palacios Ruhman, divested Allende's body of the bloodied turtleneck sweater he had been wearing throughout the siege. They also removed his blue trousers, which were perforated and had blood stains around the abdomen. They dressed him in dark gray pants, scavenged from one of the cadavers inside La Moneda, and Allende's own gray turtle-neck, the stains on which they covered by putting him into his gray tweed jacket and fastening the bottom button (the President had removed the jacket during the battle and left it on his work table). Then the SIM men seated him on the red velvet sofa against the wall that faces Morandé Street, propped him against the back of the sofa, placed in his hands the machine gun he had been using almost an hour and a half earlier, and pressed the trigger just once. Allende's head split in two; part of his brain, blood, and pieces of hair flew upward and stuck to a tapestry more than three yards above on the wall behind the sofa. The scene was now set. Because the body was already stiff from rigor mortis, it had not been easy to arrange on the sofa; the SIM men had to use force to straighten the President's legs, leaving them wide apart to stabilize the body. The arms were left hanging slightly apart from the torso.

It was 3:30 P.M., more than three hours after the fire at La Moneda had been started by the exploding rockets from the Hawker Hunter jets. The 5th Brigade's firemen (whose fire engines had been standing ready since 12:20 P.M., when the aerial bombardment ended and flames appeared over the Government Palace) finally received permission to fight the fire. The fire station is less than 300 yards from the Palacio de La Moneda, on Nataniel Street, on the ground floor of the building occupied by the offices of the American news agency UPI.

Jaime Egaña, captain of the fire brigade, said afterward: "A moment we'll never forget was when the fire engine left the station; the doors opened and the soldiers posted themselves in various places. When we came out, the soldiers shot in different directions all at once to cover our advance."

When they got to La Moneda, the firemen saw that the conflagration had spread all over the Morandé Street area, to the second and third floors and the whole north façade of the Ministry of the Interior (on the right, entering by the main door on Moneda Street), and the Presidential Palace (on the left). It would take them until ten o'clock that night to put out the flames.

The order for the firemen to intervene had come from the Defense Ministry, after General Palacios had given notice that everything was ready in the President's private sitting room. But, pressed by the fire which threatened to reach the room where they were preparing the deception, General Palacios was too hasty in giving the Defense Ministry the all-clear signal. At least two firemen entered the Salón Independencia and were shoved out at machine gun point. But they got in far enough to see one of the soldiers putting a gun on the knees of the corpse seated on the sofa, while another was placing President Allende's combat helmet and gas mask beside him. After this, all the firemen were notified that they couldn't enter that room because "President Allende shot himself and nothing can be moved." As they fought the fire, the 5th Brigade firemen were warned that they were under "military jurisdiction" and were not to "tell anyone what you have seen inside this area."

When the Infantry School soldiers entered the second floor of La Moneda for the second time, after the civilian opposition had crumbled, they behaved with uncontrolled brutality, slapping and kicking their captives, striking them with the butts of their guns, forcing them to lie face down on the floor with their hands on the back of their necks, and running on top of them with heavy combat boots in order to pass through the corridors. Among the captives, the SIM men managed to find a witness.

This man was Dr. Patricio Guijón Klein, who since November 1972 had been a surgeon on the medical team of seven attending the Chief Executive. He was not a member of a Unidad Popular party; he had agreed to be Allende's doctor merely because it was a step up professionally. That afternoon he had been trapped in the palace with the rest of the medical team. His fate was to be the witness of a suicide.

By 10 P.M. the President's body was already in the Military Hospital to be put in a coffin and to be viewed by a team of doctors from the Army, Air Force, Navy, and military police, who would then copy out on a death certificate what had been established hours earlier by the detectives of the Homicide Squad. The detectives had been summoned at 4 P.M. by General Ernesto Baeza Michelsen, commander of the military troops who had invaded the center of Santiago beginning at 6 A.M. that day. This was one of several serious mistakes made in the confusion of the afternoon.

From the central command post at Peñalolén, General Pinochet had issued an order through General Oscar Bonilla. According to a tape recording made by a ham radio operator, this was the order:

"General Bonilla here. General Bonilla to Vice-Admiral Carvajal. Orders from Pinochet. General Bonilla on behalf of the commander in chief: Imperative that as soon as humanly possible the chief physicians of the Army, Navy, Air Force, and military police medical corps, including the Santiago coroner, certify the cause of Mr. Allende's death . . . so that the politicians will not later blame the military for his death. . . . I repeat, as soon as humanly possible. . . . Do you read me?"

"I read you. Chief physicians of Army, Navy, Air Force, and also military police, plus Santiago coroner, to certify cause of death of Mr. Allende . . . so that . . ."

"Yes. . . . Chief physicians of each institution including military police. . . . Over and out."

The military leaders' teamwork was highly uncoordinated that afternoon. Brigadier General Ernesto Baeza Michelsen made contact much earlier with Brigadier General Sergio Arellano Stark, his immediate superior, and leader of the troops occupying the whole of Santiago Province. Baeza seemed to have concluded, logically, that after the military blitzkrieg in which thousands of civilians had been shot and killed throughout the country, the military's word was not going to be worth much in Chilean public opinion. For this reason he must have decided that certification of the suicide ought to come from the civilian police. To that end he called the Homicide Squad to La Moneda, disobeying Pinochet's orders to have the military doctors present. The Homicide Squad team proceeded to:

1. Draw up and execute a deposition about the "scene of the incident," just as they found it when they entered the Salón Independencia in La Moneda around 4 P.M.

2. Examine the suicide-type wound in Allende's head, and *nothing more.*

3. Waive circumstantial investigation at the scene of the incident.

The Homicide Squad team, led by Inspector Pedro Espinoza Valdés, whose political ideas were openly unsympathetic to the overthrown government, began their "job" at 4:20 P.M. and finished it at 6:10 P.M.

An hour after this, General Pinochet, through General Oscar Bonilla, continued to insist on the presence of the military physicians and, furious, asked why the "certificate of suicide" still had not reached central headquarters of the occupation troops in the capital. A ham radio operator tuned in on and recorded this conversation over the military radio-telephone system, between General Bonilla and Air Force General Nicanor Díaz Estrada, who was in command of Post 3, the coordination unit inside the Ministry of National Defense:

"Nicanor, listen. We need to know if the chief health officers and the city coroner have identified the body and made the deposition yet. This is very important. *They should not take him to the morgue to do an autopsy because it's a nest of extremists and they may try to steal the body . . .*"

"Roger. We gave the order for a *secret* transfer to the Military Hospital. The coroners have been summoned to the Military Hospital. I gave orders for the deposition to be brought here to General Staff, but they haven't brought it yet . . . *it's been an hour and a half . . .* but we still don't have any news . . ."

"Okay, Nicanor. Tell Herman Brady to vouch for the absolute security of the Military Hospital. This is important . . . over to you, Nicanor . . ."

"I took care of that."

"Thanks, Nicanor."

It is clear that the leaders of the troops invading Santiago were very concerned to keep the assassinated President's body well out of sight of all personnel outside their institutions. Their concern was so zealous that the next day they would not let his widow, Hortensia Bussi, have a last look at her husband.

The following account was given to the Mexican journalist Manuel

Mejido, correspondent of the newspaper *Excelsior,* by Allende's widow on September 13 in the Mexican Embassy:

"The next day [Wednesday, September 12] they told me over the telephone that Salvador was in the Military Hospital and that he was wounded. I went there, and although I openly identified myself, the soldiers wouldn't let me in. Afterward I spoke to a general who greeted me with these words: 'Madam, I was the friend of Salvador Allende. Let me offer you my deepest condolences.' Only then did I learn that he was dead.

"This general, whose name I don't know, promised me a Jeep and an officer to escort me to the Group Seven Airfield of the Chilean Air Force, where he said I had to go. But then another general came out, I didn't know him either, and told me to go there in my own car, because there weren't any vehicles or officers available.

"I decided to make the trip in the small car belonging to my nephew, Eduardo Grove Allende. At the airfield they told me that Salvador's body was on an Air Force plane. Before boarding it I spoke by telephone with my daughter Isabel, but she couldn't come with me because she didn't have a safe-conduct.

"I boarded the plane. Imagine the scene I saw: a coffin in the center, covered with a military blanket, and on either side my other nephew, Patricio López, and Salvador's sister, Laura Allende. With me were the Presidential Army aide Roberto Sánchez and Eduardo Grove. We flew toward Viña del Mar. The airplane landed at the Quintero Air Base. The flight was smooth, there were no problems. Then they took Salvador off.

"I asked to see him, to touch him, but they wouldn't let me . . . they said the box was soldered shut. In two cars following the hearse we went to the Santa Inés Cemetery. The people watched us curiously. They didn't know what it was all about, or whose body was in the hearse. There were many soldiers and military police, as if they expected a crowd. We five who went with Salvador walked in silence to the family crypt, where a month ago we buried Inés Allende, Salvador's sister who died of cancer.

"Once again I insisted on seeing my husband. They wouldn't let me, but they removed the outer lid, and all I saw was a cloth covering the coffin. I didn't know whether it was the head or feet. I wanted to cry. The officers kept me from seeing him. They repeated that the coffin was soldered shut. Then I said in a loud voice to the officer escorting me: 'Salvador Allende cannot be buried in such an anonymous way. I want you at least to know the name of the man you are burying.' I grabbed some flowers from nearby and threw them into the grave and said: 'Here lies Salvador Allende, who is the President of the Republic, and whose family they wouldn't even allow to accompany him to the grave!"

THE CONTRADICTIONS

The preparations in the Salón Independencia of the Chilean Government Palace were so hasty that the various participants committed some crass errors—errors that would enable any third-rate detective of the Santiago civilian police to see right through the scenario. But the Santiago civilian police are not interested in discovering who killed President Allende. The present director of investigations of the Chilean civilian police is the same general who gave the order to investigate to Inspector Pedro Espinoza and the Homicide Squad technicians who were summoned to La Moneda to examine the suicide-type wound in Allende's destroyed head. The general, Ernesto Baeza Michelsen, was named director of investigations on the very afternoon of September 11.

However, under the psychological pressure of the events of September 11, the inspector and his subordinates did not think clearly enough to rectify a mistake made by the SIM agents. It was preserved for posterity in the "police report" prepared at La Moneda and read on September 20 by General Baeza Michelsen to a press conference of those journalists who survived the military invasion of Santiago on the eleventh. It states:

"The corpse was seated on a garnet-red velvet sofa against the west wall between two windows looking out on Morandé Street, with the head and torso *slightly inclined toward the right, upper limbs slightly extended, lower limbs stretched out and somewhat separated.*"

And something else important for any investigation is added:

"*. . . The projectiles causing suicide were shot from the weapon placed between the knees and the barrel pressed against the chin. . . .*"

What type of weapon was used by Salvador Allende, according to this police report?

"AK-type machine gun, Serial No. 1651, Soviet make, inscribed with the following words: *'For Salvador, from his comrade-in-arms Fidel.'* "

That is to say, it was a large-caliber firearm with tremendous fire power.

Any police reporter (and I was one for a long time for *La Tercera*, a Santiago newspaper) has plenty of experience of suicide deaths by firearms as well as of suicides seated on a chair or other piece of furniture without any armrests. This allows us to reconstruct the events beginning with the Homicide Squad's assertion that Allende committed suicide by resting an AK-type machine gun on his knees, sitting on a fairly wide sofa, that is, a sofa without any lateral support.

Because of the height of the sofa seat (we reporters were well acquainted with the sofa in question), and also to steady the machine gun's stock with his knees when he sat down to commit suicide, Allende would have had to put his weight on the points of his toes. This would have resulted in a tensing of all the muscles in the legs, and his torso leaning forward, arms very flexed, head resting on the machine gun's barrel point. It would have been what one might call an "uncomfortable" position of "unstable equilibrium" frontward.

By pressing the trigger in this position and shooting off half his head with two bullets, the "suicide" would have experienced a terrific jolt in his body, separating the knees, and the machine gun would have dropped to the floor, while the body would have leaned forward and to the right, falling to the floor next to the sofa.

None of this happened. Allende's case seemed to have been very "special." His body became *rigid immediately after the shots,* the spread legs were already rigid, to keep from falling off the sofa, and best of all (so that there would be no doubt): the machine gun remained in the alleged suicide's lap.

(This detail is contained in the actual legal deposition made by the Homicide Squad, and in the statements made by General Javier Palacios Ruhman on September 22 in Bogotá to the Spanish news agency EFE: "I approached the body. The President was sitting in the middle of the red-upholstered sofa *with the machine gun in his hands,* his helmet and gas mask to one side, his glasses on the floor. The face was swollen and the skull was split in two, like a watermelon." Please observe how General Palacios, in his desire to give more details, reveals the inconsistencies: the body was "seated" in the "middle" of the sofa, the head was destroyed "like a watermelon" by a machine gun—and yet death and rigor mortis came instantly, causing him to remain seated with the gun in his hand, after the tremendous impact of two bullets of the caliber of a Soviet AK model!)

The most serious discrepancy of all was a difference of *two hours* between the actual death of President Allende and the time of death given in the Homicide Squad's deposition.

This error is contained in the final lines of the police report, according to the version published in the Santiago daily *El Mercurio* on September 21. It says:

"Time of death, at 18:10 when the examination was completed, was estimated at six hours previous"—12:10, two hours before Allende actually died.

Of course, the police under Inspector Espinoza's command cannot be blamed. When they arrived at La Moneda, there was fighting all over the city and it was still not clear which side was going to win. So although the police must have realized that there was something highly irregular about Allende's suicide, they acted professionally and merely put in writing, in the deposition, the entire scene, exactly as they found it. The police experts, in acting as they did, thus left "a door open" for their own role should the military be defeated later by the civilian forces.

But it isn't only the Homicide Squad deposition that reveals inconsistencies. Let us begin with the most important, the statement of Brigadier General Javier Palacios Ruhman, chief of the armored and infantry troops that attacked the Palacio de La Moneda

On September 22, in Bogotá, Colombia, General Palacios was interviewed by journalist Arturo Abella on the TV news program "Seven O'Clock." The transcript of his remarks follows:

"When we surrounded the Palacio de La Moneda in pincer formation, aircraft had destroyed a large part of the building. We went in without gas masks and were received by gunfire from the members of Allende's personal guard, who were shouting 'Marxism does not surrender.' We were almost blinded by the smoke, but we overcame the opposition. When I went up to the second floor looking for the President, his working offices were empty and in disorder. . . . I continued walking through the area that was not destroyed. I came to the anteroom before the large dining hall in the palace. I opened the door, and there Allende was, sitting on a sofa."

"You recognized him at first glance?"

"No. It didn't seem to me to be Allende. Beside him, or in a corner, there was a doctor named Yojon or Gijon. He was shaking and could hardly speak. He said, 'It's the President. It's the President.' The President was sitting in the middle of the red-upholstered sofa, with the machine gun in his hands, his helmet and gas mask to one side, his glasses on the floor. The face was swollen and the skull was split in two, like a watermelon. The hands were black with powder. There was almost no blood. I ordered my men not to touch anything until the coroners arrived to examine the body. Coroners came from all three branches of the Chilean armed forces. They verified that it was suicide. Photographs were taken which are now in the government's possession and will be presented on request."

"They say that there were wounds in various parts of the body?"

"Not one. Not a single one. The coroner's report shows this. There was also a bottle of whiskey in the room. I asked the coroners to determine if there was any evidence of alcohol in the body of the President. Allende had had absolutely nothing to drink."

Note that these declarations by General Palacios were made on September 22 while he was in Bogotá as head of the Chilean military sports delegation to the Fifth South American Festival of Cadets. Palacios had no knowledge of the "perfecting" going on in Chile with the story of Allende's suicide under the supervision of General Ernesto Baeza Michelsen.

Palacios, after 4 P.M. of that day, didn't speak again to Baeza or anyone else involved in the "suicide" operation. He simply returned to headquarters, which had been transferred to the Bernardo O'Higgins Military School, and spent the days before he left for Bogotá doing his part in the "cleanup of downtown Santiago."

Thus, when he made his very detailed statements in Bogotá about the incident, he was unknowingly contradicting General Baeza's "official version."

Palacios's version reveals that his troops fought defenders *who had no intention of surrendering.* If that was so, then why had Allende committed suicide?

Forty-eight hours earlier, on Thursday, September 20, back in Santiago General Ernesto Baeza Michelsen, now director general of investigations of the civilian police, released the "official report" on the material, which *completely contradicted* General Palacios's statements two days later.

1. General Baeza said that Palacios's troops entered La Moneda after it surrendered. Why the insistence on a surrender? Only if Allende surrendered would there be any justification for the suicide.

As has been established, the defenders in the Palacio de La Moneda never expressed any desire to surrender, but all morning long the rebel officers were repeatedly announcing Allende's "surrender" on the radio stations in their control, and they had even issued an official communiqué to that effect just after 1 P.M. on the eleventh.

To lend "seriousness" to the surrender thesis, on September 20 Baeza read to reporters the "deposition" of Dr. Patricio Guijón Klein (who was freed unconditionally in December 1973 by the military authorities):

The President said "give yourselves up," that "Payita [the President's private secretary, Miriam Rupert] should go out first, I'll go out last." We began to get organized. Somebody provided a broom, and I took off my white doctor's coat, which we were wearing to identify ourselves. As we were going down to the Morandé Street door to give ourselves up, I remembered that I had left my gas mask behind and went back to look for it. And just as I went to look for it, I passed in front of the door to the next room. Just in front of me, to the right, sitting on a sofa, I saw President Allende at the precise moment when he shot himself with a gun placed between his legs.

I could see his body shake and his head explode upward in smithereens. I couldn't determine whether it was one or two shots because the intensive fire going on outside prevented my distinguishing the shots made by his gun.

At once I ran to him to see if I could be of any assistance, but when I got close I could see there was nothing to be done. The damage was too extensive, and certainly caused instant death. I was completely disconcerted by this situation and realized there was nothing else to do. Since I had lost contact with our group, there was no one else in the room, and I couldn't think of anything to do but sit down beside him and wait for whatever happened.

If Dr. Guijón and the rest were going down the Morandé Street stairs, and if he had taken off his "identifying" white medical coat (usually a life preserver in such situations), why did he go back for his gas mask? Wouldn't his life have been better protected by staying with the surrendering group and not by separating himself from it?

And last, if he realized that Allende had killed himself in a room a few steps away from the Morandé Street stairs, why didn't he cover these few steps at full speed and shout, "The President has killed himself"?

Dr. Guijón's activities seem strangely unnatural, given the circumstances in which he found himself.

2. General Palacios says he found Dr. Guijón "beside him, or in a corner."

Palacios says that Guijón "was shaking and could hardly speak." But General Baeza said something else. "Dr. Guijón was next to the body of the President, and when General Palacios entered, he identified himself as Mr. Allende's personal physician and gave an account of what had happened." And to give rise to new difficulties, Baeza quotes the following from Dr. Guijón's deposition: "I was sitting right next to the President" when "the general" entered. And as it happens, "the general" (Palacios) on September 22 in Bogotá can't remember whether Guijón was "beside him or in a corner."

3. For the police to assert that a man can commit suicide sitting down in an unstable position with a machine gun held between his knees, and remain seated when dead—wait, with the machine gun *in his lap*—is grotesque. This is precisely what the Homicide Squad report says. How could *this* mistake be rectified? Guijón said that he had pushed the suicide machine gun away from himself to avoid

having the soldiers think he was a combatant and that afterward General Palacios, in an "excess of zeal" "not to move anything at the scene of the suicide," had ordered him to put it on Allende's lap, and that the civilian police, in "describing" the scene, had done only that, "describe" what they saw. The weapon was resting on the body's lap because General Palacios had ordered Guijón to put it there.

On Thursday, September 20, Baeza read this part of Dr. Guijón's deposition, and he repeated it to reporters in interviews granted the following December. This is Guijón's statement: "At a given moment I removed the weapon because I was sitting right next to the President, and there wasn't very much space between the body and myself, and the weapon was too close to me. Then I thought that if in a given moment soldiers came in they might think I meant to defend myself. So I decided to remove the weapon and place it at the other end of the sofa. *Later I showed this to the general who came in* [Palacios], *who made me put the weapon back in its place.*"

Now, that is a very good statement, but as it happens, General Palacios forty-eight hours later in Bogotá was saying something quite different: "I approached the body. The President was sitting in the middle of the red-upholstered sofa *with the machine gun in his hands, his helmet and gas mask to one side, his glasses on the floor.* The face was swollen and the skull was split in two, like a watermelon."

4. To complete this canvas, General Palacios related on September 22 in Bogotá: "I ordered my men not to touch anything. . . . Coroners came from all three branches of the Chilean armed forces. They verified that it was suicide. Photographs were taken. . . ."

Palacios did in fact order his troops "not to touch anything," but that was in the burning Salón Rojo of La Moneda. The transfer of Allende's cadaver to the Salón Independencia was accomplished after 3 P.M. not by Palacios's men but by members of the SIM team sent by General Baeza. Palacios received instructions from General Pinochet at Peñalolén headquarters to let the chief health officers of the three service branches and the military police into the room, but these officers *did not go* to La Moneda. Palacios, of course, did not know this, because after about 4 P.M. he was out of touch with the scheme.

Thus General Baeza's account contradicts General Palacios: "When President Allende's death became evident, the high command summoned detectives and experts from the Homicide Squad to La Moneda, keeping Dr. Patricio Guijón Klein at the scene of the incident. He appeared to be a suspicious member of the GAP and possibly had assassinated the Chief Executive." These policemen were the ones who took "seventy photographs" of the scene of the incident.

In conclusion, Palacios says that "coroners came from all three branches of the Chilean armed forces." General Baeza says no, that they were "technicians from the Homicide Squad." Palacios says that the "soldiers" took the photographs at the scene of the incident. General Baeza says no, they were taken by the Homicide Squad technicians, as it actually happened.

And to add a lyrical appendix to this bundle of contradictions, here are the words of the coroner's report on Allende's body, produced to eliminate all doubt about the "suicide":

"Analysis of the skin on the hands and chin showed the presence of gunpowder, caused by the use of a firearm."

This, in a simple suicide, is often conclusive proof. But what does it prove in Salvador Allende's case? He had been fighting for four and a half hours, using this weapon.

5. On September 22, General Palacios emphasized that "Allende had had absolutely nothing to drink." It is to be assumed that Palacios made this assertion after having spoken with some of the doctors who performed the autopsy on Allende's body.

However, the final autopsy report says that "Allende's body showed a 90% level of alcohol poisoning." Why was this done? Was it necessary to have a "drunken President" for Allende's suicide to be good? Did it serve the junta's project of smearing Allende's reputation?

On his return to Chile, General Palacios was met with the news that his troops had taken a "Government Palace that had surrendered." He modified his Bogotá statements and in the first week of October 1973 read them to Christian Democrat and right-wing journalists (the only survivors in the Chilean press after the rebel generals' strikes against the leftist press). This was the general's new version of the taking of La Moneda:

> At the moment of entering through the Morandé Street entrance, a white flag on a stick was seen, which later turned out to be the white coat of a doctor and which was put out by Payita at Allende's orders. At that time, approximately thirty civilians exited from the building, all members of the personal guard (GAP), and several doctors, who surrendered to our forces. When we reached the second floor of La Moneda, it was already transformed into an inferno by the effects of the fire. At the same time, we were getting surprise shots from snipers hidden in some offices.

But stubborn details kept plaguing General Palacios in his "amended" statement. In recounting his deployment inside La Moneda, he made it clear that he ran toward the Salón Rojo. That is, he did not bother to first check the rooms that were still in good condition, where there might very well be "snipers hidden" (among these rooms was the Salón Independencia, Allende's "suicide" room), and instead ran to the Salón Rojo, which was in flames, and to the presidential suite, which was also catching fire. Why? Naturally, nobody asked him.

But the general's "amended" statement does cohere with that of the witness produced by Baeza and avoids the main contradictory elements in Points 2 and 3:

> Continuing our advance inside La Moneda and opening the doors into the Salón Independencia, we came across the spectacle of Mr. Allende sitting on a sofa, dead of gunshots he had fired at himself, placing his machine gun—a present from Fidel Castro—under his chin, which caused death instantly. Inside this room we found a young man who under questioning said he was Dr. Guijón, a member of the President's medical team. He had heard Mr. Allende's shots as he was leaving the room and came back. Guijón was able to attest that after giving them the order to surrender and leave La Moneda, Allende stayed behind to commit suicide.

General Palacios was not very good at memorizing statements about facts that never happened, and his version of what Guijón said is inexact and even contradictory, though to a lesser degree than before. The main thing is that Guijón, "shaking" and babbling, as described by Palacios in Bogotá, disappears and is replaced by a Guijón with aplomb.

Still, once again, Palacios lets himself be carried away by true impressions, and he needlessly adds: "I ought to confess that I didn't recognize Allende, poorly dressed as he was when we found him, and because of the manner of suicide, which practically split his head in two. His hands were full of gunpowder from the guns he himself had been shooting from the windows of La Moneda against the attacking troops."

A little clarification is in order: Which body did he not recognize because he was so "poorly dressed"? Is he referring to the body of Allende in the Salón Rojo, assassinated by the Infantry patrol around 2 P.M.? Or the body of Allende in the Salón Independencia, "suicided" by SIM personnel between 3 and 4 P.M.?

The body of Allende in the Salón Rojo was wearing only a gray turtleneck jersey and blue pants that were wrinkled, sooty, stained, and filthy after four hours of combat. The jersey was perforated by half a dozen bullet holes in the abdominal region. This body corresponded to "I didn't recognize Allende, poorly dressed as he was when we found him."

But if Palacios meant by this that he didn't recognize Allende's body as later placed by SIM men in the Salón Independencia to simulate suicide, then he is wrong.

According to the Homicide Squad report, the body of the "suicide" Allende was dressed in a "gray tweed jacket, fastened with the bottom button; gray, high-necked pullover with dark gray geometrical figures, white sport shirt, dark gray slacks, white socks, black shoes, and *blue silk handerchief with red polka dots in the upper left pocket.*" This is not exactly a "poorly dressed" corpse.

The discrepancies even at the time were so serious that on Wednesday afternoon, September 12, General Baeza, in the presence of civilian functionaries of the police investigation, offered his resignation to General Pinochet, shouting: "It serves us right for working with such dumb sonofabitches!" What had aggravated Baeza was a press release on Allende's suicide written by Federico Willoughby MacDonald [press secretary to the military junta] and handed out to the press at 2:30 P.M. on Wednesday, September 12.

The press release had infuriated Baeza because it was full of inaccuracies which later could cause problems, above all because it had appeared as an "official communiqué of the military junta of government." According to a radio broadcast of it,

the military junta of the government of Chile officially announced that former president Salvador Allende committed suicide and that his body was buried at noon today. Their communiqué indicates that:

1. Yesterday, Tuesday, at 13:09, Salvador Allende offered to surrender unconditionally to the military forces.

2. To this end, a patrol was immediately sent to La Moneda, but its arrival was delayed by the skillful activity of snipers specially posted in the Ministry of Public Works who attempted to intercept it.

3. Upon entering La Moneda, this patrol found Mr. Allende's body in one of its rooms.

4. Transferred to the Military Hospital, the body was examined by a medical commission made up of the chief health officers of the armed forces and the military police, as well as a coroner, who determined that the cause of death was suicide.

General Baeza's fury was justified, because according to that official communiqué of the military junta, the "battle of La Moneda" had ended shortly after 13:00 hours, in circumstances that were public and well known, and moreover were sanctioned by a communiqué from the Defense Ministry the day before, September 11, that "the Palacio de La Moneda has fallen into the hands of the military forces at 14:50 hours."

At the same time, this communiqué placed Allende's "suicide" shortly after 13:00 hours. Late in the day on the eleventh, the prefect of investigations in Santiago, René Carrasco, had told foreign correspondents of Agence France Presse, United Press International, and Associated Press that "the personnel of the squad specializing in these services attested to the death of the fallen President, which occurred approximately between 13:30 and 14:00 today."

And last, the official communiqué indicated that Allende's body had been transferred to the Military Hospital to be examined by the armed forces units. This was also false, since that transfer took place around 7 P.M., *after* the Homicide Squad played the role that the communiqué had assigned to the chief health officers of the armed forces and the military police.

General Baeza shouted in front of a dozen or so senior officers of the Joint Command that "this kind of declaration makes us look ridiculous" and "thrusts back on us precisely the suspicions that we want to avert": the suspicions that Salvador Allende had been assassinated.

Furthermore, that afternoon of September 12, General Baeza had another reason to worry. The groups of armed civilians aiding the coup d'état (classed under the generic name "independent units" by the Joint Operation Military Command at Peñalolén) had, without authorization, set up a short-wave radio transmitter which, at 4 P.M. on September 11, had broadcast the news of President Allende's death with roughly the following text:

Attention Chile. . . . Attention the whole world. . . . This is Santiago thirty-three. . . . This is Free Chile. . . . Allende is a corpse. . . . Captain Roberto Garrido has executed the Communist tyrant in his own palace. Captain Garrido has liberated us from Marxism. . . . This is the Association of Free Chileans speaking. . . . This is Free Chile. . . . Allende has been executed by our glorious soldiers. . . .

General Baeza, learning about this broadcast on the night of September 11, ordered an investigation to find out where the secret radio was located. To his surprise the broadcast had come from the Defense Ministry, and furthermore his immediate superiors suggested that he discontinue investigating it.

In the end, General Baeza had only one cause of satisfaction: having been able to postpone for twenty-four hours the news about Allende's suicide, so that details could be finalized, statements made, and civilian groups prevented from stealing the President's body and discovering its many bullet wounds. He had even been able to allow time for a reporter to view the scene. By 6:30 P.M. on the eleventh Juan Enrique Lira, the head photographer of the most important paper in Chile, *El Mercurio,* arrived. He later wrote: "Lighted by the firemen's spotlights, President Allende was leaning back on a plush sofa, with his head completely destroyed. He had a machine gun to one side. At that time I thought that he must have fired a burst of more than two shots, from the condition of his head, but later only two empty cartridges were found."

The military chiefs also allowed Lira and other reporters from the Catholic University TV station to remain in the area for nearly a quarter of an hour, filming and taking notes.

WHAT REALLY HAPPENED

Chronologically, the events of Tuesday, September 11, actually took place in this order:

9:20 A.M. President Allende's three military aides left La Moneda, after he had told them that "the generals betraying Chile have announced that they will attack this presidential palace five minutes from now. You are free to act according to the dictates of your conscience. I will be staying here inside La Moneda, and I will oppose them to the last bullet." This conversation was witnessed by Drs. Enrique Paris (a Communist) and Eduardo Paredes (a Socialist), various journalists of the Unidad Popular, and some of the ministers who stayed with Allende. When the military aides left the palace and entered the Defense Ministry a block away, the National Agriculture Society radio station made its first spurious announcement of Allende's surrender.

11 A.M. When the Air Force bombing promised for that hour did not materialize, the radio stations in rebel hands again announced Allende's surrender. But the truth was that Allende had asked the generals to hold off the bombing for ten minutes, so that "the women

and whoever else wants to can leave this place before the last battle."
Allende gathered together everybody, civilians and soldiers, in the
Winter Courtyard. There, addressing himself to the members of the
palace guard of military police—fifty men—and to military police
Director General José María Sepúlveda Galindo, Allende told them
that whoever wanted to could leave La Moneda. He added that the
only thing "I ask is that you give up your arms when you leave the
palace. . . . Those of us who are going to oppose the military rebellion
will need them." All the officers and soldiers left La Moneda as soon
as they were disarmed by the civilians, who had to keep them at
gunpoint to avoid any kind of betrayal. (Sepúlveda Galindo defected
from President Allende that morning. He was later given a diplomatic
post by the military junta.)

11:10 A.M. The first women left La Moneda, among them reporters
Frida Modak and Verónica Ahumada. The President had been trying
since 9:30 A.M., when the rebel troops surrounding La Moneda had
fired the first shots at the palace, to make the women and "the men
who don't bear arms" leave the building. At 9:25 A.M. Allende, in the
Salón Toesca, called everyone in the building together to warn them
that the "traitor General Baeza Michelsen has announced to me that
they are going to begin the attack on La Moneda in two minutes."
Allende made a short speech, the gist of which was: "Just as no
revolution can triumph if its leaders do not know how to assume their
responsibilities at all times and to the bitter end, it is also true that
useless deaths contribute in no way to the cause of the revolution.
Hence, I fervently beg all the men to help me convince the women to
leave the palace, because those of us who stay are going to fight to the
bitter end."

Minutes after 11 A.M., Allende had spoken with General Baeza
Michelsen by telephone to ask for "a cease-fire of ten or fifteen minutes" to allow the women to be evacuated. Beatriz Allende, the President's daughter, witnessed this telephone conversation, and she
remembers that Allende said: "General Baeza, you who have betrayed
your country, I hope that at least you haven't betrayed what a man
must be to a woman: at least respect them enough for this."

At that moment, the anxiety at rebel headquarters was tremendous. Allende's plea for a cease-fire had been misunderstood by General Pinochet as an offer of surrender. And when the first women came out of La Moneda, General Pinochet, from his command post in Peñalolén, was desperately calling Post 5, the coordinating post, in the Defense Ministry, headed by Vice-Admiral Patricio Carvajal. Their conversation, recorded by a leftist ham operator, follows:

> "Give me Admiral Carvajal . . . Augusto to Patricio."
> "One moment, please, General. Post 5 here."
> "Patricio, the sooner the President leaves, the better, with all the chickens he wants . . . all the chickens he wants . . ."
> "Not all, not the GAP . . . not all. Just now they said five women were giving themselves up."
> "From La Moneda to the plane . . . from La Moneda to the plane, old man . . . don't play with him any more . . . keep the leash good and tight . . . let's not have any problems . . . no GAPs with him . . . all GAPs are to be tried . . . keep him closely guarded because they can get him away. . . ."

At this moment, fighting was going on in the industrial sectors of Los Cerrillos and Vicuña Mackenna and downtown, between Plaza Italia on the east, the State Technical University on the west, the Mapocho River on the north, and Matta Avenue on the south (a rectangle of thirty by twenty blocks, more or less). General Augusto Pinochet, who had not been apprised of Plan Alpha One to assassinate Allende, was convinced that the ultimate object in attacking La Moneda was to put Allende on a plane at the Los Cerrillos air base and send him out of Chile.[8]

Shortly after 11:15, General Pinochet found out that there was no surrender, that the "five women" had not given themselves up, as Vice-Admiral Carvajal had told him, but instead those women and some male civilians had simply evacuated La Moneda and that the fighting was still going on. Pinochet ordered a new cease-fire and asked to speak with President Allende. Only Allende's half of the conversation remains: "I do not make deals with traitors, and you, General Pinochet, are a traitor."

At this point, General Pinochet requested assistance from Vice-

Admiral José Toribio Merino, head of the insurrection in the Navy and one of the four members of the self-proclaimed "government junta." Over the telephone Merino demanded that Allende resign, to which Allende answered: "Surrender is for cowards, and I am not a coward. The real cowards are the lot of you, conspiring like gangsters in the dark of night."

Despite persistent attempts on the part of Generals Pinochet and Baeza and Vice-Admiral Merino, Allende refused to give himself up, and at the same time declined to make any deal with them, "because I am your superior and I cannot make deals with rebel subordinates." This led Allende to imagine that it might be useful to conduct a "second-level" negotiation, and he charged Fernando Flores, ex-Treasury Minister, Daniel Vergara, Undersecretary of the Interior, and Osvaldo Puccio, his private secretary, to undertake an "embassy" to the Defense Ministry to discuss with the generals the terms of a "political settlement" of the situation.

At 11:30, these three left La Moneda and were conducted under military escort to the Defense Ministry a block away. There, they asked to see Generals Pinochet, Leigh, and Mendoza and Vice-Admiral Merino. Merino and Leigh were opposed to the parley, while Pinochet and Mendoza wanted to negotiate. To force events, block the parley, and go ahead with Plan Alpha One, General Leigh gave the green light for bombing La Moneda. Without ever having spoken even to the commander of that post, that is, while they were still sitting in the waiting room, Allende's three envoys were the terrified witnesses of the bombardment of La Moneda by the Hawker Hunter fighter planes.

The air attack began at 11:56 A.M., going from north to south, from the Mapocho River toward Bernardo O'Higgins Avenue. For the tens of thousands of Santiago citizens living near Constitution Square, where the Chilean Presidential Palace is located, 11:56 A.M. on September 11, 1973, marked the beginning of a nightmare.

What did the two pilots feel as they flew their planes toward the palace? The Santiago daily *El Mercurio* published an interview with them on Saturday, November 24. *El Mercurio* asked:

"What did you feel when you found out you had to bomb La Moneda?"

"I was very concerned. It was a shock. After all, I had to attack my own country, but there were no moments of hesitation or fear. We are always ready to obey any order. The precision? That's thanks to constant training over targets smaller than the Government Palace, 200-liter barrels or parts of tank chassis. In this case, the rockets have a greater degree of precision than the bombs and were launched from the Mapocho River, some 800 yards or so from the target, at a height of 500 yards and a speed of 250 yards per second."

"Why were only two pilots and two planes used?"

"Because that was enough."

"How did you feel psychologically after the air attack?"

"Good. Satisfied at having carried out the mission. Impressed by what we had done. But in no way did we feel sorry about it, not at all. We were all glad."

The *El Mercurio* story says that, summoned by their code names, two pilots of the Chilean Air Force were selected for the bombing. "The order of the high command was crystal clear: Target: La Moneda." The newspaper adds: "From 8 A.M. the Hawker Hunters had begun to land at Los Cerrillos airport [which is next to a Chilean Air Force base] from various bases around the country."

The two fighter craft made nine strikes between 11:56 and 12:15. Eighteen rockets struck the two-hundred-year-old building. The upper floor was badly damaged on the north side (where the President's and the Minister of the Interior's offices are) and on the entire west wing. The smoke and the flames from a raging fire set off in the northeast part could be seen from several kilometers away.

Between 12:15 and 12:20, from the Alameda corner of the Defense Ministry, General Javier Palacios waited tensely for the "surrender" signal. But it never came. He ordered a "demolition" attack by the Sherman tank cannons through Morandé and Moneda streets. At the same time, he deployed the Infantry School's and the Tacna Regiment's infantry in pincers, behind the tanks and through Teatinos Street. Intensive machine gun fire and two shots from bazookas from inside La Moneda demonstrated to the attackers that the defenders had no intention of abandoning the struggle. The advance of the 2nd Armored Regiment tanks was halted by General Palacios, because they could not move forward with the infantry under the intense fire coming from the palace. At 1 P.M. General Palacios asked General Pinochet what to do, since it was impossible to advance with his troops and take La Moneda without another air attack. General Pinochet ordered him to cease firing for the time being.

13:05. General Pinochet consulted with Vice-Admiral Patricio Carvajal at Post 5 in the Defense Ministry and ordered him to send Osvaldo Puccio, President Allende's private secretary, back to La Moneda with a note containing the conditions of unconditional surrender. Pinochet asked Carvajal to explain in the note that "the President will have safe-conduct to leave the country with his family and whatever other personnel he may want." But Carvajal did not write that in the note. He sent Puccio to La Moneda with the terms of an "unconditional" surrender and with instructions that "the President should give himself up to the commander of the armored troops" (it must be remembered that the final phase of Plan Alpha One, which Carvajal knew about, but not Pinochet, envisioned the rapid transfer of Allende to the 2nd Armored Regiment's headquarters, to carry out the presidential "suicide"). At the same time, Vice-Admiral Carvajal ordered the other two envoys sent by Allende, Fernando Flores, and Daniel Vergara, to be sent as prisoners to the Bernardo O'Higgins Military School in the upper district (east) of the capital.

Osvaldo Puccio was taken toward La Moneda in a military Jeep. But the intensive fire from La Moneda and the Ministry of Public Works (near the palace, on its east side) forced the Jeep to stop.

13:10. General Palacios ordered the Sherman tanks to resume their advance, firing their cannons, and gave his infantry the order for a "final attack" on La Moneda. A curtain of machine gun bullets covered the walls of the palace, along with the explosions of the tanks' cannon fire. This allowed the infantry to go forward and at last reach shelter from the defenders' gunfire beneath the walls of the building.

13:15. As a result of the intensive machine gun and cannon fire, the journalist Augusto Olivares Becerra, the director of National Television and a personal friend of Allende's, fell defending the palace.

Thanks to eyewitnesses who survived the holocaust, Genaro Carnero Checa, president of the Peruvian Journalists' Association, was able to publish in the Lima daily *Expreso,* December 11, 1973, a reconstruction of the last day of Augusto Olivares's life. An extract from his story follows:

"The last time I saw Augusto Olivares was in the President's office in La Moneda, before Allende told me to leave," I was told in Havana by Joan Garcés, one of the President's closest collaborators [Garcés left La Moneda around 11:15 A.M. on the morning of September 11, along with the women and other civilian functionaries of the government whom Allende had personally asked to leave "to avoid useless sacrifices"].

"He had a machine gun in his hands and was saying to the President: 'We're going to turn La Moneda into another Alcázar de Toledo, but in reverse—antifascist.'

"Other people, now in Lima, have told me about Augusto Olivares's last hours of fighting, as well as the ordeal of his wife Mireya [Mireya Latorre, a television and theater actress, radio announcer, the daughter of the Chilean genre writer Mariano Latorre] in rescuing her husband's body from the authorities. They are unimpeachable sources, extraordinary witnesses, who have asked me to withhold their names for obvious reasons.

"Olivares phoned his wife at 6:45 A.M. on the eleventh. 'Things are going very badly,' he told her. 'In a few minutes we're heading for La Moneda. A kiss and lots of luck.'

"It was around 2 P.M. and Mireya hadn't heard anything but rumors about her husband's fate. Meanwhile, President Allende, machine gun in hand, was fighting inside the palace, which was being bombarded on all four sides. A gigantic cloud of smoke could be seen from the farthest neighborhoods in the capital. 'I'm certain Augusto is there,' Mireya told one of our witnesses. 'I know him well enough. He won't abandon Salvador for anything, and if he dies, my husband will die with him.'

"The Palace phones by now weren't working and Mireya waited in vain for another call. I was the first person to tell her: 'Journalist friends told me. Augusto died in the Gallery of the Presidents on the second floor of La Moneda, in the heat of battle, with his gun in his hands. Allende had the courage and dignity to ask for a moment of silence for his friend's death.'

"But we couldn't confirm his death or locate his body. Night fell as we continued our dreadful search. At the Central Post for Public Assistance, and at the Military Hospital and the Legal Medical Institute, they denied his body was there. The vast quantity of corpses hindered attempts at identification.

"At dawn, a telephone call confirmed the awful news. It was from an Army colonel, who intimated to Mireya that although there was to be a total curfew the next day, she would be allowed to bury her husband. But she could have no more than two hours and the burial had to be entirely private—this last stipulation, in the middle of that strict curfew, was almost funny. A military vehicle would be sent before 11 A.M. that day, Wednesday the twelfth, to 'permit the operation.'

"The promised vehicle never arrived. In the afternoon we decided to rely on the good will of a driver who worked for Channel 7 TV, of which Olivares had been director. At the risk of his life, the driver got us as far as the building. He didn't have the necessary pass to be out on the streets like this, so on the route to Public Assistance, where Augusto's body lay, our vehicle was stopped many times. Our only credential was Mireya's famous face, known from her many theater and TV appearances. She got us through the patrols. The streets of Santiago were completely deserted, shrouded in an ominous silence broken only by sniper fire and the occasional chatter of machine guns.

"Once we got to Public Assistance, Mireya approached the director and some other doctors. They were in quite a state—unnerved and dismayed by the incredible number of casualties. 'We've already lost count of the corpses.' At the funeral homes there was a great deal of turmoil, and it was a tremendous battle to get one of them (the Santa Lucia) to agree to sell us a coffin (at 78,000 escudos!). But it was impossible to find a hearse. We finally persuaded a driver at Public Assistance to let us use an ambulance to transfer Augusto's remains to the Legal Medical Institute. He was the same driver who had rescued Olivares's body at La Moneda and brought it to Public Assistance. Mireya bravely went in alone to find her husband in the room full of corpses. The coffin, inside the ambulance, was taken to the Legal Medical Institute. Because the gravediggers and crematory workers were not on the job, we stayed there until the next day, when we had Augusto cremated."

13:40. Shortly after Augusto Olivares was killed, Infantry School soldiers broke into the first floor of the palace, through the main entrance on Moneda Street. A successful skirmish with the defenders enabled them to maintain this bridgehead.

13:52. The telephones were still working when Jorge Timossi, head of the Cuban news agency Prensa Latina, got through from his offices in the capital to talk to Jaime Barrios, director of the Central Bank and President Allende's economic adviser, who was with the group fighting off the rebel assault. Barrios said to Timossi: "We will fight until the end. Allende is right nearby, firing his machine gun. It's just hell—the smoke is smothering us. Augusto Olivares is dead. The President sent Flores, Vergara, and Puccio to parley a couple of hours ago—it seems that the President wants written guarantees of the workers' social victories—I don't think he'll resign. . . ."

Jorge Timossi couldn't get any more details because just then telephone communications were cut off. The phones in La Moneda were dead.

14:00. Eight minutes after this telephone call, Infantry School soldiers were taking the main staircase leading to the President's offices.

Six or seven minutes later, President Allende was dead.

Around 14:45, some forty minutes later, the soldiers completely overcame the civilian resisters. General Palacios drew back the bloody flag covering Allende's body and communicated to his commander in chief: "Mission accomplished. Moneda taken. President dead."

Sixty seconds later, the radio stations, all controlled by the rebel generals, announced the fall of La Moneda.

Inside the palace, ten civilians were dead. Of the thirty-two survivors, fourteen were wounded.[9] General Palacios ordered the wounded to be taken in military custody to the Central Post of Public Assistance. Miriam Rupert, President Allende's private secretary and the only woman among the defenders, pretended to faint. She was put with the group of "prisoners for the Central Post." At the Post, where confusion reigned owing to the huge number of dead and wounded, she managed to steal down a corridor, dress herself as a "doctor" in a white coat, climb aboard an ambulance going out to collect the wounded, and escape.

Inside La Moneda, Dr. Enrique Paris made a fatal mistake: he allowed himself to lose his temper. From the floor, where like the other prisoners he was lying face down, his legs open and his hands on the back of his neck, he shouted: "Assassins! You killed the President!" The soldiers took him to General Palacios. There he was recognized. Paris, in a rage, shouted that he saw how they killed the

President. Palacios ordered Paris to be taken to the Defense Ministry, a building less than 200 yards away.

Four days later, on September 15, Dr. Paris reappeared, a babbling wreck, in the National Stadium, which had been converted into a concentration camp. His eyes did not focus. He was confined to a section of roofed boxes in the National Stadium, with only twenty other people. He was heard repeating, "I am Quiñones the bull . . . the bull," and his companions heard him sobbing. In the middle of the afternoon, Dr. Paris, or what remained of him, leaped over the railing of the presidential box. He dislocated a leg. The soldiers ran toward him and struck his head with the butts of their guns. Dozens of blows. His companions watched the brains of Enrique Paris scatter on the floor of the National Stadium.

But let us return to September 11, in the Palacio de La Moneda, or at least in the ruins of the Palacio de La Moneda.

Forty minutes after the radio stations announced the fall of the palace, and while the SIM team was preparing the "suicide" scene, the generals broadcast the following communiqué over the radio network:

"The occupation of La Moneda has made secure the authority that has been imposed by the armed forces and the military police of Chile for the good of the country. It brings forth new hope for the country this springtime, and we ask citizens to show their loyalty to Chile by flying the flag in front of their houses. This liberation and reordering of Chile is nothing but a cause for joy in this month in which we commemorate the men and women who sacrificed themselves to give us our freedom."

The situation deserves the remarks made by the Chilean writer Fernando Alegría, professor at Stanford University in California, in the December 1973 issue of *Ramparts* magazine:

The junta released a communiqué that appeared in the newspapers. They said that Allende committed suicide and added that there were heavy traces of gunpowder on his hands which suggested, according to the same communiqué, that the President had been firing for a long time. Knowing Allende as I did, however, I am convinced he died fighting, with a machine gun in his hands. He was determined to fight on in La Moneda. If the junta is using the word "suicide" metaphorically to describe the fact that Allende stood alone facing an entire army, then I can accept the official communiqué, although I find their use of metaphors deplorable.

2 Why Was the General Assassinated?

> Don't put up roadblocks for us. The worst thing would be if we were to fail not because we are inept but because some artificial roadblocks are put in our way. If that were to happen, the people of Latin America would have no recourse but violence. If so, the day will come—not that I want it to—when no North American will be able to set foot safely in South America. This is the great political responsibility that the U.S. has.
>
> SALVADOR ALLENDE, interview with *Time* magazine, April 19, 1971

By the end of President Eduardo Frei's administration in 1970, the common people's hopes for the "revolution in freedom" promised in 1964 by his Christian Democrats had been shattered. The people were looking elsewhere for the solution to the economic crisis afflicting their country. Accordingly, the two dominant sectors of Chilean society, the American multinational companies and the oligopolies, had a double perspective on the newly elected President, Salvador Allende, his program, and his political coalition. They saw him both as a threat to their power and as a possible "bulwark of containment" for the workers' desires to rid the country of U.S. imperial interests and to curtail (perhaps even to overthrow) the power of the oligopolies.

The U.S. government showed its interest too, but the two organizations involved were not of one mind. While the Pentagon possessed enormous influence in the three branches of the Chilean armed forces, the CIA had close ties to the leadership in the Christian Democratic and the National parties and to the most reactionary sectors of the

Chilean oligopolies. The CIA had always shown surprising ignorance about the mind of the Chilean high command, which led them to commit serious errors in two major coup plots. Not before late 1972 did all of the groups unsympathetic to Allende's government—the Pentagon, the CIA, American multinationals, Chilean oligopolies, and the Chilean armed forces—come together in a coordinated plan with a prudent and, as it were, scientifically determined timetable to carry it out. This lack of coordination meant that between the election on September 4, 1970, and September 11, 1973, Salvador Allende and the coalition of leftist political parties supporting him had to deal with six attempts at a military overthrow of the civil administration: September–October 1970; March 1972; September 1972; June 1973; August 1973; and September 7, 1973.

It was partly the manner in which Salvador Allende exploited the dominant sectors' double perspective of him that allowed him to disarm their conspiracies, solve political crises, and keep his administration afloat. But it was also the peculiar manner in which Allende tied the military to himself just after his election to keep himself in office that at the same time shaped his final overthrow. This delicate balance began with the Schneider case in September–October 1970.[1]

THE SCHNEIDER CASE

On the night of September 4, 1970, Salvador Allende emerged as the winner of the presidential election by the small margin of 30,000 votes out of 3 million cast for the three different candidates. Allende had been the candidate of the Unidad Popular, a coalition of leftist parties. From the moment he was elected, various schemes to prevent him from taking office began to be concocted. These were cut short by the events of Thursday, October 22, 1970.

That day proved in the long run to be tragic, because Allende was to interpret its events as "the sign" that the Chilean armed forces were an "institution unique in Latin America" because they were influenced neither "by North American imperialism nor by the Chilean oligarchy" and for that very reason "did not constitute a danger factor" for the process of socioeconomic transformations proposed by the Unidad Popular. This error was the starting point from which Salvador Allende embarked on a series of mistakes in his dealings with the armed forces which eventually facilitated their final bloody attack on the civil administration on September 11, 1973.

This is what happened on October 22, in the language of the police report of military police Major Carlos Donoso Pérez, in charge of the 24th Commissariat of military police in Las Condes (eastern Santiago):

At approximately 8:20 hours, while General René Schneider Chereau, commander in chief of the Army, was being driven to his office in his official car chauffeured by Corporal Leopoldo Mauna Morales westward along Martín de Zamora Street, he was intercepted opposite No. 4420 of that street by a vehicle which collided with the general's and which was surrounded by five individuals, one of whom, making use of a blunt instrument similar to a sledge hammer, broke the rear window and then fired at General Schneider, striking him in the region of the spleen, in the left shoulder, and in the left wrist, occasioning wounds of critical nature, according to the prognosis of the Military Hospital, where he was taken for immediate attention.

On Sunday, October 25, General Schneider died. The incident was officially interpreted as follows:

1. General Schneider was assassinated by a band of conspirators and "paid with his life for his adherence to the Chilean Constitution."

2. The assassination was intended to serve as a pretext "for a military insurrection" that would "prevent Allende's taking office as President," but "in an exceptional display of discipline, the Army, deeply wounded by the outrage, reacted in precisely the opposite way than was hoped for by the conspirators, by reasserting their adherence to the laws of constitutional rule."

3. The plot failed, in spite of the brutality of the "extreme recourse of political assassination" employed by the conspirators.

In order to prevent the Chilean public from discovering the true story behind General Schneider's assassination, the armed forces high command and military police agreed to reveal one part of the story and to sacrifice half a dozen implicated generals by retiring them and by passing a "lenient sentence" on ex-General Roberto Viaux Marambio. Viaux was the head of the group charged with executing René Schneider. (During Viaux's trial Chilean newspapers stated that he had connections with both ITT and the CIA.)

In his presidential message to Congress of May 21, 1971, Allende referred to the armed forces' role "in the process of changes in the *Vía Chilena* toward socialism," and said that "in spite of some soothsayers and harbingers of doom who doubt their patriotism . . . our armed forces, by their professionalism and respect for the Constitution, are the *guarantors* of the present process of change."

Going a step further, Allende construed the following thesis: "For this reason I want to point out that a conscious, organized, and disciplined people of political parties who loyally understand the meaning of unity, of workers organized in their unions, in their federations, and the Central Única [de Trabajadores, an organization of the laborers and part of the office workers; it had a membership of nearly 1 million] are the granite foundation of the revolutionary process. *Just as much so are*—and I repeat and emphasize it because this process is taking place within the boundaries of the law, *are also*—the armed forces and military police of Chile, to whom I pay homage, *the people in uniform,* for their loyalty to the Constitution and to the will of the people expressed in the voting booths" (Salvador Allende, Santiago, National Stadium speech of November 4, 1971).

It must be remembered that Allende was referring, at all times when he touched on the topic of military loyalty, to the high commands. Nobody doubted the loyalty of the conscripted rank and file; they were laborers, peasants, and office workers in uniform. But the high commands were a class apart. Allende never permitted a scientific, objective discussion of this topic. Nor did he permit speculation on which sectors of Chilean society those high commands would defend in the event of a widespread crisis provoked by the emergence of a popular front demanding a share of the power and direct participation in a society until then managed by a small minority of property holders and by the representatives of U.S. enterprises.

The following incident typifies Allende's attitude toward the armed forces. At the beginning of April 1971, Senator Alberto Jérez of the Senate Defense Commission and "coordinator" between the generals and the Unidad Popular government called me to his office and told me: "As you know, at the end of this month, Salvador is going to give a master class to the Santiago military garrison. The class will be held at the Army Academy of War, before some eight hundred officers. Salvador asked me to get the best information that exists on the Chilean armed forces, and I suggested your name to do the report, so that he'll know what kind of ground he's stepping on. Salvador agrees. He knows you, and he knows you're an expert on Chilean military matters from the political angle. You've got seven days to do it."

In about twenty pages, I presented a summary of events between 1964 and 1970, including an interpretation of the situation pointing up the extreme danger to the stability of the Unidad Popular government posed by the continuance of the same high commands in the armed forces as had existed before Allende took power.

At the end of April, during the course of a leftist journalists' meeting, Alberto Jérez gave me this message: "Salvador was very grateful for your report, but he told me it wasn't useful to him, because you are talking about imaginary armed forces taken out of books by Lenin, and he is dealing with flesh-and-blood human beings. He said to tell you that the Chilean armed forces are a special breed, not foreseen by Lenin in his books. . . ."

The report I had sent to Allende was, in different form, the same information that appears on the pages that follow.

A PROBLEM FOR THE U.S.

In early 1964 the Pentagon decided to pay closer attention to its relationship with the Chilean armed forces, repairing and reconditioning them in case conditions continued to show a trend toward the danger of a worker and peasant subversion in Chile.

For the American generals of the Southern Command in the Canal Zone (who operate at a cost of $136.5 million per annum, with twelve generals and admirals commanding 10,500 troops), in charge of "protecting and administering" the programs of military aid to Latin America, the "Chile case" was, in 1964, a potential problem area.

The Chilean political and economic situation was leaning toward a serious confrontation between the workers and Chilean and American business interests. It was the last year of the presidency of a representative of the Chilean oligopolies (Jorge Alessandri Rodríguez, president of the Paper and Box Manufacturers, a trade association uniting more than $500 million worth of Chilean and North American capital*), and there were clear signs of economic disaster: an inflation rate of over 46 percent after a rate of 8 percent in 1961, 14 percent in 1962, and 45 percent in 1963. Unemployment was over 7 percent, that is, more than 200,000 unemployed out of a work force of about 2.8 million Chileans. The foreign debt had reached $1,896 million ($1,629 million of which were already expended credits and $267 million in credits outstanding). The infant mortality rate was 102.9 per thousand.

The economic gulf between the classes was extreme: 1 million peasants and workers lived on a per capita income of $380; 60,000 landholders, industrialists, and administrative managers enjoyed a mean income of $10,450 per annum.

In statistical terms, the 1964 situation was as follows, according to the studies of the Office of National Planning (Oficina de Planificación Nacional—ODEPLAN—created by the Frei administration):

Wage earners, who made up 50 percent of the work force, received 21 percent of the total annual income.

Office workers, who made up 22.8 percent of the work force, received 27.2 percent of annual income.

The self-employed, who comprised 21.8 percent of the work force, received 17.6 percent of annual income.

---

*This refers to the *activo fijo* (fixed assets) of more than sixty industrial, agricultural, financial, and commercial enterprises belonging to the oligarchic clan Matte-Alessandri.

Contractors and bondholders, who were only 1.4 percent of the work force, absorbed 26.4 percent of the income.

The remainder of the income (7.8 percent) went to the government, through its properties and direct taxes.[2]

Economic discrepancies were much higher outside the cities, where 25 percent of the active Chilean population worked. The 3 percent of agricultural landowners considered to be *latifundistas** appropriated 37 percent of the income generated in that sector, while 71 percent of rural families received only 33 percent of the income.

To maintain this status quo, the successive Radical and Conservative governments between 1945 and 1964 had structured a repressive military apparatus (the Military Police Corps, or Carabineros) which, when they threatened to be overwhelmed by the workers' struggle, would be aided by the armed forces' three branches, principally the Army. However, the basic means of "maintaining the social order" was political deception and suppression of labor unions. (Between 1945 and 1964 the unionized population of Chile had shrunk by more than 20 percent.)

Political deception was reflected in the fact that the alliance of the Conservative and so-called Liberal parties comprised 30 percent of the electoral body. The Radical party (which represented government officials and industrialists with ties to the North American copper companies, plus some *latifundistas*) made up 20 percent of the electoral body. The Christian Democratic party, which began to be important only in the late fifties, had 15 percent of the vote (it had broken off from the Conservative party in the thirties; in 1964 it was composed of the major industrial interests and a class of highest-level technicians tied to the Chilean as well as the North American oligopolies).

By early 1964 the coalition of Socialist and Communist parties had amassed 25 percent of the total vote and showed a consistent tendency

*This word has no real English equivalent. It designates the owners of vast amounts of agricultural land, most of which is uncultivated.

to recruit its sympathizers from among the hundreds of thousands of workers stricken by poverty and unemployment. The workers were pressing for a law establishing a farm workers' union, for raises in pay, for an easement to permit laborers' and office workers' unions, for an agrarian reform law, and, most important, for the nationalization of the copper, iron, and saltpeter mines, which were controlled by U.S. enterprises, as well as for the nationalization of the telephone and power utilities in the capital and the central zones, also in the hands of North Americans.

Thus the 1964 presidential race between Salvador Allende (supported by a Socialist-Communist alliance, plus the greater part of the Radical party at the lowest levels) and Eduardo Frei (head of the Christian Democratic party, plus the Conservative-Liberal alliance and a small segment of the Radical party) was conducted in an atmosphere of violent anti-imperialism, a general agreement about the urgent need for a law of agrarian reform, and a political mobilization of the masses unprecedented in the history of the country. The Christian Democrats, taking up the banner of political deception from the Radical party, even suggested the need for a "revolution," but "in freedom," which would involve the expropriation of the *latifundistas*, bank reform, the expropriation of some gigantic Chilean industrial consortia that were privately owned, tax reform, and a "new agreement" with the Anaconda and Kennecott copper companies.

The situation threatened to become critical for the dominant groups in Chilean society, both North American and national. From 1945 until 1964, the U.S. government and the Anaconda, Kennecott, International Telephone & Telegraph, and American Foreign Power companies, mainly, had enormous influence over the Chilean government and the Conservative, Liberal, and, above all, Radical members of the Chamber of Deputies and Senators. For instance, the Radical President Gabriel González Videla, after leaving the presidency in 1948, was named president of the Chilean subsidiary of Radio Corporation of America and vice-president of the French and Italian Bank. Between 1948 and 1964, Gabriel González Videla had risen from being a lawyer of modest means to one of the richest men in Chile. Another typical case is that of Rodolfo Michels, the most important man in the Radical leadership during the same years. Michels was in charge of administering the funds annually contributed by the Anaconda Company to finance the Radical party. All of the projects for laws on "foreign investment," and copper, iron, saltpeter, telephone, and electricity contracts, before being presented to Congress by the Radical administrators and their successors, were first discussed in the Anaconda offices at the Chuquicamata mine. When Michels "retired" from political life and was named vice-president of Anaconda in Chile, he was replaced by the "treasurer" of the Radical party, Constantino Tallar, who at the same time was the "contractor" of Anaconda's residential and industrial construction work.[3]

In 1964, with radicalism splintered, and faced with strong grass-roots support for Allende's leftist coalition, the U.S. government and its multinational corporations were in a quandary: whom could they use to look out for their interests? The Radicals had no chance to pull together a coherent group with real access to La Moneda and the Parliament. Inquiries were sent to Chile: Robert Haldeman, president of Braden Copper (a Kennecott affiliate), which held the El Teniente copper mine concession in O'Higgins Province, by late 1963 had had conversations with the head of the Christian Democrats, Eduardo Frei (a lawyer serving the oligopolistic group of Osvaldo de Castro, closely linked to the American company Anglo Lautaro), who had already declared his candidacy for the 1964 presidential elections. He had requested financial aid from Kennecott for his campaign in exchange for a formal promise not to nationalize the copper mines and to formulate a technical agreement that would mutually benefit Chile and Kennecott. Haldeman informed his superiors that "in my opinion" Eduardo Frei is a "person to be trusted," who "believes in what he says." Kennecott, Anglo Lautaro, and ITT (whose executive team included one of the most important men in the Christian Democratic leadership, Guillermo Correa Fuenzalida, who was in turn the chief executive of the financial-industrial group of Banco de Chile, which managed capital assets of more than $600 million) as well as other multinationals and the U.S. government were interested in the results of the 1964 presidential campaign, and believed that Frei's election would be to their benefit.[4]

Twenty million dollars to finance Frei's campaign were collected and administered by the International Development Foundation, a U.S. government agency. The plan was to accede to popular pressure for agrarian reform and farm workers' unions, as well as to reach "new accords" that would look like nationalizations with Anglo Lautaro for saltpeter, American Foreign Power for electricity, ITT for the telephones, and Anaconda and Kennecott for copper.

David Rockefeller of the Chase Manhattan Bank advised on the economic steps to take "to guarantee measures favoring capital proceeding from the U.S." "Coordinator" between the Rockefellers and Eduardo Frei was Engineer Raúl Sáez (as of July 11, 1974, Chile's Minister of Economic Coordination, a post especially created for him).[5]

The $20 million was not a bad investment for the United States. Frei won the presidential elections with 56 percent of the vote. But Allende raised his percentage of the vote from approximately 25 to 39 percent. This was worrisome to American interests. American University in Washington, D.C., began an in-depth investigation of Chilean society, inserted into what came to be called "Plan Camelot." They recommended a series of measures to "avoid the peril of popular subversion in Chile." These measures revolved around a refitting of the Chilean armed forces' capacity to cope "in an extreme situation."

At about this time, Roy Hansen, a sociologist at the University of California, was preparing a scholarly study on the subject of the Chilean armed forces high command.[6]

Roy Hansen arrived in Chile in late 1964 and made contact with Álvaro Bunster at the University of Chile (the latter would also be drafted for Plan Camelot; curiously, he was later appointed ambassador to Great Britain during Allende's administration). Through Bunster's sister Ximena he obtained the status of investigative sociologist.

Hansen's scientific operations were, of course, centered on the Chilean armed forces. For this purpose, he got in touch with the secretary general of the Chilean Army's Academy of War, Colonel René Schneider Chereau. Colonel Schneider gave Hansen unlimited access to the Academy of War's library and study plans, and arranged personal interviews with the corps of generals.

As Hansen's study progressed, he discovered that the Chilean Army had a superstructure suited to a far larger corps than the one they managed (one general to every 1,000 men, that is, 32 generals to approximately 32,000 men, and one colonel to every 200 men). When he also discovered that the "decisive force" in the country's military system was the Army, he concentrated his investigation on it. The result of Hansen's work, which the Chilean Army labeled "secret," was entitled *Military Culture and Organizational Decline: A Study of the Chilean Army.* A copy of his study was shelved in the "classified" section of the Chilean Army's Academy of War library, another went to the University of California sociology library, and the rest went to the Pentagon.[7]

In 1964, in Roy Hansen's view, the Chilean armed forces command elite were clearly in danger of disintegration as a result of their total lack of participation in the country's important decisions. In spite of the fact that the opinion of the Chilean armed forces' command had been decisive in the country's political development, for the last forty years they had been used merely as a "terrorizing specter." At the same time, they were given an undignified third-order role in the system of government and, what is more, were placed in sixth or seventh rank economically. Hansen said that since the 1924 military coup (by the Santiago garrison to force the oligarchic majority in Parliament to pass reform laws for the workers' salaries and health and retirement benefits, to prevent a "Bolshevist insurrection" of the masses), the Chilean military elite had not found it necessary to intervene directly in politics, and this had had the effect of relegating them to the attic in successive civil administrations.

Hansen "foresaw" that the high commands, to protect themselves from further decline, would have a marked tendency in the near future to take an active part in politics and in national decisions made by the controlling circles.

Investigating what the generals thought about the rest of the society they lived in, Hansen reached these conclusions: The generals had a profound contempt for civilians, whom they considered useless, corrupt, and ignorant. Some of them believed that the Parliamentarians, the civil politicians, and many officials high in the state's hierarchy "had no idea what Chile is, how it must be defended from external aggressions and internal subversion." It was also the generals' opinion that "the Fatherland" could be defended only by the armed forces, because civil politicians were incompetent. They felt that civilians held the military in contempt but would turn to it whenever they were unable to control the "subversion of the masses." Hansen's statistics on the political opinions of the high command were the following: 10 percent were right-wing, 80 percent were centrist, and 10 percent were left-wing. But he added the explanation that for the Chilean high commands, "leftist" meant Frei's Christian Democratic program of agrarian and banking reform and new contracts with the North American companies. For the generals, the coalition of political parties that had supported Salvador Allende was the "extreme left," and none of them supported it.

In the first half of 1965, when the Pentagon wanted to put into practice a part of its long-term plan to prepare the Chilean armed forces as reserve forces for maintaining the structure of Chilean middle-class society in the case of a disaster with the civil politicians, there were serious problems. This part was Plan Camelot, whose intention was to study, classify, and weigh all "the elements of social, political, and economic pressure against the established system" to achieve "a system to control those pressures." When it began to be applied, the militants in the leftist parties at the University of Chile denounced it. The scandal was so bad that even the Christian Democrats, for appearances' sake, supported an investigation in Parliament. The leftists in Parliament, plus a segment of the Christian Democrats, described

Plan Camelot as a "foreign power's plan of espionage against Chile," and Washington itself was forced to issue a statement in June 1965 that "we have suggested to the corresponding authorities that the application of Plan Camelot in Chile and Colombia be suspended."[8]

But the work in the Chilean armed forces was not suspended. The U.S. military mission (whose offices are inside the Ministry of Defense in Santiago, off limits for Chilean civilians) began "advising" the Academy of War curriculum and recommended that all upper-class men at the Bernardo O'Higgins Military School (which trains officers for the Army) and the Captain Avalos Aviation School (which trains officers for the Air Force) ought to spend a forty-day instruction period at the U.S. Army's Southern Command in the Panama Canal Zone.

This "recommendation" from the Pentagon to the Chilean high command was put into operation in 1968 by the then director of the Bernardo O'Higgins Military School, already the Pentagon's "trusted man" in the Army, Brigadier General René Schneider Chereau, who had been so helpful to Roy Hansen.

At the same time, Schneider, a professor in the Academy of War, was active in introducing new courses on economics, politics, government administration, foreign commerce, the politics of industrialization, the history of the Chilean political parties, agrarian and urban reform, banking policies, and so on. That is to say, an entire curriculum in "public administration" was intended as an important part in the instruction of the Chilean Army's future generals. In the same way, intensive studies of Marxism were begun through courses on Marx, Lenin, and Mao Tse-tung.[9]

From 1968, Professor Schneider, after long work sessions with the members of the U.S. military mission in Santiago, began to develop "the modern theory of national security," which consisted of maintaining that the real meaning of the phrase "the armed forces are the guarantors of national security" had a double character: security with respect to external enemies, and security with respect to internal enemies, and that in "the present conditions of Chile" the "internal" enemies of national security are much more dangerous, real, and latent than the "external" enemies. And who are those "internal" enemies? According to Pentagon theory as transmitted through General René Schneider, they are all those who, taking advantage of popular discontent resulting from social injustices and abuses by the possessors of wealth, are trying to remove Chile from the "Christian Western world" in which it was born and is destined to continue living. Among these "internal" enemies, naturally, those "who advocate Marxist socialism" hold the place of honor.

Similar courses and theories were being developed at the same time in the Navy, Air Force, and military police, all under the aegis of the "North American intelligence advisers" and all through senior officers like Brigadier General René Schneider Chereau.

While the Pentagon gave top priority in Chile to the betterment of its relations with the native armed forces, Frei's government was too preoccupied with its relations with U.S. companies to heed the generals' material requests. But three years of preparation to be "masters in the arts of war and civil government" had prompted the generals to ask for a larger share of the wealth generated by the work of the Chilean laborers and peasants.

In 1969 a new social and economic crisis began to emerge. Five years had passed since Frei's call for a "revolution in freedom," and its failure was all too evident. Economic development had been stagnating, with growth of the GNP dropping in 1967 to 0 percent; in 1968, .6 percent; the projection for 1969 did not look better than .7 percent. Food prices were rising: in 1967, a rise of 14.5 percent; in 1968, 25.5 percent, and the 1969 projection was 30.7 percent. In the same year, the mean remuneration of 1,300,000 urban and agricultural workers was *35 times less* than the mean income of some 62,000 employers and landowners. Agrarian reform, which had promised to create 100,000 new landholders, had been able to expropriate less than one-third of the large estates. The foreign debt had risen from $1,896 million in 1964 to a total of $2,765 million in 1969, while U.S. and other foreign enterprises were taking out of the country, through profits, depreciations, amortizations, and interest payments, *more than one million dollars a day*. During Alessandri's administration (1958–1964), this annual outflow was $170 million, but before the last year of Frei's administration, it had gone up to more than $344 million. Andrés Zaldívar, Frei's Treasury Minister, reported in November 1969 that cash outflow to foreign countries would reach $450 million for fiscal 1969. On the other hand, the Christian Democratic government had paid $186 million to American Foreign Power, holder of the Chilean Electric Company, for machinery that was worth less than $40 million; it had promised $1 billion to Anaconda for a "pacted nationalization" of Chuquicamata, the largest copper mine in the world, for equipment that was worth less than $170 million. A similar accord had been reached with Kennecott, paying $80 million for 51 percent of the installations whose value did not exceed $70 million in the El Teniente mine.*

All of this, made known to the Chilean people by leftist journalists and nationalistic publications, had provoked a vast anti-imperialist sentiment which was being expressed in constant agitation by laborers, peasants, office workers, and students, demanding the expulsion of the U.S. copper companies from Chile and the expropriation of all industrial enterprises with a majority of capital held by U.S. companies, which had been producing the phenomenon of "industrial denationalization" in Chile during the Frei administration.

The peasants' struggle for land had gone to the extreme of appropriating some large estates by force, while farm worker unionization had grown from 3,000 peasants in 1964 to nearly 120,000 in the last month of 1969. In the cities, workers' strikes for better wages were triple those during the previous administration. Professors and university and high school students were constantly agitating for educational reform on the upper levels. The situation was explosive enough for Eduardo Frei to ask Nelson Rockefeller not to visit Chile on the

---

*This subject is treated in greater detail in my book *American Imperialism in Chile*. The figures were cited in a constitutional accusation against Eduardo Frei in June 1973, which was not successful because there was a government minority in both houses of Parliament.

Latin-American tour that resulted in his famous report on Latin America. In this report, Rockefeller would recommend that the U.S. government promote the taking of power in Latin-American countries by the progressive body of officers of the new generation, since they were the most coherent organization in Latin-American societies. The "progressive body of officers" to whom Rockefeller was referring included the high commands training in the Chilean Army's Academy of War under the advice and supervision of the U.S. military mission.[10]

Around mid-1969, in the middle of this social ferment, Brigadier General Roberto Viaux Marambio, commander of the First Army Division stationed in Antofagasta, solicited "the opinion of the younger officers" (colonels, lieutenant colonels, majors, and captains) and wrote a letter of petition to the Army's commander in chief, Sergio Castillo Aranguiz, to be presented to Eduardo Frei. General Viaux's letter said that "national security and internal peace in our country" depended on the armed forces, and "in our judgment" the Frei administration, like its predecessors, had not concerned itself with keeping a modern army in working order, "well equipped and taking real part in important national decisions." The letter demanded that a new government policy toward the armed forces be put into effect, that senior officers' salaries be adjusted to conform to "their high social status and national responsibility" (in the letter, Viaux complained that "a general of the Republic earns less than a competent worker at the Chuquicamata copper mine," which was true), that adequate war matériel be purchased, and that the higher echelons of the military hierarchy be given a prominent participatory role in the economic, political, and social development of Chile.

General Viaux was confident that his letter would lead to a new dialogue with President Frei, because he had discussed it beforehand with the head of the Army's General Staff, Division General René Schneider Chereau. The latter had even made suggestions about the "participatory" role of the generals in the economic and political life of the country.

Frei, however, did not listen to René Schneider, but he did listen to Sergio Castillo, the commander in chief of the Army, an intimate personal friend and a "Freista" above all else. General Roberto Viaux was relieved of his command of the First Division on Saturday, October 18, 1969, and recalled to Santiago. On Tuesday, October 21, Viaux awoke as head of a military insurrection localized in the Tacna Regiment in Santiago, with the support of the Junior Officers' School, the Academy of War, and part of the 2nd Armored Regiment. At noon on October 21, it was clear to the reporters covering the incident that General Viaux was counting on the covert support and sympathy of the majority of Santiago's officer corps, and that, technically, if Viaux suggested it, there was nothing to prevent the overthrow of Eduardo Frei and his replacement by a military government without a shot being fired. However, after a phone conversation with the head of the Army General Staff, René Schneider, General Viaux issued a statement in which he emphasized that "my movement is not against the President of the Republic," but rather was a last resort "to call attention" to the necessity of putting the Army in the place it deserved.

The next day, October 22, General Viaux ended his rebellion, having elicited the following concessions: The commander in chief of the Army, General Sergio Castillo, would retire and be replaced by Division General René Schneider Chereau. General Viaux accepted forced retirement for himself, since General Schneider's presence as commander in chief guaranteed that his petitions would be heard.

General Schneider forced Frei to carry out part of Viaux's original petition: in January 1970, the generals' salaries were raised from an equivalent of six times the minimum wage to twelve times the minimum wage. (The minimum wage is fixed by law each year for state employees and private enterprise.) That is, the generals became part of the 2 percent of Chilean households with the highest income. They had belonged to the 10 percent with the highest income before. The military budget was raised by 50 percent for the following fiscal year, and plans to expand the number of officers in the three branches of the armed forces, the military police, and the civilian investigatory police were studied. (These plans were not put into effect until 1971, under Allende's administration.)

It was agreed that for their part the corps of Army generals would study long- and short-term "plans of action" to put into practice General Viaux's demand that "the armed forces be given a real responsibility in solving important national problems." During 1970 this plan was deferred by the generals themselves so they could concentrate on the means of intervening "in search of social peace," should the political struggle for the presidency erupt into violent confrontations between the various political factions, a situation that kept threatening throughout the year until September 4, the day of the presidential elections.

ALLENDE, THE NEW PRESIDENT

In April 1970, the presidential campaigns were providing a few surprises to the "experts" who had decided that Salvador Allende was "politically dead." The Socialist Senator who was the Unidad Popular's candidate had already been defeated in three presidential elections, in 1952, 1958, and 1964. However, public opinion polls showed that in the north and south of the country, in the industrial concentration at Concepción and in Santiago, the capital, sympathy for Allende, especially among the laborers, peasants, and office workers, assured him of more than 35 percent of the vote. Since there were three candidates (the other two were former President Jorge Alessandri and a Christian Democratic Senator, Radomiro Tomic), there were "great possibilities" that Allende would win by a narrow margin.

In the last week of April an important meeting was held at the house of Patricio Rojas, President Frei's Minister of the Interior. It was attended by Andrés Zaldívar, the Treasury Minister; Patricio Aylwin, a Christian Democratic Senator; Pedro Ibáñez, a National Party (conservative) Senator; and the director of the Paper and Box Manufacturers, Arturo Matte Larrain. The topic of conversation was how to prevent Salvador Allende from becoming President should he win the election.

The Chilean Constitution decreed that if the winning presidential candidate did "not obtain the half plus one of the vote," then, fifty days later, the Parliament "could proclaim President whichever of the candidates had obtained the first two pluralities." That is, Parliament could elect the "runner-up." The meeting's participants decided to launch a public opinion campaign to get "Allende's runner-up" elected. To provide a veneer of "national legitimacy" to this maneuver, the participants agreed to ask the Army's commander in chief, General René Schneider Chereau, to declare publicly that the armed forces would "guarantee" the election of the runner-up, if necessary.

Patricio Rojas talked to Schneider, and through Andrés Zaldívar they got Agustín Edwards to tell the director of his newspaper, *El Mercurio,* to interview the commander in chief. The interview appeared on page one of the May 8 issue and established the following points:

1. The Army will guarantee the constitutional verdict.

2. The Army is the guarantor of a normal election, in which the candidate elected by the people or by the Chilean Congress in plenary session will assume the presidency. (This was a key point: Schneider was saying that the military would guarantee the presidency to whoever won 51 percent of the vote in September—impossible for Allende —or to the runner-up if the first [Allende] got less than 51 percent.) In saying this, Schneider complied with the Christian Democrat/Conservative collusion's request. But he went beyond them, and spoke of "guaranteeing" only a "normal election." This opened the possibility that the military would find an election in which Allende won more than 51 percent of the votes "abnormal," would annul it, and would call new elections.

"Political intervention is outside all our doctrines. We are the guarantors of a legal process on which the entire constitutional life of our country is based.

"If abnormal events occur [internal disruption], our obligation is to prevent them from obstructing what is intended by the Constitution." (In these two points, Schneider makes it clear that the military will not take the side of any political party, but that they will act should the system of North American imperialist and Chilean big business control be threatened.)

"Whoever is very restless about certain ideas, certain tendencies, or certain political activities and wants to participate in them had better take off his uniform and embrace them as a civilian." (Schneider was here warning a small percentage of middle-level officers who showed some sympathy for Allende's candidacy. He was also calling attention to the threatening recurrence of progressive ideas among the officers, after the great internal cleanup of 1961–1962 when those suspected of sympathizing with "socialist ideas" were forced into retirement.)

But when September 4, 1970, arrived, the political situation was very different from what had been envisioned. The election results were predictable enough (Allende with 1,075,000 votes—36.3 percent; Alessandri with 1,036,000 votes—34.9 percent; and Tomic with 824,000 votes—27.8 percent). But Allende's relatively skimpy victory was greeted with a great explosion of enthusiasm by his million sympathizers. That night there were parties in the streets and demonstrations in Santiago, Valparaíso, Concepción, and the other important cities. And, totally unexpected, large sectors of Christian Democratic youths and workers came out to join the Unidad Popular demonstrations, making a kind of spontaneous "anti-imperialist front." All this would have clearly made it a rash and brutal move to elect, fifty days after the fact, the runner-up as President of Chile.

In addition, Radomiro Tomic (who did not know about the intended ploy of his party leaders) visited Allende at his home at noon on September 5 to "salute him as the winner and future President." Allende, before hundreds of newspapermen, embraced Tomic and answered, "Your moral gesture consolidates our friendship of more than thirty years."

Obviously a new way would have to be found to dissolve Allende's victory. All day Sunday, September 6, secret meetings went on between Senators Pedro Ibáñez and Francisco Bulnes (on behalf of Alessandri) and the Ministers of the Treasury, Andrés Zaldívar; Defense, Sergio Ossa Pretot; Economy, Carlos Figueroa; and the Interior, Patricio Rojas (on behalf of the Frei government). The commanders in chief of the Air Force, General Carlos Guerraty; Navy, Admiral Jorge Porta Angulo; and military police, General Vicente Huerta; and the head of the Santiago garrison, Army General Camilo Valenzuela, were having a separate meeting of their own.

Immediately afterward, two members of the military made a proposal to General Schneider. It was a very simple one: to convince Eduardo Frei that it was necessary to prevent, at any cost, the ratification of Allende's victory in Parliament. This was to be accomplished by means of a military insurrection which would result in Frei's resignation, the appointment of a governing military junta, and the calling of new presidential elections between only two candidates after a six-month period. To warrant this military insurrection, a plan of social chaos was proposed, involving "financial panic" and a "wave of terrorist acts."

General Schneider was agreeable but made two stipulations: one, that he would not become a member of that military junta and would retire from active duty at the moment of the planned insurrection; and two, that the U.S. military mission had to be informed of these plans, to obtain "their support" or "the benefit of their experience."[11]

That Sunday afternoon, the conspirators put their plan into action, beginning with a gigantic network of telephone calls warning people that "the Marxists will wind up with all the money" and that they should "withdraw all savings and deposits in bank accounts." On Monday morning, September 7, the branches of the commercial and federal banks, and the savings and loan associations, opened to long lines of depositors who wanted to withdraw their money. Two weeks after the elections, 611 million escudos (some $50 million) had been withdrawn from current accounts in the private sector of the commercial banks and the State Bank; 54 million escudos (about $4.5 million) had been withdrawn from savings in the State Bank; the withdrawal against adjustment bonds was 11 million escudos ($900,000); and the savings and loan associations suffered withdrawals of 322 million escudos (over $26 million).

The large oligopolies began to demand full payment for sales of raw materials previously made on installment to medium-sized and small businesses. At the same time, the large oligopolies stopped buying from the medium-sized and small businesses. This situation was intended to set the interests of these two categories against those of the laborers, peasants, and office workers who sympathized with Allende.

The "financial panic" was completed with the flight of foreign currency, dollar speculation on the black market, and the artificial increase of trips abroad, all in illegal maneuvers protected by Frei's Ministers of the Treasury and the Economy.

The sale of dollars for trips abroad, which from January to August 1970 had averaged $5.3 million per month, rose to $17.5 million in September and $13.6 million in October. The official price of the dollar was 12.2 escudos, but on the black market it reached a high of 70 escudos.

On October 13 the directors of the Confederation of Small Businesses and Manufacturers reported on "the percentage of decrease in business activity: Santiago, 53 percent; Arica, 28 percent; Antofagasta, 20 percent; Coquimbo, 83 percent; Valparaíso, 30 percent; Colchagua, 50 percent; Concepción, 33 percent; Los Angeles, 53 percent." In alarm they pointed out that "in the whole country, sales have gone down 38.4 percent" and "we have work only for the next fifteen days and resources for wage payment for twenty more days."

On September 23, performing his role in the plot, Frei's Treasury Minister, Andrés Zaldívar, gave a speech over national radio and television citing terrifying statistics about the financial calamity and reporting that "the economic situation of the post-election period stemmed from psychological factors" and that "the more than probable results of this situation would be a complete and generalized economic disaster."

The "financial panic" part of the plot had been achieved to perfection. What then kept the conspirators from succeeding in their aim to prevent Allende from assuming power?

Through Arturo Matte Larrain, one of the owners belonging to the gigantic Paper and Box Manufacturers, the conspirators had established a bridge between President Eduardo Frei and ITT. Along with the CIA, ITT was giving its support to a coup that would prevent Allende's ratification by the Chilean Parliament. Matte Larrain's contacts were the Americans Robert Berrellez and Hal Hendrix, both ITT public relations officers.

On September 8, Matte Larrain informed Frei that ITT was lobbying in Washington to get the U.S. government to support a "military junta" that would prevent Allende's ratification, and that a general plan of "pressure" had already been agreed on by the various U.S. private industries in Chile. According to the plan, banks would not give new credits or extend those already approved; the companies would delay in delivering products, cash remittances, replacement parts, and the like, would withdraw all technical assistance, and "would pressure savings and loan associations to declare bankruptcy." According to a memo dated September 17, 1970, sent by ITT representatives in Chile, Hal Hendrix and Robert Berrellez, to E. J. Gerrity, senior vice-president in charge of public relations for ITT, in New York, the State Department had given its green light to Ambassador Edward Korry to do all possible to prevent Allende from taking power. Berrellez and Hendrix had asked Matte to assure Frei that ITT was ready to contribute money or whatever else was necessary.

According to the same ITT memo, Frei's response was along the following lines: he felt he could not shatter his image as a democrat, so if the situation continued to develop, he hoped that he would be thrown out and sent into exile for a while. He would not do anything to prevent the financial and economic collapse from cultivating public receptivity to a military coup that would reorganize things. However, he refused absolutely to do anything to attract public suspicion to himself. He felt he had to guard his public image.[12]

Matte Larrain, through ITT's Hendrix, was asked to persuade Frei to take a more active role. Frei never decided to take that step.

At the same time, Brigadier General Valenzuela, commander of the Santiago garrison, had contacted retired General Viaux to form a "crash team" to instigate acts of terrorism throughout the country. Viaux's group was aided by Enrique Schilling, private secretary to Radical Senator Julio Durán, as well as by a growing group of university students led by the lawyer Pablo Rodríguez Grez.

The terrorists began work in mid-September, depending for protection on director general of military police Vicente Huerta, and for technical advice on two members of Army intelligence (SIM).

The scheme was successful except that Frei was not actively collaborating, and the victorious candidate, Allende, was rapidly establishing contacts with the Chilean armed forces to "clarify his program." Edward Korry, the U.S. ambassador, began to get nervous and sent highly insolent messages to Frei, one of them saying, "Tell him it is time to put his pants on."

For his part, Allende let the generals know (through Manuel Torrez de la Cruz, Herman Brady, and René Schneider) that those who opposed his ratification were making a mistake, for the following reasons: never in Chilean history had the runner-up been elected in a plenary session. The million Chileans who elected him would not accept such a decision. "My program" is one of "developing state capitalism" and is not socialist. "The reforms" of "my program" are "the only peaceful way left for this system."[13]

Allende's declarations, on another front, had been repeated to the Christian Democratic leaders who were not implicated in the military coup: Renán Fuentealba and Bernardo Leighton, both of whom carried great weight with their party's leadership. From there arose the idea of making Allende sign a "Statute of Democratic Guarantees," to be incorporated into the Chilean Constitution and to serve as Allende's certificate of "non-Marxist" conduct. On October 8 this statute had already been drawn up and approved by both the Christian Democrats and the Unidad Popular. The statute ensured that at least a majority of Christian Democratic legislators would vote for Allende on October 24, giving him enough ballots to be elected.

As Allende's conversations during the first week of October were bearing fruit with the Christian Democrats, his messages and conversations with the military leaders were also showing their effect. Schneider had kept the U.S. military mission in Santiago abreast of everything that happened; this information was relayed to the Pentagon. The Pentagon evaluated the situation, and in early October the U.S. military mission informed Schneider that "the whole plan is canceled." On October 15, Schneider gave a talk on the subject at the Army's Polytechnic Academy, repeating the instructions the U.S. generals had relayed from Washington:[14]

1. We should not act stupidly in such a delicate moment in the constitutional life of Chile. The armed forces cannot at this time "detain evolution and change." Our duty is "to accept them," to take care that they develop in an orderly fashion and without disturbing the peace.

2. "Pessimism and loss of faith" can lead us into believing that "the Marxist enemy is at the door" and into mistakenly "going to extremes" to fight him.

3. A very significant group of Chileans "is not at this time disposed to allow to be snatched away from them an election victory that they believe will change the course of their lives." Our duty is to let these people make their experiment, but without harming others, without harming our Fatherland or our institutional life.

4. "Senator Salvador Allende has given us assurances" that he will remain within the bounds of the Constitution and the laws, that his "program of change" will not pose a threat to our Western, Christian way of life. The Senator has said something to me personally with which I concur: at this point in time, a government like Senator Allende's is the only type of government that can prevent a violent and tragic people's insurrection from exploding.

5. We, the armed forces, who are the guarantors that this society will continue being "Western and Christian," will have to "wait and

see what happens." The future will tell us whether we must intervene to put things back in their proper places, or whether Senator Salvador Allende will keep his promise to "guide" the people's restlessness and "prevent the insurrection of the have-nots."

The Chilean Army's commander in chief had passed the word on to the Army high command. It was also passed on to the director general of the military police and the commanders in chief of the Air Force and Navy. When Jorge Porta Angulo relayed it to his corps of admirals, four of them met with Allende to ask him if what was being said in the armed forces about him was true. Allende confirmed all the ideas Schneider had divulged. Admiral Porta Angulo resigned his post and was replaced by the commander of the First Naval District (Valparaíso), Vice-Admiral Hugo Barrios Tirado.[15]

What had happened in the first week of October 1970 was that the Pentagon had said *no* to a military coup in Chile. The Chilean generals were left with the awkward task of dismantling the already functioning coup machinery. The Pentagon's decision made a tremendous impact in the CIA, which had hoped to go ahead anyway. The lack of coordination among the Pentagon, President Nixon, and the CIA was to create a fragmentation in the team of conspirators, by now reduced to retired General Roberto Viaux's "crash team."

Robert Berrellez's and Hal Hendrix's memoranda to the vice-president of ITT in New York, beginning in September 1970, have made this lack of coordination with the Pentagon famous. In a memo dated Santiago de Chile, September 17, and sent to Edward Gerrity in New York, Hendrix and Berrellez reported: "Late Tuesday night (September 15), Ambassador Edward Korry finally received a message from the State Department giving him the green light to move in the name of President Nixon. The message gave him maximum authority to do all possible—short of a Dominican Republic-type action—to keep Allende from taking power." The same report added that we should "bring what pressure we can on USIS in Washington to instruct the Santiago USIS to start moving the *Mercurio* editorials around Latin America and into Europe."

The report added that Arturo Matte Larrain believed that Eduardo Frei had not yet made up his mind, that "a subtle but firm enough pressure must be brought to bear on Frei," and that "the *Mercurio* chain is hitting at Allende and the Communist party with effect."[16]

That is, on September 15, President Nixon appeared to be giving the "green light" to the conspiracy while the Pentagon was still analyzing the situation.

On September 30, Gerrity sent word to Messrs. Merriam, Neal, and Ryan of ITT that in Chile, Jack Guilfoyle, a New York ITT vice-president,

was advised of the following by Enno Hobbing of the CIA:
Hobbing was visited yesterday by Gregorio Amunategui, who is an Alessandri representative. Gregorio had come from Santiago and his message to Hobbing from Alessandri was—keep cool, don't rock the boat, we are making progress—.
This is in direct contrast to what Broe recommended.[17]

On October 9, the ITT vice-president in Washington, William Merriam, sent a report to John McCone, a former CIA director, in which he wrote sarcastically that he was "rather surprised" to learn that "the Nixon Administration will take a very, very hard line when and if Allende is elected," and disappointedly remarked that "this is the first heartening thing I have heard."[18] Obviously, there had been quite a shift in policy from that cited in the September 17, 1970, memo from Hendrix and Berrellez to ITT's E. J. Gerrity, stating that Ambassador Edward Korry had been advised to move in the name of President Nixon to prevent Allende from taking power.

By that time, it would appear that the Pentagon had given Nixon its opinion and had ordered its man in Santiago, Schneider, to defuse the coup. But ITT persisted. On October 16, Edward Gerrity in New York heard from Hal Hendrix that "the chance of a military coup is slim but it continues to exist.

"A key figure in this possibility is former Brigadier General Roberto Viaux." But he warned: "It is a fact that word passed to

Viaux from Washington to hold back last week. It was felt that he was not adequately prepared. . . . Emissaries pointed out to him that if he moved prematurely and lost, his defeat would be tantamount to a 'Bay of Pigs in Chile.' "[19]

Hendrix was not telling Gerrity everything. On October 3, Hendrix's associate, Robert Berrellez, had met with Roberto Viaux and his brother-in-law Raúl Igualt at the Santiago Country Club to discuss the news that Washington wanted Viaux to cancel the coup. Viaux told Berrellez that he had heard from General Schneider that the project was canceled. Berrellez was of the opinion that there was a traitor somewhere, and persuaded Viaux to go ahead. The general said that a phony kidnaping of the commander in chief, René Schneider, was being comtemplated to create two or three days of tension. This would be followed by the overthrow of Frei and the appointment of a military junta headed by Camilo Valenzuela. Berrellez said the kidnaping should be a real one. He also reported to Hendrix that Viaux seemed furious at Schneider and agreed that if there was a traitor, it had to be the commander in chief of the Army.

On October 21, after General Schneider had already dismantled the coup, Hal Hendrix had told his superiors in New York: "Now there is general resignation that Allende will win easily in the Congress. . . . In spite of the forementioned, there remains in Chile a faint whisper of hope—or wishful thinking—that a military coup will be staged to prevent Allende from assuming the presidency . . . some civilian and military personnel continue to look toward former Brigadier General Roberto Viaux to lead a military action."[20]

That same day, the group directed by ex-General Viaux was preparing the last details of the plan to use the "traitor Schneider" to create the social chaos which would lead to a military coup.

On the morning of October 22, Viaux dispatched a team to "liquidate the traitor." General Schneider was shot inside his Mercedes-Benz. He died three days later, after the Plenary Congress had elected Salvador Allende President.

On October 25, Hendrix reported to New York: "Contrary to the general expectation, the military did not move against Allende over the weekend. It was believed that the killing of Schneider was the prelude to the coup."[21]

Since the Pentagon had told the Chilean generals *not to move,* they did not move, even after the assassination of their commander in chief.

Allende agreed with Schneider's successor, General Carlos Prats González, to "investigate the Schneider case in such a way as not to provoke a rift in the armed forces"—in other words, not to investigate the real causes, the true extent of the Chilean generals' complicity in the coup and with the Pentagon, as well as the participation of Frei's Cabinet ministers. Prats would vouch for the Army's "loyalty" to Allende, if Allende would not force him to investigate. This was the first of several dangerous agreements Allende made with the Chilean generals that moved him into their line of fire.[22]

The armed forces agreed to sacrifice Vicente Huerta, the director general of the military police; Admiral Hugo Barrios Tirado, commander in chief of the Navy; and Carlos Guerraty, commander in chief of the Air Force. They were replaced by José María Sepúlveda Galindo, military police; César Ruiz Danyau, Air Force; and Raúl Montero, Navy. These three, together with Carlos Prats, urged Allende not to replace the rest of the generals (as was the custom every time the President of the Republic changed), in order to "protect institutional stability and cohesion." Once again, Allende acceded.

However, Allende took advantage of the military's reluctance to allow the truth to be revealed by exploiting General Schneider's assassination as the supposed proof that "over and above all things, the Chilean armed forces are professional and respectful of the Constitution and the laws." Allende thus converted Schneider into a symbol of "loyalty to the Fatherland." He did this so successfully that, judging from later events, he even convinced himself of it. He had lost sight of the truth: Schneider had been obeying Pentagon orders until his death, and the Pentagon machinery inside the Chilean armed forces remained intact. Allende was agreeing to leave it intact. This was to prove a fatal mistake.

NOW WHAT?

The assassination of the Army's commander in chief proved traumatic for the great majority of the senior officers in the armed forces. The middle- and upper-level officers who were not aware of the real plot analyzed the incident with a peasant simplicity: the general was assassinated because of the politicians' ineptness.

The image of Roberto Viaux, the general in retirement, who until October had stood for "the Army's rebirth," was for many officers popped like a soap bubble. But once again, the reason given was: Viaux had been corrupted by his contact with politicians.

Within the officers' corps of the Army, Air Force, and Navy, the beginning of Allende's presidency coincided with an upsurge of violent anticivilian sentiment. This manifested itself at some improvised gatherings at the Santiago Officers' Club (curiously enough, situated next to the Brazilian Embassy) in the question: "And what happens if we take these clowns' bread and butter away, and keep it all ourselves?" As the days went on, the question acquired the reflection and outline of a counterquestion: "Are we prepared to take charge of the whole works?"

Suddenly, to an outside observer, the Pentagon's apparently innocuous 1964 undertaking to introduce courses in economics, politics, industrial development, agrarian reform, and so on in training the Chilean armed forces was amply justified. A colonial country's armed forces had been prepared to cope with a possible crisis in colonization brought about by the failure of the civilian organizations dependent on the oligopolies, or by excessive pressure from the laborers, peasants, and office workers to disrupt the system. This very set of circumstances was gestating in early 1971.

At that time, primarily in the Army, the "eggheads" began to emerge as important figures. They were a group of generals, colonels, lieutenant colonels, and majors at the Academy of War who had been paying close attention to "the national reality" and its "problems" since 1970. These officers were advised by the Pentagon through the U.S. military mission in Santiago, which directed their study of higher economics, macrosociology, microsociology, and related subjects.

The "eggheads" had a brilliant spokesman in Major Claudio López Silva, who had a degree in sociology; in 1970 he published a paper entitled "Las Fuerzas Armadas en el Tercer Mundo" (The Armed Forces in the Third World) in *Memorial del Ejército de Chile* (Chilean Army Briefs) No. 356, on the recommendation of the journal's director, General Pablo Schaffhauser, who was to become chief of the Army General Staff the following year. López Silva's thesis is summarized in these ideas:

1. In the Third World the military has a strong tendency to participate in politics.

2. The Third World's armed forces are the only social organization that is cohesive, capable, and efficient enough to cope with the socioeconomic problems of underdeveloped countries (this is, of course, the same thesis put forth by Nelson Rockefeller in his 1969 report).

3. "Communism" is a real enemy, but "on innumerable occasions" the small groups of "oligarchs" that dominate a society have used the "specter of Communism" to pressure the military to intervene in politics, overthrow governments, and thus enable the oligarchs to recover their position as exploiters.

4. The chief cause of political unrest in Latin America is poverty. Poverty is produced by an unjust distribution of wealth. If wealth comes to be equitably distributed, "there will be no subversion in Latin America."

5. The United States has an obligation to prevent subversion in Latin America by aiding us with development programs.

6. The correct way to confront the threat of Communism is by achieving agrarian, banking, and industrial reforms that are just to both "the laborer and the industrialist."

7. Only the armed forces have shown themselves capable of effecting change in Third World societies without creating "social chaos."

8. In Latin America, the armed forces are the only cohesive organization that can keep these countries within "the Western bloc of nations."

9. The problem of economic development in each country has ceased to be one belonging solely to the politicians or certain civilian groups. It is basically a problem of "national sovereignty," which fundamentally relates to the country's armed forces. A weak country has a weak military apparatus. An economically strong country has strong armed forces. Thus, when politicians prove incompetent to develop a country's economy, the military is obligated to intervene to prevent the national sovereignty from being endangered.

10. "The Constitution and the laws" are not "unalterable social entities" but rather legislative guidelines that can change, adapt, or "destroy themselves," according to what is convenient for a nation's security and its internal and external sovereignty.

Based on these "ten commandments," the "eggheads" came out at the end of 1970 with the thesis that the economic, political, and social structure of Chile was in a profound state of crisis, from which it could save itself as "a Western nation" only if the armed forces as a "political and armed" organization were to take charge of leading the entire society. General Herman Brady Roche and Colonels Washington Carrasco and Mario Sepúlveda Squella, all leading figures in the SIM (Army intelligence) with training in U.S. military intelligence schools, were a species of "intellectual leaders" coming out of the "egghead" movement who presented a novel explanation of the Allende phenomenon to the rest of the generals and senior officers. This was discussed minutely throughout 1971 in the three branches of the Chilean armed forces.

This interpretation was: "Allende is not a threat to the kind of society which we, the armed forces, desire. On the contrary, Allende provides a certain security at this critical moment." And they argued thus: the new President of the Republic knows that he will remain in office only if he respects the Constitution. On the other hand, his political enemies, in the National party and the "Freista" wing of the Christian Democrats, would do everything possible to destroy the Constitution, since it had shown itself incapable of preventing the victory of a leftist coalition like Allende's. Now, then, what do we, the armed forces, need most right now? We need only one thing: *time.* Time to prepare, to train our officers for the moment we take over the whole society's machinery. This time is being given to us by President Allende, who will be careful not to step outside the bounds of the Constitution or to alienate us. He is going to let us take part in whatever aspect of government administration we want, and he will try to disarm the masses' attempt to organize, overtake the forces of order, and resort to "popular insurrection." He will thereby help to ripen conditions for the opportune moment, when the armed forces will enter the scene and establish "a new social order, without politicians, without class hatred," and "keep both the bosses and the workers on the leash."

The "eggheads" further told their incredulous colleagues that "we must get closer to Allende, fraternize with his politicians, attend his meetings." And they added: we have to show him that we are "Allendistas," and, desperate as he is owing to his lack of maneuverability in his plans for nationalization and expropriation, he will draw these military "Allendistas" into the administrative machinery. The military will be their real base of support against the assault of the *latifundistas* and "recalcitrant" oligarchs as well as against the assault of the masses who will keep trying to push them into a situation resembling that of the Bolsheviks in 1917. All this will leave us in a perfect position to intervene successfully when it becomes necessary. However, the essential thing is to *gain time,* and only Allende can give us this.

The "eggheads" won over most of the senior officers, thereby averting the threat of a military insurrection, when they clearly stated that "our fundamental enemy is Communism," "our basic task is to prevent Communism from taking over Chile on the crest of a popular insurrection." With Allende in the presidency, "Communism is still very far off." Yet the danger existed that afterward, much later, in the development of events, not even Allende would be able to avert the Communist threat. "At that time, we will have to intervene, not before."

During 1971–1973, Generals Herman Brady Roche, Orlando Urbina Herrera, Guillermo Pickering, Pedro Palacios Camerón, Rolando González Martins, and César Raúl Benavides and Colonels (afterward generals) Washington Carrasco, Mario Sepúlveda Squella, and Sergio Arellano Stark were considered to be "loyal men" by Salvador Allende and his closest collaborators—in the case of Herman Brady, even "Marxist."

(When Chancellor Clodomiro Almeyda, of the Socialist party, traveled to Havana on an official visit in July 1971, his small entourage included Colonel Washington Carrasco, who gained the sympathies of the chancellor and his political advisers as a "progressivist" who showed "promise" as a revolutionary. On September 11, 1973, Carrasco, by then a general, was chief of the Third Division stationed in the industrial city Concepción. In that area on the day of the coup, in a mere three hours, from 5 to 8 A.M., 250 industrial and agricultural union directors were liquidated.)

Through Senator Alberto Jérez of MAPU (Movimiento de Acción Popular Unitaria, Movement for United Popular Action) and later of the Christian Left (Izquierda Cristiana), a member of the Senate Defense Committee, and a sort of "coordinator" between Allende and the generals, the "egghead" officers managed to persuade Allende of the validity of the "economic frontiers" theory, which may be summarized as follows: The armed forces are the guarantors not merely of a country's physical boundaries but also of its "economic frontiers," that is, economic development, and for that very reason they must "uphold the executive power" with all of their "technical, organizational, and disciplinary capability" by acting in positions of the highest responsibility in the structure of the economy.

Already by November 4, 1971, in the National Stadium speech marking the first anniversary of his administration, President Allende was paying homage to the "loyalty and discipline of the armed forces and military police." At that time he unveiled their theory: "I underline the way they [the armed forces] have joined the process of defending our economic frontiers and their presence in steel, iron, copper, and the Nuclear Energy Commission. This establishes Chile as a nation to be envied by many countries of the world."

By this time, senior officers on active duty had been placed by Allende in 265 important jobs in the national economic structure, including the Production Development Corporation (CORFO—Corporación de Fomento de la Producción) and the Office of National Planning (Oficina de Planificación Nacional), the prime movers of economic development in Chile. Officers on active duty in the Air Force, Navy, and Army were members of the directorates of the nationalized copper mines at Chuquicamata, El Salvador, and El Teniente.

But the "eggheads" did not restrict themselves to advancing their strategy of "preparing themselves to govern at the opportune moment." They also added an "intelligence" component to their preparations: in key organizations of the country's economic administration, they secretly infiltrated dozens of Army, Air Force, and Navy intelligence officers posing as "civilians." The November 2, 1973, issue of the reactionary magazine *Qué Pasa* included an interview with the new vice-president of CORFO, Brigadier General Sergio Nuño Bawden (in 1971 appointed by Allende to manage the one-time Dupont explosives factory, a subsidiary of CORFO). General Nuño Bawden confided: "The whole of this complex field opportunely attracted the attention of SIM, and the Production Development Corporation received major attention. This resulted in some curious situations: the ex-secretary general of the corporation, when he gave himself up at the Defense Ministry after September 11, discovered that an office worker he had fired two years earlier was an Army official. Many office workers were surprised to see, after the Armed Forces Declaration, their ex-colleagues putting on uniforms."[23]

This military infiltration into the civilian sector took place not only in the economic structure of the state but also in the political realm. Officers were placed in each of the political parties comprising the Unidad Popular, in the Revolutionary Left Movement (Movimiento de Izquierda Revolucionaria), in the leftist journalists' organizations, among the reporters for the leftist newspaper and radio stations, and among the laborers', peasants', and office workers' unions.

Just as the "egghead" analysts had predicted in late 1970, the Unidad Popular government kept recruiting senior officers into the administration apparatus in what appeared to be a desperate race to keep the armed forces "neutralized."

By May 1973, when the military conspiracy was public knowledge, President Allende was still repeating the old maxims of 1971. On May 21, 1973, in his annual message to the Parliament, he read the following:

In a modern society as we conceive it, the armed forces ought to be completely integrated. I want to express the country's satisfaction at the armed forces' performance of their patriotic tasks, both theirs and that of the military and investigatory police.

In addition to playing their customary role, the armed forces joined the representatives of the popular parties and the workers' Central Única to form the Cabinet that ended the subversive work stoppage in October.

It has been the constant preoccupation of this administration to press forward and fulfill the three branches of the armed forces' plans for development, the better to guarantee the strict accomplishment of the specific tasks of national defense. To this end, during 1972, laws were passed to raise the Army's and Air Force's authorized manpower ceiling, and the Congress is currently considering a similar proposal for the Navy. To this should be added the economic support for the improvement and expansion of their infrastructures, as well as the renovation of military and logistic matériel.

This policy will be pursued to back up the development of the economy, because national security and economic development demand a harmonious union whose imbalance can only have negative consequences for the nation. For this reason the government *has placed special emphasis* on the armed forces' participation in socioeconomic programs. . . . The government will continue to promote this participation, which allows Chile to rely on human resources of *high moral and intellectual preparation.*

At the very moment Allende was making this statement, the Navy Infantry's high command in Valparaíso was training two civilian groups (Fatherland and Liberty, and the ex-Cadet Commandos) to perform acts of terrorism "to support" a "general stoppage of industrial activities" which was scheduled to be unchained "within the next sixty days." Also, in the Army's Academy of War in Santiago, Generals Sergio Arellano Stark, Javier Palacios Ruhman, César Raúl Benavides, Ernesto Baeza Michelsen, and Herman Brady Roche were discussing "a tentative general plan" to invade Santiago, break down the industrial cordons, paralyze the mobility of the Unidad Popular's union organizations, and attack and overcome the Government Palace. And in the Navy's General Staff, the chief of the First Naval District (Valparaíso), Vice-Admiral José Toribio Merino, was setting up his famous "three-thirds plan" to "execute some 3,000 responsible activists, imprison another 3,000, and exile 3,000 managers of all political persuasions" to "pacify the country" and reestablish order by forming a government of "the armed forces."

THE HARD-LINERS

However, the Academy of War and SIM "eggheads" who became the "intellectual leaders" of the armed forces' conduct during the Allende administration did not comprise the majority of senior officers. Their power rested less in their numbers than in their close contact with the Pentagon and their access to information being prepared under the aegis of the American University in Washington, which had various contacts with the Pentagon. Since late 1970 this contact had permitted the composition of a kind of aide-mémoire with respect to the main lines of the Unidad Popular government's program, which served to draw the different political views of the senior officers together around a "line of conduct," the nature of which has been sketched on the previous pages. The main points of the aide-mémoire were:

1. The armed forces consider it "correct" that the basic wealth of

the country should be in the hands of the Chilean State, because that strengthens the national economy and thereby the capability of the armed forces to equip themselves properly.

(This philosophy reached its apex in July 1972, when General Carlos Prats was charged by his corps of generals to tell Allende that "the administration of the nationalized copper companies ought to be mainly in the hands of military technicians, since it is a strategic industry," and that "a study ought to be made leading to autonomous financing of the armed forces out of profits from copper sales," which, in fact, meant that the Chilean military would become an entity on the fringes of Parliament for its own financing, a power within another power. Allende, at that time, found "the idea reasonable," but apparently did not have time to return to the topic before his overthrow.)

2. The Armed Forces support the nationalization of the copper mines, but at the same time they believe that "the North American companies who are exploiting them should be paid reasonable indemnities."

(Salvador Allende, on November 4, 1971, emphasized this in his first anniversary speech. The mines had been nationalized in July of that year, and "military pressure" for "compensation to Anaconda and Kennecott" was very strong. Allende said: "Here are four numbers the people should remember. These companies invested the sum of $30 million. In fifty years, they have taken out $4.5 billion. If the Special Court does not decide against it, two companies will be compensated, and if the Special Court does not decide otherwise, we will not compensate Anaconda, or Kennecott, or El Salvador, but the debts of those companies are $736 million and it is logically foreseeable that we will have to assume those debts. Thus, *we will be paying an indirect indemnity* of $736 million to the copper companies who over a period of fifty years took out $4.5 billion." This argument served to lower military pressure on the subject. It had, in any case, forced Chile's foreign debt upward, in one stroke, from over $3 billion to over $4 billion, and made the Chilean economy even more dependent on North American, and even European, foreign aid.)

3. The armed forces believe in the need for an agrarian reform to permit the capitalistic development of rural areas and liquidate part of the *latifundistas'* power over Chilean society. This reform will serve to support the industrialization of the country, as a new market and as a producer of industrial raw material.

(This thesis, cribbed from the Alliance for Progress created by the assassinated John F. Kennedy, had already provoked the ire of the *latifundistas* against Eduardo Frei's agricultural policy and was producing an angry new campaign by their organizations against the Chilean generals, whom they called "chickens" for allowing Allende to run the country.)

4. The armed forces believe it to be "just" that the credit institutions (banks) should be controlled by or be in the hands of the Chilean state, to better "regulate" the "democratic national growth" of the country, which historically had been obstructed by the personal interests of some powerful groups in the private oligopolies. The latter's "recalcitrant" attitude is a threat to "the stability of the entire economic and social structure" of Chilean society.

5. The armed forces believe that the U.S. banking, industrial, and commercial cartels ("the most advanced and efficient in the world") *should participate,* under a "clear and exact regulation that protects our national sovereignty," in the industrial development of Chile, because "without the capital and technology of the United States, *we will not be able to become a developed country.* "

(In May 1971, at the Lima meeting of the board of governors of the Interamerican Development Bank, the Chilean Treasury Minister, Américo Zorrilla, a member of the Political Commission of the Chilean Communist party, stated the same thesis: "In the picture of the Chilean revolutionary process, external financing as well as investment of foreign capital plays a role . . . oriented toward the priorities indicated by the necessities of our economy. . . .")

The Chilean military thesis as well as the then Treasury Minister's had a kinship with Nelson Rockefeller's 1969 Latin-American report: "The time has arrived for the United States to move consciously from a paternalistic role to one of partnership" with the Latin Americans, in which "foreign private investment can provide essential technical knowledge and capital."[24]

6. The armed forces believe that all change must take place within "our institutional system, in consideration of the democratic way of government and in solidarity with the Western bloc of nations."

From these points put forth by the "eggheads" (whom we shall henceforth refer to as the "reformist generals," to distinguish them from other groups of generals whom we will define shortly), the senior officers derived a consistent criterion to deal with the Unidad Popular phenomenon. On these same points, President Allende and part of the Unidad Popular leadership made a kind of entente cordiale with the armed forces, and the latter in turn influenced the Christian Democratic and National parties' leadership. Even the private oligopolistic associations such as the Society for Industrial Development (SOFOFA—Sociedad de Fomento Fabril) and the National Agriculture Society (Sociedad Nacional de Agricultura) accepted the criterion of "wait and see" proposed by the "reformist" generals and the Pentagon, under the general slogan "Allende can help us put out the fire."

An incident in August 1971 shows how the Unidad Popular government, its program reduced to what the military and the U.S. Pentagon wanted, had the conditional support even of its political enemies. Eximbank, a U.S. government agency, bowing to pressure from Anaconda and Kennecott, refused a credit of $21 million to Chile for the purchase of Boeing passenger planes for the National Airline (LAN—Línea Aérea Nacional), in order to "pressure for indemnification for the copper industry."

The reactionary *El Mercurio* commented on August 17: "This North American political maneuver endangers inter-American relations and constitutes a repetition of old, historical errors."

The National party, which promoted the interests of the agricultural, industrial, and commercial oligopolies of Chile, had released a declaration of irate protest the day before: "Attitudes and statements such as the ones we refer to serve only to obstruct international relations and to impede the solution of our problems. . . . They show a lamentable lack of judgment and an ignorance of the Chilean reality."

But it was *La Prensa,* the daily newspaper of the Christian Democrats, directed by Eduardo Frei's group, which most clearly defined the problem, in an editorial on August 16, 1971:

> The apparently responsible decision of Eximbank's president has all the crudeness of a provocation. . . . The American government appears once again, and prematurely, to have identified with private interests, forgetting a superior political interest. . . . In our country's government, for the moment at least, two tendencies coexist. One sector wishes to conduct the Chilean revolution inside the boundaries of the Constitution, without violence on the internal plane and without creating an international crisis. Another sector wishes to provoke a violent rupture which, necessarily, will project itself onto the international plane. It is these people who demand or announce unilaterally that the expropriated industries should not be indemnified. . . . Eximbank has begun to play up to this viewpoint, which wants nothing more than to provoke just such reactions. . . . On few occasions, if any, *has a nationalization in Latin America operated with more legality*—and even constitutionality— *or with more guarantees for the North American enterprises affected.*

The political representatives of Chile's agricultural oligopoly (already decaying after Frei instituted agrarian reform in 1967) and the commercial, financial, and industrial oligopolies knew whereof they spoke when they reproached the Nixon administration in August 1971 for having let itself be influenced by Anaconda and Kennecott lobbying. Even the industrial oligopoly's association, the Society for Industrial Development, on the same day, August 16, addressed an irate letter to the president of Eximbank in which they explained that "Chile is living through a process of profound economic and social transformation that is radically affecting our economic structure and, as a consequence, the situation of our industrialists. Therefore, our institution of trade guilds—the oldest in the Americas—finds itself pledged to *minimizing the economic cost of the transformations we are experiencing* and to fully guaranteeing that the economy develop within a framework of freedom and democracy and with full respect for the fundamental guarantees. . . ." For this reason, in the face of Eximbank's refusal of credit, "as private industrialists and above all out of respect for our noble democratic tradition, we cannot accept their subjection to resolutions of this nature, conditioning them to decisions which our government might adopt in the lawful regime which has democratically been installed in our country." The Society for Industrial Development went on to urge Eximbank to reverse the deferral of the loan to LAN-Chile.

STRENGTH AND WEAKNESS

When the Pentagon decided in October 1970 to wait and see if Allende could be managed within reasonable limits as a "fireman for the people's fire," the "reformist" generals were agreeable. Consulting with the Chilean industrial and commercial sectors, they estimated that if the experiment was not suffocated from without, it could succeed and "the structures' reform into a sturdier state capitalism" could "calm the popular insurrection."

Allende's administration had initiated a policy of "economic reactivation" for 1971 which was basically founded on utilizing the entire installed productive capacity and on expanding internal demand by means of substantial upward adjustments in wages and salaries, and the institution of price controls which, in reality, turned out to affect the oligopolies less than it did the medium- and small-sized businesses. This economic reactivation had the effect of achieving an 8.3 percent index of economic growth in 1971, a record gain. But that was the peak. If there was not an immediate influx of capital, the system would crumble, causing popular pressure to exceed the Chilean oligopolists' idea of "reasonable limits."

On another front, the "reformist" generals' pressure on Allende had managed to whittle down to a splinter the main plank of the Unidad Popular's platform, which was the reassignment of all the oligopolies in private Chilean or foreign (chiefly North American) hands. In order to actually expropriate the oligopolies, out of a total of slightly more than 35,000 industrial and distributional establishments in the country, about 266 businesses had to be transferred over to the state, to the Area of Social Property. Allende had promised to transfer only 90 of these. This left more than 50 percent of oligopolistic capital in oligarchic and North American hands. And of the 90 transferred only 53 would be totally controlled by the state; the remaining 37 would be in the so-called mixed area, in association with the same oligopolistic companies in private American and Chilean hands.

Allende had agreed to undertake this "expropriation" within the confines of "the Constitution and the laws." This made the cost of forming the Area of Social Property gigantic and transferred enormous quantities of capital to the "expropriated" owners, permitting them to maintain substantial economic and strategic power. Even for August 1971 the numbers were eloquent: they were promised a total of 10,846 million escudos for that year, the equivalent of $890 million. This was the breakdown:

Purchase of shares to nationalize commercial banks	400 million escudos
Cash payment for the expropriation of large estates	320 million escudos
Purchase of industrial oligopolies	600 million escudos
Purchase of three foreign banks	120 million escudos
Purchase of U.S. iron, saltpeter, and industrial consortia	576 million escudos
"Indirect" indemnification to Anaconda and Kennecott	8,830 million escudos

Clearly, this created a potential weakness in the government's economic plan which, in August 1971, made the Chilean oligopolists confident that they could handle the "situation" and keep Allende within "reformist change" so as to "avoid revolution." Obviously, it was important not to asphyxiate the Chilean economy, almost completely dependent on American capital, in order to achieve a "relative economic level" that would discourage the laborers, peasants, and office workers from "moving ahead in the process of transformation." But the Pentagon had been unable to convince Nixon's economic advisers to maintain "a prudent and open attitude with respect to Allende." Instead, Kennecott and Anaconda were manipulating Nixon.

At that moment, doubts began to spring up in the heart of the military high command. It had been only two months since enormous popular pressure had obliged the reactionary majority in Parliament to pledge itself to the leftist minority and unanimously approve the nationalization of the North American copper mining companies. This had not had the effect of dissipating the feeling of "anti-imperialism at the grass roots." On the contrary, it was growing every day.

A group primarily of Army generals, led by Oscar Bonilla (former aide to President Frei and closely linked politically to the Frei faction in the Christian Democratic party); Manuel Torres de la Cruz, ultra-Catholic and a sort of "father" to Chilean fascism, chief of the Fifth Division in the extreme South; Hernán Hiriart, chief of the Cavalry Division centered in Valdivia, in the South; Ervaldo Rodríguez Lasa, chief of the Third Division, centered in Concepción; Alfredo Canales Márquez; and Ernesto Baeza Michelsen began to voice opposition to the "reformist" generals' philosophy of "wait and see."

This group came to be called the "hard-liners." They contended that the "reformists" were wrong about being able to manipulate Salvador Allende, who would go "wherever the masses dragged him." In their estimation, the main task of the Army and the rest of the armed forces was to persuade the Pentagon that Allende had to be overthrown "to reinstate a democratic government like Eduardo Frei's."

Manuel Torres de la Cruz, for example, believed that Allende would not be able to restrain the destructive wishes of the Marxist elements and would do everything possible to gain time to put himself in a position to turn the country inside out.

The "hard-liners" were believed to have advocated reactivating a "plan of action" resembling that of September–October 1970. The idea was to appoint a transitional military junta, headed by Torres de la Cruz, and after a six-month period hold new presidential elections, with Eduardo Frei as the candidate of the forces of order. During the second half of 1971 and the first eight months of 1972, the "hard-line" thesis did not carry much weight with the Army, even though it had the sympathy of the commander in chief of the Air Force, César Ruiz Danyau, and his generals Gustavo Leigh, César Berdichewsky, and Carlos Van Schowen, as well as the chief of the First Naval District (Valparaíso), Vice-Admiral José Toribio Merino, and his colleagues Pablo Weber and Horacio Justiniano (the three of them being in close contact with the U.S. Navy). Justiniano, meanwhile, performed his role of "Allendista" perfectly, in Salvador Allende's eyes "a progressive man," "an admirer of the Soviet Union" and "of unimpeachable loyalty."

This group of "hard-line" generals had an advantage their "reformist" colleagues lacked: close contact with political figures, Frei in the Christian Democrat party, as well as Patricio Phillips, Pedro Ibáñez, and Francisco Bulnes in the National party.

THE CONSTITUTIONALISTS

The political struggle within the armed forces was kept balanced and marginal by a group of generals led by the Army's commander in chief, Carlos Prats González. Its best-known figures were the chief of the First Division stationed in Antofagasta, Joaquín Lagos Osorio; the chief of the General Staff, Augusto Pinochet Ugarte; General Héctor Bravo Muñoz; and Generals Javier Palacios Ruhman and Carlos Araya.

Carlos Prats was the spokesman for the "constitutionalists," whose general line was: "We will support Allende so that Allende will support us." "We will get Allende to transform our armed forces into an institution of unsurpassable preparation, having a high economic status and effective participation in government." Carlos Prats's thesis was: "We should work to form an Allende–armed forces government" based on the following division of labor: Allende would control the masses of workers, and the armed forces would control the country so that it would prosper. The armed forces must help Allende strike out at "the extremists of the right as well as those of the left."

Carlos Prats's thesis, until October 1972, or more certainly until March 1973, had the widest acceptance among the senior, middle-level, and junior officers in the Army and among the middle-level and junior officers in the Air Force and the Navy. In the corps of military police, Director General José María Sepúlveda Galindo was an enthusiastic partisan of Prats's thesis.

Precisely because of Prats's moderation, and because he allowed the "wait and see" strategy to continue, the "reformist" generals in the Academy of War, who were in close contact with the Pentagon, were Prats's faithful allies until 1973 when the "stampede" of laborers', peasants', and office workers' organizations endangered the whole system. Until then, the Army commander in chief was leading a group of senior officers toward the goal of an Allende–armed forces government, with Christian Democratic participation but excluding the "extremist" groups of the Communist and Socialist parties. This was the "constitutionalist" line.

The "reformist" generals, whose goal was to prepare themselves to rule the country and form a purely military government, or one including Allende but not the Unidad Popular parties, agreed with the "constitutionalists" that if the time came for them to take power, they could not destroy all previous changes in the economic structure and they should continue to develop state capitalism.

These debates went on from November 4, 1970, all during 1971, and ended in November–December 1972, when the thinking in the heart of the high command began to take a very different direction.

3   The Bosses Conspire and the Workers Mobilize

Last October's work stoppage was the major obstacle put in our country's path to prevent the workers from consolidating and advancing. Its immediate effect was a loss of more than $200 million.
SALVADOR ALLENDE, Third Presidential Message to Parliament, May 21, 1973

On August 15, 1971, the Santiago daily *La Nación* carried an interview with a laborer employed in the textile factory Yarur S.A. (the heart of the Yarur group oligopoly, which included the Credit and Investment Bank [Banco Crédito e Inversiones], chemical, textile, and food industries, distribution and financial companies; Chase Manhattan Bank held a substantial portion of Yarur stock). The factory had been requisitioned by the government for the Area of Social Property. Fulfilling the "annual goal" for the Area meant expropriation of copper, iron, and saltpeter companies, private banks, and textile and cement factories, in addition to some distribution companies. The controller general of the Republic, under pressure from the Yarur group and Chase Manhattan Bank, had declared the expropriation "illegal."

The Yarur S.A. laborer had this to say: "We don't care whether the requisition is legal or not. We will not give the factory back. Neither the controller nor the Supreme Court can make us. We workers know what we are doing, and we refuse to continue being exploited. What the courts say is one thing, and what we are going to do, quite another. . . . The Unidad Popular government has given us the opportunity of making decisions in our factory. Our aim is to keep moving forward, even if we have to bypass the law."

This statement reflected a very definite popular state of mind.

In the first week of September, the president of the Society for Industrial Development, Orlando Sáenz (commercial engineer, age forty, a business manager in the metallurgical industry), read aloud at a directors' meeting an alarming report from the military police statistical services that showed how the workers and peasants were sweeping away law and order by occupying agricultural and industrial property to reinforce their demands for better salaries and living conditions, and, in some cases, attempting to force the government to expropriate monopolies whose owners had received verbal nonexpropriation agreements.

As a frame of reference, the report noted that in 1969, the workers took over 118 farms; in 1970, the last year of Frei's administration, the figure climbed to 365; but now, in the first eight months of 1971, the farmers had taken over 990 farms—four takeovers a day!

The same thing was happening in industry. In 1969 there had been 23 workers' takeovers; in 1970, 133; and in the first eight months of 1971, the takeovers had extended to 531 businesses—an average of more than two a day.

For Orlando Sáenz and his colleagues, this report indicated that "social chaos could not be avoided" by attempting to influence Allende's economic and social policies. Sáenz said, "Our interests are threatened, and we are the heart of the national economy, which means that the interests of Chile are in danger."

The situation was very disturbing for the select group of industrial, commercial, and financial oligopolists. (These people totaled no more than 1,000 and owned more than 60 percent of the national productive apparatus.) Under the influence of certain generals, they had agreed to "sacrifice" some of their economic power to "save the system." But events during the first eleven months of Allende's government showed that while the President was trying to fulfill the agreement he had made in October 1970 to maintain limits to his program of change, the people's organizations were transgressing those limits (for one thing, they didn't know about Allende's compromise) and were pressing for the completion of the entire program, which was the "expropriation of the economic power of North American imperialism and the national oligopolies."

For the Society for Industrial Development, "the time had come to cut this situation short." Orlando Sáenz got in touch with Benjamín Matte, president of the National Agriculture Society (the *latifundistas'* trade guild), and with Jorge Fontaine, president of the National Confederation of Production and Commerce (Fontaine belonged to the *El Mercurio* oligarchic clan). They were all agreed, along with their respective directorates, that they had "to back Allende into a corner," beginning with a massive publicity campaign to turn popular support away from the government, and afterward overthrow him constitutionally.

To set this antigovernment offensive into motion, Sáenz and his economic advisers were able to rely on an economic fact that gave them tremendous maneuverability. The Unidad Popular government had been able to reduce inflation (from 1970's 32.5 percent to 1971's 20.1 percent) thanks to its "economic reactivation" policy, which consisted of price controls, mobilization of the entire national productive apparatus to full capacity, raising low wages and salaries to levels higher than the inflation index, and keeping high wages at levels equal to the inflation index. However, this economic reactivation contained one serious danger, owing to Chile's oligopolistic, dependent economy. Once it reached the limits of expansion, if a parallel accrual of large capital did not take place, a shortage of products (created by excess demand) and a resulting rise in black market prices could return control of wages and salaries to the oligarchy, in whose hands it had traditionally been.

At the same time, the price freeze, being based on the costs of the large oligopolistic manufacturers whose production was much larger, also left them a "reasonable profit margin," though it affected severely the small and medium-sized businesses, whose unit costs were much higher owing to smaller production.

The only way out of this economic deadlock, from the Unidad Popular's point of view, was to set up a strong Area of Social Property by transferring private oligopolies to the state, thereby changing the entire system's productive structure (thus avoiding a shortage) and setting prices at the level of the production costs in small and medium-sized businesses. The "surplus" profit received by the oligopolies, which would no longer be in private hands, could be then plowed back into the economy in the form of capital growth and social services, improving the conditions of the lowest strata in the population.

But the potential size of the Area of Social Property had been limited from the start by Allende's compromise. At the same time, private businesses had restricted their capital growth (1971 would end with an 11 percent decline in private reinvestment). On another front, the price freeze had pushed many small and medium-sized businesses to the verge of bankruptcy. Already in September the effects of a shortage were beginning to be felt throughout the system, and a black market was beginning to emerge.

The Society for Industrial Development team now initiated various plans to destroy the Allende government's popular platform.

Point One: Use any means to prevent the formation of an Area of Social Property larger than the limit, keeping it innocuous as a force in the national economy. Eduardo Frei was recruited to arrange for the presentation to Parliament of a constitutional amendment ensuring this "legal freeze" (the parties influenced by the oligarchy and the American multinationals controlled the majority vote). The job was assigned to a Christian Democratic Senator, Juan Hamilton, and his colleague Renán Fuentealba.

Point Two: Attract the support of the medium-sized and small businessmen (104,000 retailers, 34,000 industrialists, and 150,000 families in agriculture), with such slogans as "better prices for your products," assurances against "expropriations" (something none of these people had to fear), and "commercialization" without state control. All this would doubly benefit the private oligopolies.

Point Three: Fight against any sort of people's organizations that support state price controls (supply and price juntas), production control (committees to oversee production and so on), or control of reactionary conspiratorial activities (committees of popular unity, which had been disbanded by the Unidad Popular parties as a concession to the reactionaries in September–October 1970), and describe them as "organizations of Marxist dictatorship" whose goal was to "strangle democracy."

Point Four: Turn private investment and speculative capital toward the black market (in 1972–1973 more than $100 million was put into this by the oligopolists) in order to unleash runaway inflation, resulting in economic chaos and government loss of popular support.

Point Five: Set up an intensive propaganda campaign to prove that the breakdown of the economy was caused by "the failure of Socialism," hiding the central factors of shortage of investment capital, government agencies' inability to plan, and lack of control of the apparatus of the bourgeois state itself to resolve the crisis "in favor of the groups with the least resources" instead of "favoring the Chilean and foreign private oligopolies."

Point Six: In a period of six to eight months (beginning in October 1971), effect the deterioration of mass support for the government, and then demand a plebiscite. Allende would, of course, lose; he would then either step down or yield to the economic requests of the Society for Industrial Development, the National Agriculture Society, and the National Confederation of Production and Commerce.

To help implement those six points, they could rely on the intact economic and political power of the oligarchy (less than one-fourth of their businesses had passed into the hands of the state, and for these they had been paid); on a majority in the Parliament; on complete influence over the Judiciary and the controller general of the Republic; on newspapers that accounted for more than 80 percent of the country's daily circulation; on radio stations that reached more than 50 percent of the country's listeners; and last, they could rely on the most important thing: the armed forces' "neutrality."

The "reformist" generals, via Orlando Urbina Herrera and Washington Carrasco, had let Sáenz and his associates know that "if you want to change presidents according to the Constitution, by a plebiscite, we won't get in your way." The "constitutionalist" generals, via Augusto Pinochet, had let the same be known. The "hard-liners" supported the plan because it fell right in with what they had been scheming since September 1970.

Nevertheless, the "reformist" generals insisted that an "error of judgment" existed in their agreement with the Society for Industrial Development. In their estimation the time had not yet come to "get nervous"; Allende's ability to "calm the workers and make them see reason" was not yet exhausted.

The National party leaders, headed by Onofre Jarpa, and Senators Pedro Ibáñez and Francisco Bulnes, as well as Deputies Patricio Phillips and Fernando Maturana; the Frei faction of the Christian Democratic leadership, chiefly the former defense minister, Juan de Dios Carmona, Senators Juan Hamilton and Patricio Aylwin, and Yarur group employee Felipe Amunátegui Stewart were commissioned by the Society for Industrial Development, the National Agriculture Society, and the National Confederation of Production and Commerce to set the propaganda campaign in motion.

On October 1, 1971, the Society for Industrial Development opened fire by distributing a "balance sheet" on the Unidad Popular's record: the government's prestige had been adversely affected and its political judgment called into question; important industrial groups were being harassed and their rights abrogated; public opinion was disconcerted and confused; and, worst of all, none of the desired objectives had been achieved.

THE EMPTY POTS

The preliminary statistics of November 1971 showed that consumption of poultry, pork, sugar, and potatoes had increased by 16, 18, 37, and 55 percent respectively. On the other hand, the productive apparatus had reached its limit. A market shortage of those products was affecting large numbers of office workers, medium-sized and small businessmen, and their families who were not eligible for the direct supply line through unions and union federations.

In Santiago especially, the lines of people going once a week or every fifteen days to buy poultry or sugar were enormous, and a black market was springing up.

On November 4, celebrating his first year of government, President Allende spoke to a capacity audience of 80,000 in the National Stadium. He did not omit mention of the shortages: "There has been a temporary shortage of some products, owing to the increased buying power of the masses, owing to the tendency of certain sectors to buy more than they need. If they need three or five kilos of meat, and they find some, they buy ten or twelve kilos and store it in their freezers. There is psychological pressure for people to buy more than they need. We also ought to point out that there is speculation going on in several districts. . . . In the case of meat, for example, at the beginning of this administration more than 200,000 head of cattle left Chile" (shipped out by *latifundistas* to provoke economic chaos on a large scale).

The "psychological pressure" was coming from the mass media owned by the private oligopolies and their political parties. They had inaugurated a daily news campaign designed to create a buyers' panic in the population.

In the same speech, Allende tried to calm hundreds of thousands of farmers, laborers, and office workers who were helplessly watching the private oligopolies continue to run the economy, creating a black market and cornering large hoards of staple products. The workers themselves had finally resorted to taking over businesses caught stockpiling and demanding their expropriation. They also occupied the estates of *latifundistas* used as training camps for fascist groups with military advisers from Navy Infantry, the Air Force, and the Army's Paratrooper and Special Forces Schools. Allende termed these "indiscriminate takeovers" and labeled them "leftist extremism." He said: "This is why we will not accept this pressure. We have said this with the honesty of revolutionaries. We are against all indiscriminate takeovers of rural properties, as these create anarchy in our production capacity and will end in setting one peasant against another, or all peasants against small farmers. . . . We are against the takeover of living quarters, which hurts the workers who saved their money to buy them. We are against workers' takeovers of small and medium-sized factories. Expropriation and the requisitioning of businesses must follow a government plan and not the anarchy of the willful impulse of a few."

It is interesting to note how, in three years of government, neither Salvador Allende nor the leadership in the Communist and Socialist parties ever agreed to mobilize the masses fighting against the Chilean oligopolies and North American multinationals. As far as they could, they always sidestepped the workers' demands. The workers, with an instinctive political wisdom, kept pressuring Allende and the Unidad Popular to expropriate the oligopolies in one fell swoop. This, they felt, was essential if the government's economic plan to change the country's productive structure was to succeed. In 1971 this expropriation was still possible, even if concessions had to be made at the same time in "long negotiations to gain time" with Anaconda and Kennecott. But Allende allowed this opportunity to pass in his zeal to "keep the armed forces quiet," even though he knew that their solidarity at that point was very delicate and that they would be in no position to attempt a coup with any hope of success. Probably if the masses had been able to mobilize in a more spirited and organized way instead of in the loose and halfhearted way they did, the "front of anti-imperialist and anti-oligopolist struggle" would have taken on a very different dimension.

Those on the side of the imperialists and oligopolists, however, were very well organized indeed.

Throughout November 1971, the Christian Democratic and National party leaderships were promoting a public demonstration to express "the people's protest against the hunger afflicting our homes." On the afternoon of December 2, Santiago's hillside suburb, where 90 percent of the people with the highest incomes in Chile live, unleashed a parade of 50,000 women flanked by young commandos from the

Christian Democratic and National parties and the nascent fascist group Fatherland and Liberty. The overwhelming majority of these women were well-to-do—wives of high-salaried employees, managers, senior executives, and industrialists. As symbol of their protest, each carried an empty pot and a ladle. By banging the two together, they created a deafening, terrifying noise. Descending toward the center of Santiago, the women provoked a confrontation with the military police as they tried to surround La Moneda. For two or three hours, until night fell, downtown Santiago was the scene of a pitched battle between military police and the women demonstrators.

These were the well-dressed, attractive, refined women whom one had always seen at theater and movie galas, or in elegant restaurants, neatly wiping their lips on napkins before sipping vintage wine. That day, raging in the streets, they were screaming obscenities against Allende, such as "Allende maricón, ya no sirves ni para el colchón" (Allende you faggot, you're not even good in bed anymore). I saw several attack boys who shouted "Viva Allende," striking them with pots and ladles. In one case, two women trapped a boy of about fifteen, held him down on the ground, ripped his pants at the waist, and began to strike at his genitals, while another was screaming, "Castrate the sonofabitch!" and trying to pull the boy's genitals out of his pants. Only the arrival of a military police patrol saved the boy.

The Empty Pots March forced Allende to declare the city of Santiago an emergency zone, and it remained under martial law for several days. This demonstration concluded the first phase of the campaign to overthrow Allende using "legal means."

This event, which occurred almost simultaneously with Fidel Castro's visit to Chile, prompted the Cuban leader to assert that the March of the Empty Pots signaled the beginning of the confrontation between the mass of the Chilean people and the oligarchy and imperialism. His words, not taken very seriously at the time even by leftist politicians, were to prove grimly prophetic as the months went by.

THE AREA OF SOCIAL PROPERTY

On February 9, 1972, the Christian Democratic and National party majority in Parliament carried out the orders given by the Society for Industrial Development a little over four months earlier: they approved a constitutional amendment to "fix norms for the Area of Social Property." The amendment's authors had been Senators Juan Hamilton and Renán Fuentealba. (Juan Hamilton was a lawyer for the construction industry magnates Soza Cousiño and the Klein iron oligopolists, who, although they were Chilean, kept all their capital in Switzerland and Canada. The Kleins were highly favored by the Frei regime. They financed a chain of luxury hotels on the Spanish Costa Brava in order to help the economic endeavors of the Christian Democrats.)

Hamilton and Fuentealba's "constitutional amendment" was a veritable time bomb: President Allende was obliged to promulgate it, since not to do so would break the letter of the Constitution politic, something his opponents were hoping would happen so they could dismiss him from office. On the other hand, Allende could hardly promulgate it, because it made a mockery of the Area of Social Property, vitiating it as an implement for activating and controlling the national productive apparatus. A summary of this constitutional amendment is contained in these points:

1. "For the purposes of administration" and for "technical reasons," it permitted restoring the nationalized copper companies to Anaconda or Kennecott. That is, it permitted reversing nationalization.

2. It left as "conclusively an area of private property" such enormous oligopolies as Paper and Box Manufacturers, the main business of the Matte-Alessandri group. (In Chile, there were eleven oligarchic clans who owned the largest and best part of the national economy, in close association with American principals.)[1]

3. It exempted from expropriation "petroleum and petroleum by-

products distribution," which meant free trade for Esso Standard Oil, and the English and Dutch company Shell Oil, which monopolized that market in Chile, in association with industrial groups such as COPEC (Compañia Petrolera Chilena, belonging to the family of the National party Senator Francisco Bulnes Sanfuentes, another of the eleven oligarchic clans).

4. It outlawed all transfers of private oligopolies to the state property prior to October 20, 1971. This left the Area of Social Property reduced to practically zero, pending parliamentary approval of those transfers, in "case by case" discussions.

5. It obligated the government to submit for Parliament's approval every new case of a business to be expropriated. Since reactionary elements controlled the majority vote in Parliament, it was easy to predict that the Area of Social Property would never grow, unless the government won a majority in Parliament in the March 1973 congressional elections, when half the Senate seats and all the Deputies' seats would be open.

This impudent defense of North American and Chilean monopolistic interests was the Parliament majority's way of backing Allende's government into a corner: if he approved the amendment's promulgation, he took the bottom out of his economic scheme; if he refused to, he was going outside the Constitution. This was phase 2 in the campaign initiated by the Society for Industrial Development.

A MINISTER GENERAL

During all of February, March, and the first week in April, the campaign unleashed by the Christian Democrats and the National party "to defend consumers against shortages and price hikes, the black market, and Unidad Popular sectarianism" reached fever pitch. It had taken effect in many sectors, and in elections for new leaders in employee unions, Unidad Popular candidates had been defeated by Christian Democrats and even National party candidates. Senator Luis Bossay Leiva, founder of the Radical Left party, abandoned the government coalition and took his party over to the opposition, stating that "we cannot act as accomplices to a process that has to go outside the bounds of the Constitution and will not solve the problems of the masses." Luis Bossay Leiva and other leading members of the Radical Left party had received support from the oligarchy to "form their party," a splinter of the Radical party. Their activities and their connections with the oligarchy were denounced in the Chilean daily, *Última Hora*.

On April 6, Allende responded with a master stroke. He reorganized his Cabinet, with the surprise appointment of a brigadier general on active duty, Pedro Palacios Camerón, as Minister of Mines. Allende meant this gesture to show his opponents how he was going to deal with "civil resistance," and that he had the armed forces "in the palm of his hand"—and as happens in all societies where one class dominates another, whichever holds the armed forces is the dominant class. Except that the armed forces were really held by the bourgeoisie, while the Allende government was meant to represent the proletariat. How were the armed forces of one class meant to support the pretended rule of the other class?

When Allende first broached to General Carlos Prats González the idea of the need for a military man in his new Cabinet, Prats said he would take it up with his corps of generals. The "reformists" were agreed with the "constitutionalists" that it was a good idea to accept this offer for a short time, so that "one of us can get some on-the-job training." General Palacios was appointed to Mines, exactly the area that most interested the "reformist" generals. They wanted to learn all about the organization, administration, and performance of the nationalized copper industry.

However, the generals' discussion of whether to accept this offer was not as simple and unproblematic as it seems in the telling. Less than thirty days earlier, two of the "hard-liners" had committed the blunder of attempting a coup without informing the General Staff. The Unidad Popular's intelligence services in the civilian police had found out about it, and the high command, headed by Prats, had no choice except to take disciplinary action against the conspirators.

At Temuco in March, Colonel Julio Canessa Roberts had been caught putting together an attempt to sabotage farm production with the connivance of the local *latifundistas*. He hoped to present Allende with the *fait accompli* of having quartered his own regiment in Temuco as well as some regiments from Valdivia and Osorno, so as to force the President to "respect the Constitution." Canessa was a patron of the local branch of the fascist group Fatherland and Liberty, whom he was providing with paramilitary training and arms for target practice, while at the same time he protected the smuggling of .22-caliber automatic weapons from Argentina for the arsenals of Fatherland and Liberty and the National party's Rolando Matus Commandos.

The civilian police denounced these activities to President Allende. Allende denounced them to Prats. The generals decided to defuse Canessa by transferring him to the Junior Officers' School in Santiago.

The generals were aware that Canessa was part of a much larger team formed by Brigadier General Hernán Hiriart, chief of the Cavalry Division in Valdivia, and Brigadier General Alfredo Canales Márquez, of the generals corps in the Santiago garrison. All of them were "hard-liners" who wanted a coup "here and now," followed by a military junta of government for six months and a turnover to a "new President chosen in democratic elections." Of course none of this was communicated to Allende.

In early April, when the question of including a military man in Allende's government came up, the "hard-liners" were against it because "it would mean that we are supporting a Marxist." Prats and the "reformists" managed to convince them that the Allende government was not strictly Marxist, and that the armed forces were still in a position to withdraw their minister whenever it suited them, to show "public and outspoken repudiation" of Allende's policies.

In his annual speech to the workers on May 1, 1972, President Allende warned the people that a struggle was going on behind the scenes. Referring to the Hamilton-Fuentealba constitutional amendment, he defined it as an attempt "to annul the victories achieved in the Social Area in the economy" and that "behind that attitude lurks the threat of dismissing . . . the President of the Republic. This does not disturb me personally. It concerns me because it is my obligation to defend the Constitution."

He added: "What makes me uneasy is that the bases of the Chilean Constitution are being undermined. They want to change the game; they want to plunge this country into a very difficult and intense struggle." He continued by defining his "obligations" as President, the order of which perturbed his listeners:

"It is my obligation—and I intend to fulfill it—to defend the precepts of the Constitution.

"It is my obligation to avoid confrontation.

"It is my obligation to reject all physical, economic, and social violence.

"It is my obligation to prevent a bloodbath in Chile.

"It is my obligation to defend the victories of the workers and the Chilean revolution."

For the workers listening to Allende, his vow to defend the Constitution hampered them daily in their efforts to expand their growing organization and to stop sabotage, black-market speculation, and the daily abuses that the oligopolists carried out through their fascist bands trained by armed forces personnel against the entire country's economic apparatus. And the judges, the military police, the Parliament, the letter of the law, and "constitutional precepts" all served to protect the saboteurs and obstruct the task of guarding and increasing the workers' productivity.

TO ADVANCE OR NOT TO ADVANCE

While on the one hand Allende was urging the workers to organize into supply and price juntas, peasants communal councils, production committees, committees to oversee production, and so on, to "defend the revolution," on the other hand the workers could see only too clearly how, through control of their organizations via the political leadership of the Unidad Popular, these organizations were being forced to paralyze the masses' mobilization. The workers were being prevented from preparing for the real confrontation that they could see coming: the people against the armed forces of the bourgeoisie and the imperialists.

At the heart of the government, an intense discussion was going on about this. The Minister of Economics, Pedro Vuskovic (an independent leftist, and a member of the Socialist party as of 1973) stated, as he would later write in a document published by *Revista de la Universidad Técnica del Estado* (State Technical University Review) that the essence of the difficulties lay

in everything meant by the class character of the bourgeois state, into whose still-prevailing boundaries the new achievements have been channeled. Its whole structure, including the judicial framework and even the administrative apparatus, has been shaped to attend to the interests of capitalism and dependency, to preserve the oligopolies' control, to exclude any means of access or worker participation. New demands conflict with this, and a large part of the workers' efforts falls on barren ground, sharpening a contradiction that *will be resolved only when this bourgeois state has been replaced by a state with a different character, a people's state.* Manifestations in that direction can be seen in the participation of workers in the management of industries in the Social Area, in their decisive presence on the administrative councils and other mechanisms; in the recently initiated forms of extending this presence to different levels of administrative decisions; in the still-embryonic forms of their control over the private area; in the organization of the workers and the people into supply and price juntas, to exert greater control over the process of distribution; in the communal organizations, the "industrial cordons," and many other initiatives, some of them expanded by the workers in their response to October's reactionary offensive. All of these constitute other such manifestations in that direction, which it is *essential to deepen and broaden immediately, both to confirm the character of the revolutionary process and to solve our immediate problems* [italics added].

Vuskovic stated (and only a minority of the leaders of the Socialist party and the MAPU agreed with him) that the only way to prevent collapse when the bourgeoisie and the imperialists resorted to "their strategic reserve for control" (the armed forces and the military police) was to "initiate a huge mobilization of the masses with concrete objectives to control the production apparatus and to prepare themselves for a military confrontation between the classes."

And he shaped his theory by saying, as he would later write at the end of 1972:

In this period, the advances toward achieving the Program have been large enough to motivate the most irate reaction from the imperialists and the bourgeoisie, but are as yet insufficient to forestall the national bourgeoisie's possibly using the economic power they still retain for all sorts of economic obstruction and sabotage. That is, the economy is not being directed with enough political control to ensure concentration on constructive tasks. On the contrary, it is the battlefield of an unresolved political struggle that is converting economic activity into an instrument of the same struggle. It goes without saying that in every economic problem today it is not difficult to discern deliberate action on the part of the imperialists and the bourgeoisie.

Vuskovic was saying that the bourgeoisie had set itself the goal of making the government's economic policy fail, to remove popular support from it first and afterward to overthrow it. And "in spite of the number of businesses incorporated into the Social Area, the nationalization of the banks, and the expansion of agrarian reform, the bourgeoisie continues unlawfully to retain enough economic power to be able to attempt this task with some possibility of success."

He went on:

They have this power, in the first place, because the Area of Social Property has not yet been completed in terms of the goals foreseen [that is, instead of expropriating 266 oligopolistic businesses, a compromise goal of 90 had been established]. Important oligopolies or strategic activities remain in the hands of their capitalist proprietors, constituting a large source of income and an instrument of domination over other businesses.

In the second place, the Social Area has not been able to make itself strongly enough felt in the presently dominant sector, which can impose working terms and according to their decisions generally control the conduct of businesses which, according to the Program, are and will continue to be part of the private area of the economy. Also there are not yet, in the private area, effective means of worker control. . . .

In the third place, a real redistribution of income and the process of accumulation of capital in the workers' favor has not yet been achieved in any definitive way.[2]

Vuskovic expected that these statements would convince Allende and his principal supporters, the leadership of the Chilean Communist party, of the commanding necessity to "leap forward," using as a base "a gigantic offensive of the masses," and taking advantage of the fact that "the reactionary forces and the armed apparatus of the bourgeois state do not yet have enough cohesion to attempt an armed counterrevolution." If we do not act now, his thesis ended, it will be too late, and the economic crisis will give the bourgeoisie and the imperialists a pretext for armed insurrection.

However, the thinking of the Communist party went against Vuskovic. Orlando Millas and Luis Corvalán were adamant: "We cannot do that. Our task right now is to prevent our enemies from being provoked," they added. Along with Allende, they believed that it was a good idea to "take into consideration the Santiago generals' arguments, since they've let us know [in May 1972] that they are very worried about the huge rise in inflation, the disorder in which some workers in the city and country have taken over businesses, and the drop in production in the private area."

On June 17, Allende changed his Cabinet. The two most prominent departures were Brigadier General Pedro Palacios Camerón from Mines and Pedro Vuskovic from Economy.

General Palacios Camerón was withdrawn from the Cabinet after the generals of the Santiago garrison were forced by the "hard-liners" and the "reformists" to agree that "we cannot allow a member of the armed forces in the Ministry when we know that the new Cabinet will be dominated by the Communists. It gives a bad image to our armed institutions, which are basically and philosophically anti-Marxist."

Pedro Vuskovic left because the Communist party demanded complete control of the economic part of the new Cabinet, to put into practice their policy of "national coexistence." Through Orlando Millas, who would become Treasury Minister and, later, Minister of the

Economy, the banner of Salvador Allende's new "political sleight of hand" would be stated in these words: "To move toward socialism, and later to build socialism, what must come first is the development of production in all areas of the national economy. Without this, there is nothing."

The leadership of the Chilean Communist party and Salvador Allende had unveiled the idea of freezing the process under the motto: "Consolidate what we have, first, to advance later." But "what we have" was unfortunately exactly what Vuskovic had described: substantial economic power in the bourgeoisie, a Social Area powerless to prevent the sabotage of production, armed forces constantly preparing for a "final taking of power," and a working class whose revolutionary momentum was being reined in and dissipated. These factors combined to make the workers the prey of a daily propaganda campaign in the mass media, owned by the oligarchy and imperialists. The newspapers and radio-television stations were succeeding in accomplishing the purpose of isolating the workers from their natural allies, the peasants and the lower middle class.

A NEW MILITARY PLOT

The political, legislative, judicial, and trade guild forces set loose to overthrow Salvador Allende legally began very early on to receive the support of organizations run by the CIA in Chile. Money was available not merely from the "slush fund" and "publicity and advertising" items in the Chilean oligopolies' budgets but also from multinational companies like ITT (which was reprimanded in May 1972 by the Chilean government for tax fraud and for having openly taken part in the conspiracy of September–October 1970) and from Anaconda and Kennecott, who had declared all-out war on Allende's government, including an "embargo" on shipments of Chilean copper to foreign ports, which took effect in Europe on September 30.

The scheme consisted of bringing about the breakdown of the economic system, conducting psychological warfare via the mass media, penetrating the armed forces, and preparing paramilitary "terrorist" groups to abet the deterioration of the economy.

Two of the fascist terrorist groups were conspicuous for their organization and financing: Fatherland and Liberty, and the ex-Cadet Commandos. From different beginnings they came to have the same financing, advising, and training.

Fatherland and Liberty was founded by a lawyer, Pablo Rodríguez Grez, who had been a member of Alessandri's campaign committee in 1970. Grez had connections with the financial interests of the Matte-Alessandri group, the Edwards clan, the Radical Democrats, and Anaconda, by virtue of his having once been a director of Forestry Industries (Industrias Forestales S.A.). Roberto Zúñiga, the millionaire owner of penny-arcade machines in Santiago, donated money to Fatherland and Liberty when it was being founded. Another important member was the journalist Rafael Otero Echeverría, a noted defender of the North American multinationals. In 1959 Otero had managed to cause some trouble for the Cuban news agency Prensa Latina. The Yarur group supported Fatherland and Liberty from its inception; for example, from 1964 to 1970 Otera received a salary as press director for Yarur radio, a job he did not hold.

Fatherland and Liberty was charged by the Chilean government with industrial sabotage and terrorism. Its CIA contact was Keith W. Wheelock, then secretary of the U.S. Embassy in Chile, named on page 540 of *Who's Who in the C.I.A.* (a 1972 publication of the Democratic Republic of Germany) as the author of a series of activities designed to overthrow certain governments.

However, Fatherland and Liberty's connections with the Chilean high command were none too good, particularly after Rodríguez Grez served as defense attorney for ex-General Roberto Viaux Marambio when he was tried for the October 1970 "betrayal" assassination of General René Schneider Chereau. At this time Grez had a notorious falling out with the Army high command. Only the Navy Infantry lent wholehearted support by providing training and large-caliber arms to the organization. *Última Hora* and *El Rebelde* reported that in the Army, Fatherland and Liberty was able to secure a foothold in Atacama Province through the commanding officer, Lieutenant Colonel Oscar Haag Blaschke, who allowed them to smuggle in arms from Argentina and Bolivia. In Santiago, they managed to recruit Colonel Roberto Souper Onfray (commander of the 2nd Armored Regiment until June 29, 1973) to their cause; Onfray confessed his association with Fatherland and Liberty after the failure of the coup.

Fatherland and Liberty maintained close relations with the southern *latifundistas;* eventually they were given control of the National Agriculture Society radio station in Santiago. In addition, that oligopoly's president, Benjamín Matte, was one of Fatherland and Liberty's leading members. The industrialists, for their part, contributed the good offices of the Society for Industrial Development's president, Orlando Sáenz. In a letter from Grez to Orlando Sáenz published in *Última Hora* in August of 1973, Grez thanked Sáenz for "the services lent earlier by you to our cause."

The second group, the ex-Cadet Commandos, was formed after the director of the Bernardo O'Higgins Military School, Colonel Eduardo Labbé, refused to render military honors to Fidel Castro on his December 1971 visit to Chile.

Labbé was a "hard-liner," closely associated with Generals Alfredo Canales Márquez and Hernán Hiriart. When these officers' plot was discovered in March 1972, Labbé was sent into retirement.

The ex-Cadet Commandos' main contact with the U.S. Embassy was the Chilean journalist Federico Willoughby MacDonald. He had been for years the chief of publications for Ford Motor Company in Chile. Willoughby MacDonald was intimately related to the CIA team in the U.S. Embassy (made up of Joseph F. Manus, Daniel Arzac, Dean Hinton, Frederick Lastrash, Keith Wheelock, Arnold Isaacs, Donald H. Winters, Raymond A. Warren, James Anderson, and John B. Tripton). He made contact with senior officers in the three branches of the armed forces. This job, whose original purpose was only to get support for the ex-Cadet Commandos, led to his being appointed press secretary to the fascist junta on September 11, 1973.

Willoughby's fluent English was a great asset in the generals' eyes, though not nearly so important as his useful connections in the U.S. Embassy.

The same oligarchic clans who were backing Fatherland and Liberty also financed the ex-Cadet Commandos, except that they had to spend much less money on it, because, unlike Fatherland and Liberty, the Commandos were an action group, with "commissions" and an "information bank" about the leftists' activities. In mid-1972 it was estimated that the ex-Cadet Commandos had 350 members, primarily in Santiago, Valparaíso, and Concepción. The organization was actually a satellite of the CIA in Chile, one of the components of Plan Djakarta,[3] which was uncovered in 1973, to murder Unidad Popular leaders and journalists. During the September 1973 takeover, the fascist generals made extensive use of ex-Cadet Commandos for searching out, torturing, interrogating, and murdering thousands of popular leaders.

In September 1972 the two fascist groups began to play their roles in the Society for Industrial Development's plan by undertaking to sabotage railroads, bridges, roads, and high-voltage towers, as well as by assaulting union and political leaders of middle and low rank. At that point, the economic situation was rapidly deteriorating, owing to the government's inability to control the private sector's moves to bring about a general destabilization by lowering production, halting investment, increasing speculation, and partially paralyzing the productive apparatus. By that time, the Society for Industrial Development had already given the word to its agents in the Christian Democrats, the National party, the Judiciary, the controller's office, and the various trade and professional associations directly controlled by the oligarchy, saying that "we must go on to the last phase." The last phase was total production stoppage.

One evening at a party in Viña del Mar, some officers were talking together, among them Brigadier General Alfredo Canales Márquez and Rear Admiral Horacio Justiniano. As was later reported in the Santiago daily papers, General Canales, who was drunk, confided to Justiniano: "We have the sonofabitch in the frying pan." The "sonofabitch" was the President of the Republic. He added: "This month we are going to unload the shit." Rear Admiral Justiniano was very upset because he was not in on the coup. When he returned to Santiago, he asked General Prats what it was all about. Prats conferred with his colleagues in the Santiago garrison, and they reached the conclusion that Canales was "a threat to the security of the armed forces" if he talked like that when drunk. The corps of generals was agreed that they could not make an "adequate plan to defeat the enemy [Allende's government] by attacking at an appropriate time and taking advantage of their weaknesses, if our own people are going to give it away."[4]

It was agreed to send General Canales into retirement and to "denounce him to Allende." Allende would be told that the SIM had discovered the plot in time, that it had no serious ramifications, was localized in Santiago, and involved only Canales and two colonels. This, said the generals, will maintain Allende's confidence in us, and we can go ahead as planned, without interfering with the politicians' maneuvers to depose Allende in Congress.

This fabricated "plot" was what Salvador Allende publicly denounced on September 14, 1972, as "the September plan to oust me." What he did not know was that there was still a plan, but it was the "October Plan."

OCTOBER 1972

The "October Plan," put together by the Society for Industrial Development and feverishly supported by the CIA, did not include the armed forces. It was a civilian conspiracy to bring the country to a standstill, to the brink of total collapse, and thus oblige the people to throw Allende out in a plebiscite that he would have to call as the only means of curing the country's paralysis. It had been decided that October would be a good time because popular support for the government was very feeble, thanks to the price hikes, the food lines, the shortage of all goods, and the government's inability to do anything about the situation.

On October 10, in response to a government project to form a state trucking company in Magallanes province, León Vilarín, the president of the Chilean Truck Owners Association, called for his associates all over the country to stop work "as a sign of protest against the Marxist state dictatorship." The Confederation of Retail Merchants, led by Rafael Cumsille (one of Frei's Christian Democrats), joined their strike "in defense of freedom to work." They were followed by the transportation guild of private owners of microbuses and bus-taxis, led by Christian Democrats, and the Society for Industrial Development, the National Agriculture Society, the National Confederation of Production and Commerce, the College of Lawyers, the College of Engineers, and the College of Medicine. Technicians and other employees of some not yet nationalized commercial banks joined them. In other words, all the private businessmen in the country, plus most of the professionals and a small sector of employees, had gone on strike indefinitely. They carried the banner of what they called "Chile's letter of grievances" containing political demands of various sorts all aimed at one goal: to destroy the advances made by putting the Unidad Popular's program into action.

President Allende ordered Brigadier General Herman Brady Roche, director of the Academy of War, to "intervene" with the Santiago transportation guild. General Brady, who was a "reformist," did everything possible to make sure that, contrary to Allende's request, the transportation guild's microbuses and taxi-buses would not go back to work. He maintained that there were 3,500 vehicles of that type in Santiago, that the Santiago garrison had less than 7,000 men, and that because he would have to put one soldier in each microbus and taxi-bus to protect the drivers from fascist commando sabotage, it would leave the city without a military garrison. The "reformist" generals had given Brady instructions: "Let Allende hang himself. Do not give him any assistance, but don't let it show."

But then something happened that no one, not the Society for Industrial Development or the CIA or the generals, had ever foreseen. A tremendous popular mobilization began. The Christian Democrat and National party legislators were broadcasting over the radio and publishing daily extras to the effect that "the country has collapsed," "all of Chile is on strike," "the workers are demanding that Allende resign or call a plebiscite." But on the streets, roads, farms, factories, public offices, and workers' settlements, trucks carrying cargo came into view, and vehicles carrying passengers. Thousands of silent workers with proud faces and clenched fists were walking through the streets to their jobs, every day; machines were functioning; plows were tilling the earth. The country was on the move. Haltingly, to be sure, but it was moving. The bosses and the supervisors sat at home, but the workers were walking to the factories. The great landowners remained in the city, but the peasants went out to till the crops. Laborers, peasants, and office workers, reinforced by university and high school students, had all gone out to fight the employers' lockout.

The government had decreed emergency zones (under martial law) in the twenty-five provinces of Chile, but not one soldier was seen breaking into a boss's house to force him to go back to work. At the same time, thousands of laborers were working—but only part-time, because they had to form shock brigades to repel the fascists' harassment and sabotage.

In Santiago's industrial districts, the so-called industrial cordons, first formed in June to fight fascist sabotage, began to take on a character of their own. In addition to guarding places of work against sabotage, they fought against the black market, speculation, and the scarcity of industrial raw materials. They had been conceived as "organizations for work, commerce, labor planning, and for defense against class enemies," in the Los Cerrillos industrial district south of Santiago. They had been reviled by some politicians in the Unidad Popular itself, who described them as "extremist counterrevolutionary organizations," manipulated by the "lunatic fringe."

The workers' organization against black markets and black-market speculation in working-class neighborhoods took a big step forward in October 1972 when it developed the simple tactic of distributing articles of consumption directly from worker to worker, thus avoiding the private distribution system. This was achieved through unions, union organizations, neighborhood cooperatives, and supply and price control juntas. These groups demanded that the government departments in charge of distributing consumer goods (more than 70 percent of the total for the country) give them the goods to sell directly to the people. In this way a union cooperative, for example, was able to sell its members a kilo of fowl three and four times cheaper than the neighborhood supermarket. The same thing happened at the administrative level of the factories whose managers stayed home during the owners' strike in October: the organized workers transformed themselves into worker-managers, worker-engineers, worker-administrators, and kept the companies functioning. Nearly a year later, in August 1973, the leftist section of the Socialist party proposed a platform of "action" for industrial cordons, extending this movement to the countryside. "All rural property of 40 to 80 hectares," they stated, "should be occupied and expropriation demanded. All businesses considered vital or strategic by the industrial cordons should be occupied and requisitioned. All these measures should be discussed in the workers' meetings and should involve the masses, who should carry the banners of the struggle against vacillation. By achieving these goals rapidly we will put an end to the arrogance of the owners and the fascists."[5]

The workers were really showing their strength in October. They kept industry on the move, they were taking over factories, and without owners, technicians, or managers, they were making them function. They held meetings to discuss this: "How long are we going to give the *momios* [reactionaries] to come back to work?" And this: "We should organize in armed people's brigades to overthrow our enemies permanently. . . . The military are helping the bosses by not acting . . . we have to solve the problem ourselves."

Army, Navy, and Air Force intelligence received daily reports on the "people's mobilization." They also received reports from inside "the institutions." Watching the spectacle of the country functioning without owners and managers, some senior officers expressed their admiration: "The rabble can do it." In other words: "The Allende government deserves respect—it's pulled off quite a stunt."

The strain that the October Plan had put on all parts of society had revealed the existence of a group of officers who were "Allende sympathizers." This was a serious dilemma for those who had thought the military was of one mind. It would become more serious, the intelligence reports indicated, if "workers numbering close to eighty thousand were to mobilize in Santiago province." It was food for thought: eighty thousand workers in a fighting mood, against a garrison of six or seven thousand men.

The "reformist," "hard-line," and "constitutionalist" generals met to "plan a strategy for the difficult moment." They reached an agreement to "support Allende as a political out." Why? Because that solution allowed them "to restrain the people's anger in the nick of time." The armed forces could not smash them without starting a long and expensive civil war. The military apparatus, even if it were to win, would be left half-destroyed, defenseless against its external enemies and vulnerable to its internal enemies. Their thought was that the economy was in such bad shape that if they added civil war to the effects of the present strike, "our country would fall to pieces." They also decided to support Allende because the civilian politicians had shown themselves incapable of forcing him to resign.

At the same time, the oligarchs of the Society for Industrial Development, the National Agriculture Society, and the National Confederation of Production and Commerce were viewing the same landscape of popular mobilization and the armed forces' inaction. They instructed their politicians to "make a deal," giving up their goal of ousting Allende for the time being.

Some Socialist party leaders suggested to Allende that he appoint a Cabinet in which the Army commander in chief, Division General Carlos Prats González, would serve as Minister of the Interior (a job with the rank of Vice-President), to give the government an image of strength and make it look as if it had the armed forces' support.

The proposition was put to Prats, who discussed it with his generals and the high command of the Navy and the Air Force. They decided that it was a good idea, because it allowed a number of alternatives: to control the workers' activities and their "unorthodox" organizations, so they could study them carefully, through the Interior Ministry (which oversaw the entire police apparatus of Chile); to move forward in the "constitutionalist" plan of forming an Allende–armed forces government; to allow a breather for this very serious crisis, so that they could arrive at the general elections of March 1973, which would be an "absolutely constitutional opportunity" for the Christian Democrats and the National party to get two-thirds of the Deputy and Senate seats, thereby destroying Allende constitutionally and replacing him with a "tried democrat"; to give them time to "clean up the institutions' high commands," which turned out to be harboring "foci of extremist thought"; and to establish a strategy to forward the officers' central idea of "preparing themselves to govern the country."

Such arguments were not communicated to the accomplices in the October Plan, Eduardo Frei and Onofre Jarpa. These politicians were informed that the armed forces were not yet ready to take over the country, and therefore had not been able to do anything about the work stoppage.

On November 2, Allende announced changes in his Cabinet: Minister of the Interior, the commander in chief of the Army, General Carlos Prats González; Minister of Public Works, Rear Admiral Ismael Huerta; Minister of Mines, Air Force General Claudio Sepúlveda.

On November 5, Allende left the country for two weeks, on a trip to the U.N., Algeria, the Soviet Union, Morocco, and Cuba, with short stops in Caracas and Lima. General Prats acted as Chief of State. When Allende returned, Prats dutifully returned the constitutional reins to Allende. It seemed to be Allende's securest moment.

4 The Pentagon Tells
the Generals to Go Ahead

While Allende was on his two-week tour of various countries, the Pentagon's Latin-American experts in Washington were analyzing the events of the October work stoppage. It had come to the conclusion that the popular insurrection in Chile was about to explode. By the same token, they decided that Salvador Allende was no longer in a position to control the popular insurrection. It was pointless not to help to overthrow him now and replace him with a strong regime that would dismantle the workers' organizations and thus prevent the possibility of subversion from below.

Without consulting or informing President Nixon, the Pentagon apparently decided to give the green light to the Chilean generals for an efficient, thorough, and sure-fire overthrow of Allende.

When Allende was received by General Prats on November 19, 1972, and had the reins of state returned to him, the Pentagon's envoys were already in Santiago to begin talks with the Chilean generals for the forthcoming coup. This adventure, by Pentagon decision, was not to include General Prats.[1]

The Latin-American experts' "October in Chile"[2] report had been placed before the chairman of the Joint Chiefs of Staff, Admiral Thomas Moorer.[3] And the Pentagon representatives in the U.S. Embassy in Chile, experts on the internal situation of the Chilean armed forces, got in contact with "the right men."

In November 1972, Pentagon envoys had spoken with General Gustavo Leigh Guzmán, the Air Force's second-in-command; with Vice-Admiral José Toribio Merino, the Navy's second-in-command; with the "reformist" Generals Washington Carrasco, Herman Brady, and Sergio Arellano Stark; with the "hard-liners" Manuel Torres de la Cruz and Oscar Bonilla; and with the "constitutionalist" General Héctor Bravo Muñoz.

Their message was clear: The moment has come to prepare to overthrow Allende. It is a race against time and a question of "your survival." If "the masses are allowed to keep on the way they were going in October, in a year or two they are going to run right over us."

The Pentagon envoys' line of reasoning was this: U.S. intelligence reports show that Peru is preparing for war with Chile in order to reclaim provinces lost in the nineteenth century. Reliable sources have informed us that the Peruvian generals are arming themselves with heavy tanks and will buy weapons in the Soviet Union. (Naturally, the Pentagon envoys did not inform the Chilean generals that they had planned to stop selling arms to Peru so that the Peruvian government would be forced to turn to the Soviet Union for replacements. This would provide the United States with a "strategic excuse" to begin a campaign against Peru, as soon as it had solved the Chilean problem.) Also, the Peruvian Air Force has an air transport division for their attack on Chile, and has built a modern superhighway from north to south to the Chilean border. Peru will attack in from one to three years, taking advantage of the moment when the Chilean economy has been destroyed by Marxism. Chile is not the Russia of 1917. It is not going to be able to resist this attack, and it will be defeated. Only an alliance with Brazil can put a stop to the "revanchist anxieties" of the Peruvians. But the Brazilian government has informed us that it will help Chile only if it can trust the government. It will never support the present Marxist government. Chile's survival as a nation is threatened not merely by Marxism (which wants to conquer it so that the Soviet Union can use it as a base against the U.S. and the entire civilized world) but also by external enemies who want to partition its territory and take over the rich mineral lands in the north. Peru will get support from Argentina. We (the Pentagon) could hold off Bolivia[4] (but we don't know for how long), but with the Allende government in office, the Chilean armed forces will be defeated. You generals will understand the responsibility you must assume if you know these facts.

The "Pentagon report" was a drug to many generals, who used it as the patriotic "justification" to join the plot against Allende. Very few of the generals questioned the reliability of this "Pentagon report." Among those few was General Carlos Prats González, the Army's commander in chief. An expression he once used to characterize it was "grotesque."

But what Prats thought was now irrelevant; since November, the "reformist" and "hard-line" generals were in firm agreement, which meant that a substantial majority were in favor of Allende's overthrow. Furthermore, the aid offered by the Pentagon and its announcement that Brazil's military government would also be on their side gave strong impetus to the idea that the overthrown government could be replaced by one "without fixed duration."

In the Chilean generals' last meeting with Pentagon envoys, they made a counterproposal that was accepted. They said they would give the "constitutional organizations" until March 1973 to overthrow Allende. If by that time the Christian Democrats and the National party had not been able to obtain two-thirds of the Parliament's seats and thus depose the President by a simple congressional mandate, then they would quickly mobilize for an effective, thorough, and massive military coup. The machinery was already on the launching pad.

THE POLITICAL FAILURE

In January 1973, in the city of Viña del Mar, the expanded directorate of the Society for Industrial Development met. They reviewed the failure of the previous year's campaign to overthrow the constitutional government. An official government analysis of the effects of the "October work stoppage," prepared in November 1972, was read:

The owners' strike of October pursued the downfall of the Popular government, and was a decided failure. But what did affect the country was its economic objective: to provoke disorder in the trucking industry, which transports and distributes consumer goods, raw materials, and fuel. In spite of the workers' efforts to keep the industries in operation, in spite of the young people who helped by volunteering to load, unload, and move products, in spite of the armed forces' protection, serious and even irreparable damage was caused to the economy, and to present and future productivity.

During the twenty-six days of the owners' strike, vast quantities of perishable goods were lost, among them more than 10 million liters of milk which could not be gotten to the plants. Thousands of swine and poultry had to be sacrificed for lack of feed. Seeds and fertilizers were not delivered in time, meaning that plantings were fewer and harvests will be smaller. A large number of industries, although not shut down, had to cut production so as not to exhaust their stocks of raw materials. The Paipote, Potrerillos, Ventanas, and Chagres foundries had to stop production of more than 5,000 tons of copper owing to the interruption of ore shipments from the big mines. Other factories were affected by the fuel shortage. Many construction and investment projects fell way behind. Urgent repairs were postponed because indispensable material, parts, or equipment did not arrive. All of this contributed to a substantial reduction in October's production, which will have repercussions in the year's index and in the next months.

From a financial point of view, the government lost the income from highway and bridge tolls as well as from sales taxes, its two most important sources of tax revenue. Other revenue sources were also considerably reduced. This meant that new financial deficits and additional expenditures were incurred to avoid greater evils.

In spite of everything, however, the reactionaries did not succeed. The proletariat proved stronger, as did the overwhelming majority of peasants, young people, women, and patriotic segments of small and medium-sized industry, commerce, and the truckers who defied the rebels' threats. The people, organized and aware, proved they were capable of keeping the country functioning under the most difficult of circumstances.

The lesson of October is that in spite of their vast resources and the backing of the international conspiracy [the economic blockade], the reactionaries can be overcome.

The members of the industrial oligarchy who met at Viña del Mar agreed with the government report: the country's economy had been seriously damaged, but not the laborers', peasants', and office workers' will to fight. They and other groups were still supporting the Unidad Popular's program. Although national production had been brought to the verge of collapse, the Allende government was still on its feet, and apparently in a better position than before. The bosses had managed to prevent the armed forces from helping the government, but after twenty-six critical days, in the face of the intimidating people's mobilization, the armed forces had resurfaced, in the role of Minister of the Interior.

But the bosses were also agreed that they had to keep trying to throw out Allende. During the mere twenty-six days the October strike had lasted, the bosses had paid the strikers more than $100 million (so huge an expenditure that the dollar went down to nearly half its price on the black market, owing to the huge influx of American currency, which people called "Frei dollars"). The money had come in part from important industrial groups in Brazil, Argentina, and Venezuela. And the contributors wanted results, not excuses.

The industrial oligarchy also noted that the cost of living had risen 99.5 percent by December 1972, a record inflation for Chile. The production apparatus had been badly damaged by the October work stoppage: foodstuffs and staples were so scarce that lines to buy them lasted for days in various districts in the capital. It could easily be predicted that January and February 1973 would see an inflationary stampede, a considerable deterioration in living conditions, and therefore an opportunity "to favorably influence public opinion to vote against the government in the congressional elections on March 4."

The bosses then agreed to ask for aid from the U.S. multinationals and Brazilian industrial groups to form a "campaign fund" for candidates of the Christian Democrat, National, and Radical Democrat parties, as well as those of other small right-wing groups. The "campaign fund" turned out to be huge. In a mere seven days, between Saturday the seventeenth and Friday the twenty-third of February 1973, the candidate for the Santiago Senate seat, Eduardo Frei Montalva, allegedly spent a total of $2 million on advertising in newspapers, magazines, posters, pamphlets, TV, radio, and street campaigns.[5]

But the Viña del Mar meeting of the Society for Industrial Development also discussed the possibility that "the Unidad Popular might get more than 40 percent of the vote." Although this seemed "very remote" to them, "our only way out would be civil war." The Chilean oligarchs concluded their meeting by pledging to put all their resources at the disposal of the election campaign, but at the same time not to discontinue nourishing the fascist groups Fatherland and Liberty, ex-Cadet Commandos, and so on, so that they could continue their sabotage and their infiltration of the armed forces.[6]

The Society for Industrial Development conferred with the National Agriculture Society and the National Confederation of Production and Commerce. They found themselves generally agreed on the same points.

The reactionaries' election campaign used the slogan: "Get two-thirds of the vote to oust Allende." One of the candidates for the Santiago Senate seat, Onofre Jarpa, used the slogan: "We don't need a new Parliament, we need a new government."

The election campaign was conducted by the parties of the right in such a way that soon it was common knowledge that the election was a mere pretext. Throughout February, editorials in the leftist daily *Puro Chile* were saying:

It doesn't matter to the Society for Industrial Development, the National Agriculture Society, and the National Confederation of Production and Commerce whether or not their politicians, among them Frei and Jarpa, ever get to the Senate to "legislate." They want them in to overthrow the Allende administration in a way that is cloaked in "constitutionality." Thus, for this country's right wing, obtaining two-thirds of the vote is essentially a mere accident of chance. It can happen or it cannot happen. If they get them, then Allende will be deposed after May 21. If they don't get them, they will nonetheless carry out their plot to depose him, turning to the fascist officers in our armed forces who have let themselves be seduced by their siren songs. The danger of a coup will begin on the night of March 4. The North American imperialists have already given the order to their lackeys in Chile to overthrow the constitutional government by any means. Thus the people must be on the alert. They must not let themselves be tricked by the idea that "the elections will solve the problem of power." The elections won't solve anything. The problem of power can be solved only by preparing to confront the fascists on their own ground, using their own weapons. Certainly, we must fight to make sure the enemy doesn't win a two-thirds majority in March.

That will be easy. You can see it in the streets, in the communities, in the factories, and in the peasant settlements. What is hard is the other thing, and this must be achieved. The laborers must organize, under their own leaders, as must the peasants, office workers, and other patriotic groups among the small and medium-sized businessmen, to form an unbreakable wall against counterrevolutionary fascism and swiftly destroy it, using its own methods.

This kind of editorial in *Puro Chile* caused all sorts of problems in the core of the Unidad Popular (excepting an important group in the Socialist party and the MIR or Revolutionary Left Movement, which shared the same viewpoint as the newspaper). The Unidad Popular, under Salvador Allende's personal supervision and with the complete support of the Communist party leaders, viewed success in the March elections as the only task of those people's organizations that had shown such tremendous strength in the October 1972 work stoppage. They were trying very hard to replace the leaders of the industrial cordons,* who were members of advanced groups of the Socialist party, the Revolutionary Left Movement, the PCR, and independent leftists, in favor of a staff that would adhere to the path of Allende and his Communist ministers who said that "to make a revolution is to produce."

But the industrial cordons had another idea. And that was to form "battalions of masses" to halt the armed counterrevolution. This was classified by the official publications of the Unidad Popular as "leftist childishness."

For the editors of such publications as *Puro Chile,* another problem besides emphasizing the thought of "preparing for the fight" existed: to warn the people that the fascist conspiracy had deep roots in the armed forces' high command, but without having their publications shut down for "insulting the armed forces." The leftists were being hampered in every way by the legal veneer covering the developments in the country.

---

*A kind of leftist vigilante committee—one of several people's organizations, which included supply and price control juntas, etc.

THE ELECTIONS

The election results surprised nobody. Two or three weeks before, a public opinion poll of Santiago, Valparaíso, and Concepción, taken by Eduardo Frei's group in the Christian Democrat party, showed that the Unidad Popular was going to win about 40 percent of the votes. That is, the opposition was not going to win the two-thirds needed to replace Allende with the president of the Senate while new elections were called.

The Christian Democratic and National party candidates had trapped themselves by devoting all their propaganda to getting "two-thirds of the vote."

On the night of March 4, when it was clear that the Unidad Popular had won nearly 44 percent of the vote, the masses reacted as if the government parties' coalition had achieved a landslide victory over the oligarchs' and imperialists' maneuvers to prevent the Unidad Popular program's accomplishment.

In Allende's own words, the Unidad Popular's interpretation of the election results was:

The parliamentary elections of March 4 have shown something that causes the despair and confusion of some of our opponents: the orthodox functioning of the political institutions' mechanisms through which the people express their will. Defying the schemes of those who have not stopped trying to destroy them, because they saw the elections as a "pointless goal," March 4 was a clear manifestation of defense of our democratic way of government.

On the other hand, the meaning of the election results is clarified by the historic context in which the voting took place. The government's policy has been interpreted by the massive support received by the political parties that defend it, *the largest that any government has received in the last twenty years after twenty-seven months in office.* The fourth of March has reconfirmed the Chilean way to socialism. . . .[7]

The day after the elections, the masses' enthusiasm got a bath of cold water. All the industrial cordons, communal commandos, peasant councils, and supply and price control juntas had planned meetings to "analyze the election results and take a leap forward in forming the people's power" by "better preparing to confront the armed counterrevolution." But these discussions never took place, because that day President Allende began a campaign against "the lunatic fringe" who, "objectively speaking," were playing into the hands of the imperialists and oligarchs.* The slogan "To make a revolution is to produce" was replaced by "And now, let's produce for the revolution."

Bit by bit, the echoes of October, which had been heard again in March, began to die down. The debate whether it was a "provocation" or a "revolutionary act" to prepare for the fight against armed fascism was now a moot one. As the days passed, nobody paid very much attention to the antigovernment conspiracy that seemed to be forming in the heart of the armed forces.

THE GENERALS

The week following the elections, the generals in direct touch with the Pentagon envoys had several meetings to plan their next moves. One thing was clear: the civil politicians had failed. For that very reason, the generals felt they must undertake to discharge the Pentagon's orders: do the whole job out in the open, without shielding themselves behind the other power groups, the Chilean oligopolists and the North American multinationals.

The truth was, the generals and admirals were no longer afraid. While the politicians had devoted January and February to the election campaign, the generals and admirals had set themselves to "studying" and "thinking." They had examined the history of Chile during this century. They had looked at the Latin-American and the world situation. They had delved further into the histories of the workers' movement, the peasants' movement, and the leftist parties

*See Chapter 5, especially on the hated "gun control searches."

in their country. They had studied the economic problems and the periodic crises in the nation's system. They had looked for inspiration —and they had found it. It came in the form of a National party pamphlet entitled "The New Republic," which was simply the platform of the candidate defeated in 1970, Jorge Alessandri Rodríguez, the most conservative President Chile had had in the previous thirty-five years.

The main ideas "The New Republic" put forth were:

"Only an authoritarian government" which imposes "order and discipline" and "rejects political maneuvering" will be able to solve Chile's problems.

"It is a question, then, of replacing the divisive class struggle with a vigorous national conscience, united in solidarity."

"The contribution of foreign capital to our economic development makes investment grow without having to postpone social benefits for a population who needs them."

"Unity, solidarity, and the higher motivation of the Chilean people will be possible only if these are preceded by a vigorous rebirth of the national spirit." For example, "Young people will study more and march less."

"There are many factors which conspire against nationalism. The most important of these is brought in by international Marxism, represented in Chile by the Socialist and Communist parties."

But the pamphlet's quotes didn't express everything the generals thought. For example, they did not state that the generals believed that the "breakdown of our society" had begun to be a serious factor not just in 1970, with the inauguration of a government representing "factors that conspire against nationalism," but much earlier, since 1964, when "the Christian Democrats, a party that has clear and possibly unpatriotic international links, let loose the forces of disorder with peasant unionization, excessive agrarian reform, and a populism that raised the people's aspirations."

The pamphlet's quotes also didn't say that the generals thought that the process of "breakdown" had been going on for such a long time that by now the entire society was corrupted by the lack of "national unity." It was the "politicians of all parties" who, in their eagerness to be elected or in their desire to seem "progressive and advanced," were responsible for the situation, and for that reason, the country needed "a total overhaul." Neither did the quotes reveal that the Chilean generals cherished the Pentagon's assessment of them as "the only cohesive organization in the nation capable of taking on the task of rebuilding the country." Since they were not involved with any civilian political coalition, they would be in good condition, after Allende's overthrow, to undertake the dismantling of all the factors of "disorder," that is, the workers' and peasants' union organizations, juntas of supply and price control, peasant councils, communal councils, industrial cordons, and political parties of the left.

The generals were agreed on the following principles:

1. The government that replaces Salvador Allende should be purely military, involving the three branches of the armed forces and the military police.

2. The new government should seek support from civilians only as technicians on specific matters and not as members of political parties.

3. All "foreign" ideologies must be eradicated from Chile by "remoralizing" actions on the part of the armed forces.

4. The economic crisis has only one solution: All Chileans must concentrate on their work and cease any political discussions; the Western countries, led by the United States, must give Chile substantial financial support.

5. To obtain this financial support, it will be necessary to offer "assurances to foreign capital," beginning with discussions on a "reasonable" compensation for the North American copper companies. The mechanism for this would be to annul the discount of the "excess" profits established by Allende. (That is, Chile would not deduct $774 million from the indemnizations set in October 1971. In other words, it would have to pay Anaconda and Kennecott a sum of around $500 million.)

The second phase of the generals' discussions took place in the first and second weeks of March 1973 and was dedicated to determining how to put their ideas into action.

As a first step, they set out to convert the "constitutionalist" generals, who were still adhering to Commander in Chief Prats's theory "to keep pressing until we get a government made up of Allende and the armed forces." Prats had informed the generals on numerous occasions, especially after October 1972, that "we must wait a while. President Allende has repeatedly said that he is tired of the parties with him, because they are not capable of leading the people on the road to social order and dedication to their work." To those officers who would listen, Prats said: President Allende "is coming to a point when he will be alone and will have no choice but to rule with the armed forces." A few days before the March election Prats told them: "Allende is a brilliant politician, with very good intentions, who wants the best for his people, and he is totally committed to preventing a bloody insurrection by extremists of the right or of the left."[8]

To the "reformist" and "hard-line" generals, Prats's declarations were nothing more than an indication of his personal ambitions. What Prats wanted, these generals declared, was to become Allende's heir apparent, to come out in 1976 as the leftist parties' presidential candidate.

Obviously Prats had to be left out of their plans, isolated from his sympathizers in the corps of generals, and dumped when the time came for the coup. The conspirators decided to approach General Augusto Pinochet Ugarte, chief of the General Staff and second in seniority in the Army. Pinochet was then ostensibly a "constitutionalist" like Prats, but the generals felt that they had to attract him to their side anyway in order to avoid any appearance of weakness produced by having to go over the heads of the Army's two highest-ranking officers.

The generals also decided to woo the military police high command. They chose César Mendoza Durán to contact first, since he had already demonstrated a strong dislike for Allende and "the Marxists."

And as far as their requested participation in Allende's Cabinet was concerned, they decided they would have to ask him to form one without officers, suggesting that "the armed forces have already accomplished the purpose of guaranteeing honest elections and pacifying hard feelings from last October." But at the same time they decided to leave all the military men in responsible government jobs where they were, for two reasons: to keep receiving through their minions fresh "and timely" information about the internal maneuvers of the Unidad Popular leaders, and to annul the influence on the troops of those officers loyal to Allende. These had revealed their "extremist" sympathies in October 1972 and were "setting a bad example" (as in the case of Air Force General Alberto Bachelet Martínez, named by Allende to the National Distribution Secretariat, who gave press interviews in which he endorsed "disordering" ideas —that is, that the supply and price control juntas, made up of the "rabble," should see to the proper distribution of food in the country. General Bachelet was thrown in prison on September 11, kept in the Air Force torture camp at Los Cerrillos air base until October, and afterward transferred to the public jail, where he died on March 12, 1974).

While the generals were discussing the details of the coup, the chief officers of the Army (the backbone of the plot) were distributed thus, from north to south:

Armored Division, stationed in Iquique, Tarapacá Province. Division commander, Brigadier General Carlos Forestier Haensgen, a "hard-liner."

First Division, with headquarters in Antofagasta, Antofagasta Province. Division commander, General Joaquín Lagos Osorio, a "constitutionalist" and an enthusiastic partisan of Prats's idea of forming an Allende–armed forces government.

Second Division, with headquarters in Santiago, Santiago Province. Commander in chief, Brigadier General Mario Sepúlveda Squella, head of military intelligence, a "reformist," a violent partisan of throwing out civil politicians of any party, but seriously disagreeing with the other "reformist" generals, such as Herman Brady Roche, in the struggle to gain control of the situation, which drew him nearer to General Prats. Along with General Guillermo Pickering, head of the Military Institutes, he was the only "reformist" who openly stated that "the overthrow should take place in two stages," the first an Allende–armed forces government, the second the armed forces alone, "to avoid useless bloodshed." General Sepúlveda Squella's Santiago garrison comprised eight regiments. Of these, the Junior Officers' School, the 2nd Armored Regiment, and the Telecommunications School were commanded by "hard-line" colonels; the Paratrooper and Special Forces School by a "reformist" colonel; and the Infantry School, and the Buin, Tacna, and Puente Alto Railwaymen regiments by "constitutionalist" colonels.

Third Division, with headquarters in Concepción, Concepción Province. Division commander, Brigadier General Washington Carrasco Fernández of the SIM, a "reformist" with very close ties to the Pentagon.

Cavalry Division, with headquarters in Valdivia, Valdivia Province. Division commander, Brigadier General Héctor Bravo Muñoz, ostensibly a "constitutionalist" but really a "reformist" who had infiltrated the former group for reasons of personal ambition. He was another division commander with strong ties to the Pentagon.

Fifth Division, with headquarters in Punta Arenas, Aisén Province. Division commander, Division General Manuel Torres de la Cruz, the true leader of the "hard-liners" while appearing to be "Allende's personal friend" and a "great supporter" of General Prats.

By the first half of March 1973, the alliance of "hard-liners" and "reformists," plus the personal position of the "constitutionalist" Bravo Muñoz, had already given overwhelming control of the Army troops to the generals who had decided to accede to the Pentagon's wishes to overthrow Allende. The conspirators went about their task quietly, slowly and surely putting together all the pieces of their plot.

They were so calm that they even managed to perform their roles with the civil politicians to perfection, making them believe that they, the generals, were only the politicians' tools. This is most evident in the case of Eduardo Frei, who still believed two or three weeks after the September 11 coup that it was "his coup." He had worked feverishly from the Senate (to which he had been reelected in the March 1973 elections) to persuade the generals to overthrow Allende, so that he could afterward become President for the second time. The generals allowed him to believe they were working on his behalf, and they got what they wanted: the wholehearted support of the organizations controlled by Frei's reactionary backers. The eulogies that the Christian Democrat politicians, organizations, and journalists heaped on the "military saviors of our Fatherland" in the first days after the coup were incredible. In speeches, world tours, and books they praised "the heroes in uniform." Only months afterward, in December 1973, did they realize that the generals had been using them, that they were out of the game, and, worst of all, that they had been glorifying men who were slaughtering their fellow citizens with such brutality and in such numbers that the entire world was horrified.

NOW OR NEVER

But the Chilean officers weren't the only ones who hurriedly got together after the night of March 4, 1973. The directors of the Society for Industrial Development, the National Agriculture Society, and the National Confederation of Production and Commerce also did. And in their meetings they could only have reaffirmed the opinion first voiced after the October 1972 work stoppage failed, that is, that it would be impossible to overthrow Allende by constitutional means.

They must have decided it would be best to concentrate their efforts instead on turning the armed forces against the President. Their thinking probably ran thus:

1. Only if there were real economic, political, and social chaos would the armed forces feel it their duty to intervene and depose Allende.

2. Once Allende had been ousted, the armed forces would take charge of maintaining social, political, and economic order, and the

bosses would then devise a new way to develop the country.

On March 28, twenty-four hours after Allende, accepting the generals' suggestion, had again changed the composition of his Cabinet to remove all representatives of the armed forces, Orlando Sáenz, president of the Society for Industrial Development, had *El Mercurio* publish an article by him which contained the two main tenets of the oligarchy's thinking.

Sáenz said that the departure of the armed forces from the Cabinet proved that "they have repudiated the government," because the government meant to bring chaos on the country. This oncoming situation threatened the national security and sovereignty. He stated that "the Marxists' goal is to destroy Chile," and therefore the severe economic crisis afflicting Chile should not surprise anyone. The only solution was a "unifying" government, "strong and efficient," which would "make the state an arbiter, and not a suffocating monopolist." This "unifying government" would include the active participation of the "trade guilds"—that is, the oligopolies. With the voice of a prophet, Sáenz pointed out that it was very important to "be prepared," because "the coming days will be very difficult, serious, and critical," and "who is to win in Chile will be decided, whether Marxist chaos or democracy." He urged all "democrats" in the country to fight tirelessly, until "Marxism is overcome," and voiced the hope that "the President of the Republic will listen to us."

Sáenz, representing the Society for Industrial Development, had asked Eduardo Frei, who in late May had been elected president of the Senate and was thereby "in direct line of succession" should Allende be declared "unfit" for the job, if he would undertake a special task, in conjunction with his former Defense Minister, Juan de Dios Carmona. This task was to begin "precise, frank, and direct" conversations with General Oscar Bonilla Bradanovic, to devise a scheme to overthrow Allende and to ask him, as "the good friend of both of them," to speak to Generals Carlos Prats and Augusto Pinochet to propose the same ideas.

For his part, Jorge Fontaine, representing the National Confederation of Production and Commerce, got in touch with Senator Onofre Jarpa, the National party president, as well as Senators Patricio Phillips and Pedro Ibáñez Ojeda, to "approach" the commander in chief of the Air Force, César Ruiz Danyau; the commander of the First Naval District, Vice-Admiral José Toribio Merino; and Division General Manuel Torres de la Cruz. The three politicians were told to speak frankly to the generals and admirals, and promise them "a big publicity campaign" pushing for "a government of the armed forces." The Society for Industrial Development, the National Confederation, and other industrial associations would propagate the idea of "military power" as opposed to "popular power." They would take charge of creating constant problems in transportation, trade, and production, so that the national productive apparatus would be completely paralyzed, worse even than in October 1972. They would follow whatever suggestions the generals might make for the use of their news media (*El Mercurio,* Channel 13, the Catholic University's TV station, and the Minería, Balmaceda, Cooperativa, and National Agriculture Society radio stations, as well as others throughout the country) to "undermine the prestige" of anybody they wanted, if that would help them achieve their ultimate goals.[9]

They would also guarantee the generals "a rapid decrease in Allende's prestige with the workers," because the trade unions controlled by the Christian Democrats and the National party would "promote an increase in strikes for higher wages and salaries."

The directors of the national oligopolies did not stop at the politicians, however. They also approached the president of the Supreme Court, Enrique Urrutía Manzano, an expropriated *latifundista* and a shareholder in half a dozen industrial monopolies. They asked him to begin a campaign of declarations impugning the "legality" of the government's actions and to talk to "whichever of the senior officers you can," to influence their decision "to liberate us from Allende's government." They did the same with the controller general of the Republic, Héctor Humeres, asking him to double his efforts to outlaw all state acquisitions, requisitions, or interventions in the oligopolistic industries.

By the end of March 1973, the Chilean oligarchy and the U.S. imperialists had once more set up all their pawns at the starting position for a new campaign against the Chilean government. But, unlike previous occasions, this time *all* the pawns in the system were really in the starting position.

5 The General Is Not an Honorable Man

> You will always have my unconditional loyalty, Mr. President.
> AUGUSTO PINOCHET UGARTE, commander in chief of the
> Chilean Army, in response to a question asked him by
> President Salvador Allende over the telephone on Septem-
> ber 7, 1973, the day of the Navy's attempted coup

Nineteen seventy-two had been a brilliantly successful year in the Chilean armed forces' relationship with the Executive Branch. The appropriation for military expenditures had reached a record high of $360 million, 4.6 percent of the country's Gross National Product. Percentage-wise, this put Chile ahead of other Latin-American countries (except Cuba) in military expenditures. Even in total figures, Chile's $360 million was substantial, only behind Brazil's $1,105 million and Argentina's $889 million, in the list of defense budgets from Mexico on south.[1]

In addition, training at U.S. Army camps in the Panama Canal Zone had been intensified, and there was a much larger enrollment of senior and junior officers from Chile.

That was not all. A large portion of the massive defense budget had been allocated to improve Army and military police light weapons arsenals, which put the Chilean armed forces on a much better footing to "fight internal subversion" (according to Canal Zone training sessions). President Allende had even activated a project for an extensive zone on the Argentine border, in Malleco, Cautín, and Valdivia provinces, under the exclusive control of the armed forces. In addition to starting pilot projects in timbering and farming, the Army and Air

Force used this land as a training ground for "combined operations of antiguerrilla warfare."

And since 1970 President Allende had kept to an agreement with the generals not to modify in any way the military academy's curriculum, training, and culture programs, which had been developed for the most part by the United States Army in Washington.[2]

And even more: during 1971, on the initiative of the Allende government, senior officers' salaries took a substantial jump. For example, brigadier generals went from twelve to sixteen times the minimum wage, a raise 33 percent above that received by the rest of the workers in the country. In 1972 brigadier generals' salaries went up to twenty-one times the minimum wage, an increase 31 percent above that received by the rest of salaried Chileans. Thus, during the first two years of Salvador Allende's government, the generals' salaries rose at an overall rate 75 percent above the increases received by other Chilean workers. This put the generals in a bracket with the 50,000 Chileans of the highest income in a total work force of almost 3 million.

But 1972's boons had not been limited to matériel, "antisubversive" training, and personal economic increments. The generals' "responsibilities toward society" had increased. In mid-1972, following a joint inspiration of the "reformist" and "hard-line" generals, Juan de Dios Carmona was asked to pave the way through his party, the Christian Democrats, for the passing of a gun control law which would put civilian possession of arms under military supervision. Allende thought it was a sound idea, and the Unidad Popular parliamentarians joined the Christian Democrats and National party in passing National Law No. 17.998.

In essence, the text of the law allowed military authorities to order a troop search of any domicile for arms, at any time or place, under any circumstances.

In signing this law, Salvador Allende said: "This is an instrument in the hands of the people for fighting the fascist saboteurs, because the Chilean armed forces are a guarantee of constitutionality and integrity." Later events were to reveal that quite something else had been accomplished. On the instigation of Division General Manuel Torres de la Cruz, in March 1973 the generals decided to use the gun control law for six main purposes:

1. To evaluate the actual fighting capability of the workers and peasants by undertaking widespread and humiliating searches against them.

2. To estimate the quantity of arms in the possession of leftist political and people's organizations.

3. To train the troops of the three branches of the military in operations against the civilian population.

4. To train in coordinating joint operations of the Air Force, Navy, and Army.

5. To measure the Unidad Popular's capacity for political response.

6. To train the troops psychologically so that they will "begin to see the workers, peasants, and students as their enemies."[3]

The generals began to apply the gun control law with a vengeance. Arms searches in factories, union locals, peasant settlements, leftist party headquarters, and even the private houses of popular leaders gradually began to increase in frequency and in discourtesy. During April, May, and June there were about three arms searches a week. In July the rate rose to one a day, and in August there were more than forty-five.

The character of these searches is revealed by the July 1973 statistics. Out of a total of twenty-four, ten were against factories, three against government offices, four against Unidad Popular party offices, three against people's education centers—and only two against armed fascist groups.[4]

The generals' searches seemed curiously ineffectual in halting the illegal use of arms. In July 1973, 128 attacks using arms and explosives were made on Unidad Popular leaders and party offices as well as on bridges, electric power scaffolding, and Unidad Popular newspaper offices. The fascist organizations, including Fatherland and Liberty, had publicly taken credit for more than 70 of those attacks. But, with the exception of those two searches, the various fascist local headquarters and their leaders' houses were never inspected. Out of the 128 attacks, 122 were attributed by the Army, Air Force, and Navy authorities assigned to investigate them to "persons unknown."

A not unusual case was the attack on the house of Rear Admiral Ismael Huerta, Allende's Minister of Public Works, on November 12, 1972. A bomb was thrown into the admiral's house at 1238 Uno Poniente Street in Viña del Mar. The bomb, wrapped in a copy of the ultrareactionary daily *La Tribuna,* did not explode. After its discovery, it was detonated, proving to have contained a large amount of dynamite. Three months later the civilian police found the "saboteur" —a member of Fatherland and Liberty. When the detectives took him to Huerta's house to reconstruct the crime, the admiral shook the saboteur's hand, patted him on the back, and invited him to have a cup of coffee. And in front of the detectives, he told him not to worry about the matter, that he himself would speak to the man's lawyer and have everything taken care of.

A report on this extraordinary occurrence got back to President Allende. The bombing was clearly a self-inflicted attack to create the appearance of "social chaos" by an attempt on the life of a rear admiral in the Cabinet. But, inexplicably, Allende ordered that the incident not be publicized. (After the coup, Admiral Huerta became the military junta's Minister of Foreign Relations.)[5]

But the misuse of the gun control law became even more outrageous. In early August 1973, Manuel Torres de la Cruz decided to test the six points of his theory, to prepare the terrain for the final coup. The general mobilized approximately 2,000 infantry from the Army, Navy, Air Force, and military police at the Punta Arenas garrison, his headquarters as commander of the Army's Fifth Division. He had them surround and search the Punta Arenas "industrial district." General Torres deployed tanks, recoilless cannon mounted on Jeeps, armored siege cars, helicopters, and strafings from fighter jets. The operation's novelty was that it was conducted under a "joint command" supervised by General Torres. The Air Force's infantry and equipment were commanded by General José Berdichewski; the Navy's, by Rear Admiral Horacio Justiniano; and the military police's, by General Hernán Fuentealba.

The operation of encircling the area, subduing the workers, and proceeding with the search began in the freezing cold dawn and continued for more than eight hours. The main target was the Lanera Austral textile factory, where at the time there were not more than twelve workers, seven of them women. The soldiers charged in, smashing doors and breaking windows with their rifle butts and shoving the workers into the courtyard. For six hours, the prisoners were forced to lie face down on the frozen ground, hands on their necks, while the soldiers searched every corner of the factory. They jabbed the women workers with the points of their machine guns, shouting: "Where are the guns, you shitty whores?" One worker, whom the attack had caught off guard in the toilet, was dragged out with his pants down around his knees and almost smashed to death against the floor by their rifle butts, while the soldiers shouted, "This is so that you'll learn to obey, Commie faggot!" Another worker, Alberto González Bustamante, caught as he turned off the hot water in a shower stall, was shot in the back and killed. The SIM chief in Punta Arenas installed himself at the scene of these incidents to interrogate the arrested workers, and he offered them this alternative: "If you sign a statement testifying that we found tons of concealed arms, we won't accuse you of resisting the armed forces. If not, we'll charge you with that and you'll rot in prison." They also threatened the women with rape. But none of the threats was carried out, and none of the workers signed the declaration. This gigantic military operation had harvested all of one .22-caliber Star revolver of Argentine manufacture, belonging to the night watchman.

The operation, especially because of the murder of Alberto González Bustamante, caused a great public outcry from leftist organizations. Mario Palestro, a Socialist Deputy representing the San Miguel community in the Pedro Aguirre Cerda District of Santiago, delivered an irate speech in the Chamber of Deputies, charging that "General Manuel Torres de la Cruz is a disgrace to our country's armed forces . . . he is a madman, an assassin."

The Socialist party leaders demanded that Allende fire General Torres. Allende spoke to the then acting commander in chief of the Army, General Augusto Pinochet Ugarte, to "urge" him to dismiss Torres. General Pinochet replied that it was his understanding, as well as that of the corps of Army generals, that "the commander of the Fifth Division has the complete confidence of the Army General Staff," and for that reason, nothing could be done. Pinochet, in a gesture typical of the double role he played after July 1973, suggested: "We must wait a while, until the waters calm themselves, to clean out those officers with political ideas, Mr. President." Prats, then Minister of Defense, no longer wielded any influence with the Army and was not even consulted by Allende. Allende decided to go along with Pinochet's advice. And instead of Torres's being fired, the Army General Staff brought legal action against Socialist Deputy Mario Palestro for "serious injuries and insults to the Army of Chile."

On August 29, *El Mercurio,* the newspaper belonging to the Edwards clan headed by Agustín Edwards Eastman, vice-president of Pepsi Cola in New York (currently in charge of sales to the Soviet Union), published a feature article on page 2 entitled "General Torres de la Cruz and the Activities of the Fifth Division." The text included these passages:

Manuel Torres de la Cruz is a robust man and, although not tall, is imposing; his manner is always friendly, in a forceful way. Our first meeting with the Fifth Army Division's commander, whose headquarters are in Punta Arenas, took place on board the airplane that flew him back to his base. In Santiago he had refused to make a statement to the press, joking that he was outside his own jurisdiction. We descended directly behind him; before stepping onto the landing staircase, he turned and said with calm satisfaction: "Now you are going to see something that will interest you." On the runway at President Ibáñez Airport was a gathering of Navy, Air Force, and Army officers, including Rear Admiral Horacio Justiniano and the Air Force second-in-command, Eduardo Clavijo; the Air Force commander, José Berdichewski, would greet him hours later, on his return from abroad.

El Mercurio understood General Torres's message: the three branches of the Chilean armed forces were solidly united behind the Fifth Division commander, and because by that time many oligarchic groups knew that "the coup is going to happen any minute now," it was assumed that Torres would head the future junta. So they decided to start giving him a good public image.

General Torres had correctly evaluated the degree of dissension in the Unidad Popular's parties as well as the indecisive and suicidal position of Salvador Allende and the Chilean Communist party, when he put forth his "six-point" thesis about the large-scale arms searches. He had said: "The Marxists will not dare stop us—they are afraid of us." Events had proved him right. He had said: "They will not dare turn the people against us, because the President and his Communist supporters are afraid of them too." And again, unfortunately, events proved him right.

The armed forces' gun control searches continued throughout the length of Chile and were conducted with unbounded brutality. The soldiers destroyed machinery, the modest furniture in workers' homes, their clothing, books, tools, the Central Única's regional archives.[6] They brutally beat men, women, and even children. One Air Force battalion searched the Municipal Cemetery in southern Santiago at night, deploying a massive war apparatus including helicopters with artillery. The enemy they found were two caretakers, whom they beat up and forced to kneel with their hands on their necks for nine hours in a pouring rain. They destroyed more than fifty coffins, dumping the bodies in piles onto the ground.

The most incredible thing, from the point of view of "publicly justifying" this five-month-long "search and destroy" campaign, is that they *never* found any arms other than the guns carried by the night watchmen at the sites searched. The "arms caches" they could show as a result of these extensive mobilizations were long wooden laths, construction workers' helmets, rods made of *coligüe* (a Chilean species of bamboo, much thinner than other varieties), and personal work tools which they described as "blunt contusive instruments." Laths and bamboo poles had been used by workers to carry flags in parades and to defend themselves against the civilian fascist groups harassing the public demonstrations. A typical incident was the search of the Central Única's Osorno headquarters, which was also the home of a worker. In his inner courtyard he was raising *porotos,* a kind of white bean whose vines have to be grown on poles to get enough sun. The soldiers confiscated his garden poles (twenty-four of them, each about a yard and a half long) as "weapons."

While the soldiers were "softening and reconnoitering" the Chilean people on the pretext of "disarming those who want to do violence to our country," the generals were protecting the fascist groups, among them Fatherland and Liberty, as they smuggled in arms from Argentina and Bolivia.

In the north, the commander of the Armored Division (Sixth Division), Brigadier General Carlos Forestier Haensgen, was protecting the band of arms smugglers led by Roberto Thieme, Fatherland and Liberty's second-in-command, and by ex-Army Captain Arturo Marshall (who had been implicated in the Schneider case by ex-General Viaux in 1970). They were operating from Salta, Argentina, and Oruro, Bolivia. Like Torres de la Cruz, Forestier was a rabid Catholic; his friends referred to him as "the Nazi." He had been one of the *latifundistas* expropriated by the Allende government, and was denounced in *Puro Chile, El Rebelde, Última Hora,* and *Chile Hoy* during June and July 1973.

In the south-central part of the country, Brigadier General Washington Carrasco Fernández, commander of the Third Division (headquarters in Concepción), was protecting not only the members of Fatherland and Liberty, whose arsenal was stored in the homes of his general staff, but also the National party's Rolando Matus Commandos, and Federico Willoughby MacDonald's ex-Cadet Commandos. General Carrasco, a "reformist" with agents in the SIM, was famous for his connections with the Pentagon[7] (in December 1973 the junta made him chief of the military mission in the Chilean Embassy in Washington, putting the right man in the right place). Carrasco also had a friendship with National party Senator Francisco Bulnes Sanfuentes, an industrialist who sat on the board of two subsidiaries of W. R. Grace Company.[8]

The Cavalry Division's commander, Brigadier General Héctor Bravo Muñoz, protected the *latifundistas'* training camps in Valdivia Province. These had been set up to deal with the growing liberation movement among the peasants, who were demanding more land and uncompensated expropriation of the *latifundios,* including all farm machinery and installations. Bravo Muñoz had connections with the Pentagon through General Mario Sepúlveda Squella. Bravo Muñoz was another fanatical Catholic, but he belonged to the "constitutionalist" group, whose apparent leader was Carlos Prats González. (In July 1974 Bravo Muñoz was made Minister of the newly created Department of Transportation.)

THE LAST MESSAGE

When President Allende read his annual message to the newly elected Congress on May 21, 1973, the situation was explosive any way one looked at it. The cost of living had risen by 195.5 percent in the previous twelve months. By May 16, the reserves of combustible liquid (gasoline and paraffin) had been exhausted, and problems with the supply of liquid gas were so serious that the Mexican government, in response to a desperate plea from Allende, hurriedly dispatched a tanker to Chile to cope with the fuel requirements of the Chilean winter.

The systematic misuse of private capital in Chilean and American hands and the credit squeeze the United States had been subjecting Chile to during the Allende administration had done major damage to the economy. The following information may serve as background:

"The lines of credit from North American banks began to shrink immediately. From $219 million in lines of credit granted in August 1970, the figure dropped rapidly to $32 million by mid-1971. The same thing happened with the international banking organizations and U.S. financial agencies. Minister Orlando Millas, in his report on the state of the Public Treasury, indicated that between 1964 and 1970, Chile had arranged for credits totaling $1,031,806,000 with the International Development Bank, the BIRF (Banco Internacional de Reconstrucción y Fomento, an agency of the U.S. government), the Agency for International Development, and Eximbank, an average of about $150 million per year. In 1971 this amount dropped to $40 million and was reduced to zero during the course of 1972" (Hugo Fazio, "El Bloqueo Financiero," *Revista de la Universidad Técnica del Estado*, January–February 1973).

"Charles W. Bray, a State Department spokesman, said in New York today that 'As far as the drop in foreign loans and investments in Chile goes, it doesn't seem necessary to look for any exotic explanation.' Bray declared that Allende's unilateral moratorium on the payment of Chile's foreign debt adopted in November 1971 had 'seriously damaged Chile's credit' " (UPI cable, December 6, 1972).

"When these visits are carried out [this memorandum, written by ITT's president on October 20, 1970, refers to Dr. Henry Kissinger, Messrs. Meyer and Irwin of the State Department, Secretary of State William Rogers, and President Nixon] we should demand that U.S. representatives of international banks take a strong stand against any loan to countries expropriating American companies or discriminating against foreign private capital.

"As part of the overall action, we should ask our friends in Congress to warn the Administration that continued mistreatment of U.S. private capital will bring about a cutoff of the U.S. taxpayers' funds to international banks" (NACLA *Latin America & Empire Report*, Vol. VI, No. 4, April 1972, page 16; part of the ITT documents published by American columnist Jack Anderson).

"Kennecott Copper [owner of Braden Copper, which mined El Teniente until its expropriation in 1971] . . . is trying to throw up what amounts to an international legal blockade of Chile's copper shipments. . . . The court battle could hardly have come at a worse time for Chile, which gets about 70% of its foreign currency from copper sales. The country is already boiling with political and social unrest, and teetering on the edge of bankruptcy. Obviously, Kennecott's offensive is likely to hurt future copper sales to customers unwilling to risk legal hassles and possibly costly delays in deliveries.

"Kennecott officials are determined to keep the heat on Chile. The Manhattan office of General Counsel Pierce McCreary, who is directing the campaign, has the air of a war room. His desk is strewn with shipping reports, and on one wall hangs a large map for plotting ships' courses. From here, McCreary keeps a close watch on vessels entering or leaving the Chilean port of San Antonio, the only place from which El Teniente copper is shipped. At present he is monitoring the movements of at least six ships headed for Europe, loaded with El Teniente metal; when they arrive he wants his agents to be there to greet them with court orders" (*Time* magazine, November 6, 1972).

Of course, *Time* could not add in its article that every time a freighter loaded with copper weighed anchor in San Antonio, Kennecott in New York received reports from the U.S. Navy, which received its information from the First Naval District of Chile (Valparaíso), under the command of Vice-Admiral José Toribio Merino. This fact was first publicly disclosed by a Santiago daily, *El Rebelde,* on October 14, 1972.

"After the decision made by the majority of international credit organizations to halt all activity in favor of Chile, the copper embargo, conducted with the tacit approval of the U.S. government and Chile's Christian Democrats, joined with the financial blockade, makes a vast unified operation which is literally strangling the experiment begun after October 1970 by President Allende" (Lausanne, Switzerland, daily newspaper *Tribune,* October 17, 1972).

However, during the U.S.'s financial blockade of Chile's world trade, the Chilean armed forces continued to receive credit from the U.S. They used this to buy a completely equipped Hercules C-130 airplane ($5 million) capable of carrying 90 paratroopers, various small warships, and light equipment for "fighting internal subversion."[9]

The financial blockade was aggravated by the inflexibility of the international financial system, which, even though Chile received credits from the Soviet Union and other Eastern European countries, did not save her from the destructive effects of the cessation of American aid. This was compounded by the incompetence of some middle-level officials in the Unidad Popular's economic apparatus, including a few instances of graft as well as diversion of funds to finance election campaigns and to pay some party officials' salaries. But these factors were almost irrelevant compared to the systematic, merciless sabotage by the Chilean private oligopolists and U.S. companies.

The situation can be summarized as follows:

1. In 1972, for the first time in the history of the Chilean copper industry, the Chuquicamata mine showed no profits; instead it sustained a loss of around $5 million. Lack of replacement parts and late repairs because of the U.S. blockade were the main causes.

The Chilean Copper Corporation reported that in 1972 Chuquicamata production dropped 15,000 tons from the previous year. During the same period, the La Exótica mine showed a production drop of 4,000 tons, and the El Salvador mine, a drop of 2,000 tons.

2. In 1972 the vast textile industry SUMAR, nationalized in 1971, sustained a loss of 132 million escudos (some $11 million).

3. On June 30, 1972, the balance on hand in the DINA (National Distributor) showed a loss of 20 million escudos (around $1,666,000) and indebtedness to the government's internal revenue and social security offices in the amount of 172 million escudos ($14,333,000).

4. The Chilean Electric Company (bought by the Frei regime from American Foreign Power in 1970 for $186 million, when its installations were worth only $18 million) reported a loss of 250 million escudos ($20,833,000) for fiscal 1972.

5. In May 1973, Pedro Hidalgo, Minister of Agriculture, told reporters that as a result of the foreign blockade, half the loading cranes in a district of Valparaíso harbor were immobilized. Also, owing to the lack of replacement parts, 250 locomotives out of 500 belonging to the state railroads were paralyzed.

The economic pressure of the Chilean and foreign oligopolies had a very specific goal: to create havoc in the nation's productive apparatus and force the workers to withdraw their support from the Unidad Popular government, thus leaving it at the mercy of the coup conspirators. The Unidad Popular leaders had become embroiled in a battle for economic power that would be arbitrated according to the laws of a capitalist society; this was obviously to the advantage of the oligopolies and multinational companies.[10]

The Unidad Popular's endeavor to achieve socialist goals by capitalist means rendered it vulnerable to its enemies' ploys, as did four other factors: the financial blockade, the drop in the price of copper on the world market, the rise in food prices on the world market, and the internal pressure to import more food. In 1971 and 1972, these four factors resulted in a loss of $1,105 million. Because of the financial blockade, $200 million had to be sent abroad to ensure capital movement; the drop in the price of copper from 64 cents a pound in 1970 to 49 cents in 1971 and 1972 deprived the national budget of at least $460 million; the 51 percent hike in the world price of wheat, 88 percent in butter, 40 percent in frozen meat, and 86 percent in sugar (all New York Commodities Exchange prices) necessitated an increased spending of $275 million during this two-year period. The increase in the volume of wheat imported (300,000 tons in 1970, more than 500,000 tons in 1971) and powdered milk (3,800 tons in 1970, 38,400 tons in 1971) cost an additional $50 million in 1971 and $120 million in 1972.

If these figures are added to the $493 million due in 1973 for amortizations and interest payments on the foreign debt (doubled during the Frei administration and increased nearly $1 billion by the nationalization of the copper, iron, and saltpeter mines and the expropriation of some U.S. industries), we have a picture of serious weakness in the foreign sector caused by precisely the opposite of what Allende's detractors were charging. That is to say, the Unidad Popular was not following a socialist economic and political plan, but rather a reformist, developmental one.

The seriousness of this problem can be gauged by the fact that total income in annual profits did not exceed $1,200 million, which meant that the government was compelled to spend $1,046 million annually. This left the meager sum of about $150 million for machinery, replacements, fuel, and industrial raw materials. The result was an almost total paralysis of the national productive apparatus, pushing the country's economy into a gigantic inflationary spiral.

When one adds to this the economic pressure and influence brought to bear by multinational corporations such as ITT, Anaconda, and Kennecott, and banks such as Chase Manhattan and First National City, the picture is complete. Here are two enlightening facts:

1. In 1972 alone, Chilean oligopolists transferred more than $100 million from reinvestment to speculation. There was a 54 percent drop in reinvestment of capital in the private productive area, which comprised more than 60 percent of the total national productive apparatus.

2. In 1972 alone, the political majority in the Chilean Parliament, at the beck and call of U.S. and Chilean big business interests, made twenty appropriations for projects costing a total of 60 billion escudos (some $4.9 billion), against a budget of only 12 billion escudos (about $1 billion). In other words, Congress forced the government to issue banknotes without productive guarantees for nearly $4 billion—almost one-half of the Gross National Product! In addition, they blocked tax increases on big business, thereby passing the burden of the faltering economy to the laborers, peasants, office workers, and small and medium-sized businessmen. These people were the principal victims of the inflation created by the large-scale issues of unbacked currency.

However, the conspirators behind these "objective" conditions for Allende's overthrow had not foreseen one response. As the economic chaos was aggravated, the extent of the reactionary sabotage became clearer. The people's organizations, on the fringe of the Unidad Popular's actual party leadership, had transformed what had been christened "popular power to increase productivity" (in Allende's speeches and in Communist party directives published in 1970–1973) into a project for "popular power to create the revolution." By May 1973, it was as clear to the Unidad Popular leaders as it was to the conspirators and their allies that this movement in the heart of the Chilean working class was "independent"; it had reached its own very clear conclusions, after the experiences of 1971–1972, on how to deal with the economic, political, and social crisis in which Chile's middle-class democracy had mired itself.

Large sectors of the Socialist party, including its secretary-general, Carlos Altamirano, the MAPU (Movimiento de Acción Popular Unitaria), and the MIR (Movimiento de Izquierda Revolucionaria) had decided that what was in a state of crisis was the thesis of the Chilean Communist party and Salvador Allende himself, and that the crisis was encapsulated in the phrase "the Chilean way to socialism," based in turn on the fantasy of a supposed "peaceful transition to socialism." The behavior of the government was an impediment to the Chilean people's progress toward social revolution because of its protective attitude toward the Chilean and North American oligopolies. The entire reformist structure that Allende had precariously built was in danger of being destroyed, along with bourgeois democracy. Fascism was the alternative. The Chilean masses found themselves at a crossroad: either they themselves prepared to take on the struggle or else they could be brutalized by an armed counterrevolution instigated by the fascist powers. This caused sectors of the Unidad Popular to revert to a theory put forth years earlier by parties of the revolutionary left, among them the PCR (Partido Communista Revolucionario), but never formulated into a strategy suited to conditions in Chile. This theory was published in declarations by the Socialist party and the MIR in February, June, July, and August 1973.

As one way to avoid having the masses confront the armed counterrevolution defenseless, these two political groups tried throughout 1973—until September—to get thousands of laborers, peasants, office workers, and students to mobilize and push the government to move forward in expropriations; to demand control of the industries and businesses in the Social Area, by forcing the government to fire incompetent and corrupt officials, bureaucrats, and reformist union leaders, and to replace them with genuine representatives of the laborers, peasants, and office workers; to demand prosecution of the people undermining the national economy; and, last, to recognize and act on the necessity for a universal mobilization of the masses to be constantly on the alert against the armed forces' fascist conspiracy and to struggle to neutralize it.

This attempt at popular mobilization was hampered, persecuted, and even denounced by the political leaders closest to Allende and by the Chilean Communist party directorate. When the military finally began its takeover on September 11, 1973, the people were still inadequately prepared to defend their government. And yet it was precisely this cry of "political emergency" from large sectors of the Chilean population that had informed the Pentagon's October Report that "the popular insurrection is about to explode" in Chile. To prevent this, it was imperative that the Chilean generals overthrow Allende "as soon as possible" and "at the most suitable moment" to stop a "hazardous" confrontation with this nascent "popular power," now beyond manipulation by Allende and his political supporters.[11]

In his message to the new Parliament on May 21, 1973, President Allende, who realized better than anyone else that "the new popular power" was slipping out of his grasp, nonetheless tried to use this "phantom overrunning Chile" to frighten the oligarchy into giving him time to "channel" the people's restiveness and prevent it from turning into a violent revolution.

Allende said: "The dynamism of a revolutionary process releases repressed energies, wounds dominant interests, generates new social phenomena that can be guided *and that the government has been at pains to control.* . . . However, to bring this to a satisfactory conclusion, we need to have a flexible institutional system."

Allende proposed vast state reforms to control the "new social phenomenon" (that is, the revolution) and thereby prevent it from destroying the whole system of bourgeois domination. But the legislators had estimated that "the subversion of the rabble" was going to be achieved neither by reforms nor by Allende nor by Frei. Allende's anguished pleas went unheard:

> More than the problematic economic juncture through which we are passing, the government attributes greater transcendence to the real and serious threat that weighs upon our democracy. As a people and as a nation, few dangers seem greater, because the rupture of the civil peace would mean the failure of our collective political capacity to solve the community's problems by means other than physical violence, which some are obsessively seeking. This confrontation would occasion tragic consequences, a profound human drama, as well as catastrophic economic effects. . . .
> Today my first congressional message acquires greater reality: "If violence, internal or external, in any of its forms, physical, economical, social, or political, goes as far as threatening our normal development and the workers' victories, the greatest risk will be run by institutional continuity, the state of the law, political freedoms, and pluralism. Our people's struggle for social emancipation or free determination would necessarily adopt forms of expression very different from what we, with legitimate pride and historical realism, call the Chilean way to socialism." . . .
> It cannot be a secret to anybody that the key problem we are experiencing is the generalized crisis of the traditional order of things, while a new structure of social relations is laboriously being born. . . .
> It is not the peasants, starving for bread and justice, grabbing a piece of land to cultivate (a procedure which we do not encourage), who are threatening the peace. . . . It is rather those who take nothing, because they have everything, who are the true promoters of violence, because they are obsessively creating the conditions for a civil war. . . .

Allende went on to ask them to let him aid this social birth in such a way that the whole system would not crumble.

> The bourgeoisie's hierarchy, authority, and order have lost their supremacy in the workers' eyes, while they are trying to create, within the state's institutional regime and legal norms, an order and a discipline based on their own experience. Directive committees for the Social Area, communal peasant councils, health councils, mining councils, supply and price control juntas, industrial cordons, communal commandos, and so forth are other manifestations of this reality which have emerged since 1970. Struggling against the structure of the old ruling class, these institutions of the nascent social order

are looking, testing, criticizing and creating their own laws of work and discipline.

President Allende concluded that "the state's apparatus would have been paralyzed" by internal and foreign sabotage aimed at his government had it not been for "the workers' alliance with the armed forces and the forces of order." (This statement on May 21, 1973, shows Allende clutching at the idea that he could persuade the military high command to help him in his experiment, when in fact it was well known that the generals were plotting to overthrow him at any moment. All the leftist newspapers were carrying daily reports on the conspiracy's movements.)

Concluding his message, Allende called on the reactionary majority in Parliament to help him create a "new institutionality," while he would make an effort "to control" the laborers, peasants, and office workers who were eager for a revolution. And to emphasize his meaning he concluded his message to Parliament with a call for the workers to work and only to work—at precisely the moment when his enemies were already crouching to spring:

> The People's Government appeals to the conscience and class feeling of all the workers. Your social achievements, your political freedom, your organizations, your power to challenge the strength of national and imperialist capitalism, your ability to build a new society, are great tools. These can be destroyed by the national and international forces of reaction. These people are trying to destroy the workers' victories. In the face of such a real and present threat, the workers will not allow themselves to be exploited. Your economic improvements cannot be used by the bourgeoisie against the government and the revolutionary process. Social discipline and conscious effort must mark the path of our labor. Chile demands greater production, greater productivity. . . .

The comments made on this message by a National party Deputy (and secret member of Fatherland and Liberty, as pointed out by *Puro Chile* in February 1973), Hermógenes Pérez de Arce, were eloquent: "This message can only serve to convince us how necessary it is for our country to rid itself of this generation of demagogues. . . . Mr.

Allende ought to shut up . . . and make room in Chile . . . for those who know how to rule."

A NEW STEP FORWARD

President Allende had good reason to be desperate. The reactionary offensive was reaching extremes of violence. May 21 marked the beginning of the second month of a serious mine workers' strike at El Teniente, one of the nationalized copper mines. The strike had started on April 20 and was being managed by Frei's group in the Christian Democrats, abetted by the National party and Fatherland and Liberty.

As the reactionaries had predicted, the economic crisis had caused the proliferation of workers' strikes for higher wages, which in turn served to aggravate the economic crisis, since the Allende government was prevented by its political foes in the Parliament from placing the burden on the oligarchy by raising taxes on corporate profits and personal income. The directors of the Society for Industrial Development took direct charge of influencing the workers' strikes, mostly through the Christian Democratic union organizations.[12]

The copper mine workers' strike at El Teniente was a typical case. It began with a demand for a 41 percent increase in salaries. Through Guillermo Medina, the leader of the striking workers, the Christian Democrats took over and transformed the workers' legitimate demands for higher salaries into a weapon to undermine the Unidad Popular government. Medina was put in contact with Manuel Fuentes Wedling, a journalist who belonged to the directorate of Fatherland and Liberty. Fuentes undertook to write Medina's speeches both at the mine and in Santiago. (This was discovered after the abortive coup of June 29, which disarmed the leaders of Fatherland and Liberty and led to a search of Fuentes's home, where rough drafts of speeches Medina had given in April and May were found. These were published in *Última Hora, Puro Chile,* and *El Siglo.*)

The strike lasted more than two months. By May it had become the hub of a general strike movement being guided by the Christian Democrats to embarrass the government. On May 23, some 25,000 students belonging to Christian Democratic–controlled student centers at the University of Chile went on strike in support of the El Teniente mine workers. The same day, the Secondary Students' Federation of Santiago, also controlled by the Christian Democrats, joined the student strike. The nature of the situation became clearer when fascist and Christian Democratic shock groups in the city of Rancagua, near El Teniente, transformed a public demonstration "in support of the strike" into an attack using firearms, stones, and other blunt instruments against the municipal building and the Communist and Socialist party locals. The commander of the city's garrison, Lieutenant Colonel Cristian Ackerknecht, deployed his soldiers against those being attacked. He also had the Socialist party's local searched "for arms." The situation was absurd. While the troops were "dealing with" the Socialist party local, a few meters away, in the street, Fatherland and Liberty men were hiding their revolvers under their jackets or turning their clubs into "pennant standards."

Ackerknecht's anti-Socialist action provoked an infuriated reaction from the Socialist party's national directorate (to which Allende belonged), demanding that the lieutenant colonel be fired. Instead, the Army's acting commander in chief, General Augusto Pinochet, sent more troops to the city, commanded by an officer of higher rank, Colonel Orlando Ibáñez, and made a public statement: "I emphasize that the measures adopted by the officers in charge of the Emergency Zone on May 23 have my unconditional support, backing, and recognition."

Yet once more, in the face of political insolence from the acting commander in chief of the Chilean Army, the party directorates of the Unidad Popular remained silent.

But in spite of the enormous effort Eduardo Frei put forth to make the El Teniente strike the "detonator" for Allende's resignation or overthrow, this did not happen. There were two reasons. The generals felt that they were "not ready yet" (they had held meetings on May

24 and 25); and the popular organizations not dominated by the Christian Democrats had come back with a mobilization that started the El Teniente mine functioning again.

The case of Manuel Fuentes Wedling, the Fatherland and Liberty journalist, reveals another aspect of the conspiracy: the involvement of dignitaries of the Catholic Church. One of these was the secretary of the Santiago archbishopric and director of Catholic University's TV Channel 13, Father Raúl Hasbún, whose weekly sermon broadcasts stirred up the bourgeoisie against the working classes. In a series of articles that ran daily from June 22 to June 28, 1973, *Puro Chile* exposed the following episode, which took place in March 1973.

By order of Father Raúl Hasbún, Channel 5, an unlicensed subsidiary of Channel 13, was set up in Concepción. The government reacted by installing a legal electronic signal device to interfere with the pirate station.[13] Father Hasbún then contacted Manuel Fuentes Wedling for "help" in "solving" the problem of Channel 5's "interferences." Hasbún asked Fuentes to find "a group of daring people" to destroy the government's electronic installations in Concepción. Fuentes met with Michael Vernon Townley Welch, alias Juan Manolo, Fatherland and Liberty's armaments trainer from the CIA, and the Chileans Rafael Undurraga Cruzat and Gustavo Etchepare. They formed a commando team at the orders of Father Hasbún, to break into the house at 382 Freire Street in Concepción, where the government's electronic equipment had been installed.

On March 18, 1973, the "commandos" broke into the house and stole the equipment, in the process murdering the caretaker, a house painter named Jorge Tomás Enríquez González.

The investigation and subsequent judgment hanging over Father Raúl Hasbún as "intellectual author" of the murder and armed robbery were interrupted by the coup on September 11, 1973.[14]

Another case involved the arms smuggling engaged in by National party Senator Pedro Ibáñez Ojeda, a member of the oligopolies in Valparaíso. This group's main business was the import of agricultural machinery and the ownership of the instant coffee industry (Sí Café).

The firm of Ibáñez Ojeda Brothers (the Senator and his brother) was mainly involved in importing from Brazil. In 1972 and 1973, Senator Ibáñez Ojeda placed his Brazilian connections at the disposal of Fatherland and Liberty, so that they could import arms from Brazil. This setup functioned smoothly for more than a year, under the protection of naval officers in Valparaíso harbor and corrupt customs officials who overlooked the huge crates coming in labeled as farm machinery or raw material for the manufacture of instant coffee.

Ibáñez Ojeda's operation was only a part of a vast network in Brazil which channeled funds to sabotage the Chilean economy and supply the fascist terrorist groups. In collusion with the metallurgical and banking oligopolies in Brazil, private industrialists (for one, the printing magnate Gilberto Huber) used couriers to get money into Chile. Among these were Aristóteles Brumond, reportedly in contact with the CIA team in Brazil, and an engineer, Glaycon de Paiva, prime mover of the Institute of Social Investigations and Studies (IPES), founded with Washington advisers in 1961 to "avoid" a popular uprising in the Janio Quadros and João Goulart administrations.[15] These Brazilian groups were financial and ideological backers of the teams of "experts" from the Christian Democrat and National parties to coordinate the political sabotage of Allende's government. Orlando Sáenz was in constant touch with these Brazilians, as he was with similar groups in Argentina, Venezuela, and the U.S.[16]

A NEW MILITARY INSURRECTION

By June 1973, the leaders of Fatherland and Liberty were so impressed by their own terrorism, by the extent of their infiltration among the *latifundistas* in the south, as well as by the ample protection they were receiving from the military police and the armed forces, that they decided to set up an adventure on their own. The head of the conspirators in Fatherland and Liberty, Pablo Rodríguez Grez, planned a military insurrection in Santiago that (he hoped) would touch off the whole country like a powder keg. This would swiftly result in Allende's downfall and his replacement by a civilian and military junta consisting of the president of the Senate (Eduardo Frei), the President of the Supreme Court (Enrique Urrutía Manzano), and the commanders in chief of the armed forces.

Rodríguez Grez consulted with ex-General Roberto Viaux Marambio, who had been in the Santiago Penitentiary since November 1970 for his part in the Schneider affair. He outlined his organization's achievements. Fatherland and Liberty's terrorist activities were impressive: in January 1973, five attacks on Unidad Popular personnel or offices; 29 in February; 28 in March; 57 in April; 105 in May—as opposed to a total of 66 between July and December of 1972. Only 100 of these attacks had been investigated, with 83 persons arrested —all released by the courts of justice! The Supreme Court, by special request from the director of Army personnel, General Oscar Bonilla ("a Frei man," said Rodríguez Grez), had sent an insolent official letter to President Allende on May 26 reminding him "for the *n*th time of the illegal attitude of the Executive Branch in its illegitimate interference in judicial matters" and warning that "this is no longer a case of civil rights but one of a peremptory or imminent collapse in the country's judicial system." Rodríguez Grez also reported to Viaux that Prats's prestige inside the Army was at rock bottom. Not only was the high command involved in the conspiracy but Frei, Jarpa, and other right-wing politicians had joined too. The CIA was of the opinion that conditions were ripe to provoke a civilian-military coup. He went on to say that the *latifundistas,* through Benjamín Matte, president of the National Agriculture Society, also concurred that the time had come to overthrow Allende. And, lastly, he said, Fatherland and Liberty could count on "the loyalty" of at least one Santiago regiment, the 2nd Armored, since its commander, Lieutenant Colonel Roberto Souper Onfray, was an active member of Fatherland and Liberty and also the brother of a regional director of that fascist organization.[17]

Viaux, who was openly being protected by the Supreme Court, which had reduced his sentence for planning Schneider's assassination from twenty to two years, concurred with Rodríguez Grez's estimate of the situation and suggested a plan. According to what Rodríguez Grez later told Benjamín Matte, which Matte indiscreetly repeated to a group of friends at his house a few days before the June 29 uprising, the plan was: first, to somehow create a scandal involving General Carlos Prats, to "make him commit moral suicide," forcing the armed forces to say "enough is enough" with their commander in chief; second, to attack La Moneda with the Armored Regiment's tanks, thus presenting the Santiago officers with a *fait accompli.*

This plan was really an improved version of Viaux's attempted coup of October 1970. Fatherland and Liberty bent itself to its task, concentrating entirely on preparing the two "detonators": ruining Prats's reputation and turning the tank brigades of Santiago against La Moneda.

On Tuesday morning, June 26, Fatherland and Liberty set up a "street incident" with the complicity of a Santiago regiment. The decoy was a somewhat masculine-looking woman named Virginia Cox. At an hour when most of the Santiago hillside suburb's cars were on their way into the city, Prats's car would be harassed and threatened several times with collision by two other cars, while from a third, Virginia Cox would annoy the general to the point of exasperation. It was hoped that Prats would think Cox was a man (which in fact happened) and would attack her, causing a huge traffic tie-up. The men driving the other two cars would kindle the onlookers' indignation, so that the general would be beaten and, if things went especially well, even killed. (This entire incident was prepared by the CIA, through the journalist Manuel Fuentes Wedling, a member of Fatherland and Liberty.)[18]

Things went more or less as planned. At noon on June 26, after General Prats's car left the Santiago hillside suburb, for twenty blocks it was crossed in front of, bumped, and sometimes even pushed by two other cars. Virginia Cox was in a small car making vulgar faces and hand gestures at Prats and shouting "Old faggot" at him. Enraged, Prats intercepted her car and drew his service revolver, aiming it at her head. It was only then that the general realized that his tormentor was not a man. By that time, more than a hundred angry people had surrounded the scene. One of the Fatherland and Liberty provokers shouted, "Faggot general, you're just like Allende—you only dare with women!" By great good luck, a taxi driver in the crowd seized the general by the arm, shoved him into his cab, and drove off to the Ministry of Defense. The taxi driver later told reporters: "I realized that the crowd wanted to lynch the general . . . if I didn't get him out of there, they would have killed him. There were fellows there shoving him. Everybody was shouting all kinds of things at him and egging the others on too. . . . To get my cab out of there, I had to floor the accelerator and plow through some people who were trying to block our path."

General Prats's car was left behind; the air was let out of the tires, and the roof and windshield were lettered in yellow paint with the words "Chicken generals—Prats faggot." From the very beginning of the incident, reporters had been covering it for the Minería radio station, which belonged to the industrial oligarchy, and for *El Mercurio*. The reactionaries' newspapers, radio stations, and TV channels began to broadcast the story incessantly from the afternoon of the twenty-sixth on, taking the angle "General Prats attacks a woman who stuck her tongue out at him," calling him "a coward" in their reports, "a person who should not be the head of our glorious armed forces."

The next day, *El Mercurio*'s page two carried a very long article signed by Carlos Vicuña Fuentes, a reactionary intellectual. Entitled "A Call to Sensible People," the article said, in a nutshell, "the country cannot put up with the present situation any longer," "our armed forces are the moral reserve that will save our country," we "need to have a military government take the nation's reins" and, "after a prudent interval, give control back to a select group of people of proven wisdom and intelligence."

The same day, June 27, a regiment captain in the officers' mess at the 2nd Armored Regiment tried to persuade his fellow officers that "we ought to go to headquarters with the tanks and tell that faggot Prats to get out, and make Allende resign." But the conspiring generals, occupied with their own coup plans, were not sympathetic to Fatherland and Liberty's efforts. The captain was arrested by the unit's own SIM men and taken to the Defense Ministry. The next day, the unit commander, Lieutenant Colonel Roberto Souper Onfray, sent a message to the directorate of Fatherland and Liberty that he had been relieved of his command and would have to turn over his post to Colonel Roberto Ramírez on the twenty-ninth.

Rodríguez Grez and Benjamín Matte replied that he should incite his unit to rebel. So, on June 29, at 9 A.M., after shooting those officers who opposed them (eight men died), the 2nd Armored Regiment manned six Sherman tanks, surrounded La Moneda, attacked the Defense Ministry, and freed the captain taken into custody on the twenty-seventh. But the rebels had committed one slight error: Allende was not inside La Moneda, but at his home on Tomás Moro Street, in the hillside suburb on the other side of the city.

From 9 to 11 A.M., Souper's tanks fired more than fifty rounds, while Fatherland and Liberty and Lieutenant Colonel Souper waited for the rest of the Army to revolt. They waited in vain. No other regiment in Santiago joined them. No radio station was taken over by soldiers. Not even Eduardo Frei, president of the Senate, or Urrutía Manzano, President of the Supreme Court, said a word. What had happened?

It appeared that Fatherland and Liberty's entire plan was based on "the hope" that the rest of the military units would revolt; it did not take into account the fact (of which Fatherland and Liberty was unaware) that a "real coup d'état" was being prepared in the corps of generals, and it was not yet ready.

The problem was that the most important conspirators, the generals and admirals, did not yet have assurances that Augusto Pinochet, the second-ranking general in the Army, was completely in favor of the overthrow operation. Even after their general strategy had been mapped out, according to calculations by Generals Sergio Arellano Stark, Herman Brady Roche, Gustavo Leigh, and Vice-Admiral José

Toribio Merino, they had not yet even started conversations with General César Mendoza Durán of the military police (although Mendoza was supposed to have been "contacted" in March, the generals had postponed the conversations until they had a complete "military" picture to present to him; by June this still had not materialized). The planned procedure was meant to be coordinated with an intense "political campaign beginning in July, to be completed in September," the purpose of which was to put Allende "outside the law" in the eyes of Parliament, the judiciary, and the controller, and to "win over public opinion."

When, on Allende's orders, General Prats went to the Santiago Military School (the Defense Ministry was under siege by Souper's tanks) at 9:45 A.M. on June 29 to "put down the mutiny," the generals had already gathered to discuss the situation and were in agreement about doing so. General Prats, without knowing it, was leading one group of conspirators to put down another group. With the conspiring generals' help, he got the various regiments in Santiago to mobilize to quash the uprising.

Prats himself went to head up the Junior Officers' School because it was under the command of the ultrafascist Colonel Julio Canessa Roberts. General Augusto Pinochet led the Buin Regiment, whose commander was a "constitutionalist." General Oscar Bonilla was sent to the rebel regiment, the 2nd Armored. Bonilla, a "hard-line" conspirator, was one of the few people capable of convincing the rebels to put down their arms "to wait for the right moment."

Later, on the way to La Moneda, General Prats was joined by General Guillermo Pickering, a "reformist," head of the Military Institutes. Meanwhile, the chief of the Santiago garrison, "reformist" General Mario Sepúlveda Squella, ordered the Infantry School (commanded by a "constitutionalist" colonel), the Telecommunications School (commanded by a "hard-line" colonel), and the Paratrooper and Special Forces School (commanded by a "reformist" lieutenant colonel) to advance on the rebels attacking La Moneda from the northeast and south.

General Prats had requested that President Allende order the military police to keep away from the operation of "blockading" the rebels. Allende agreed and limited the military police to guarding his house on Tomás Moro Street.

In a desperate effort, the Fatherland and Liberty fascists dynamited the Radio Portales transmission plant, which belonged to the Socialist party. But their situation was hopeless. At 11:30 A.M. the rebels surrendered on the streets next to La Moneda, while three tanks commanded by Lieutenant Colonel Souper escaped toward 2nd Armored Regiment headquarters, only to surrender to General Oscar Bonilla.

Pablo Rodríguez Grez, Benjamín Matte, and other directors of Fatherland and Liberty took asylum in the Ecuadorian Embassy.

At 8 P.M. that day, Friday the twenty-ninth, in front of the Palacio de La Moneda, President Allende called the people together to give them "a report on the events." The assembled workers, some 20,000 of them, shouted such slogans as "Arms for the people," "Power to the people," "Dismiss Congress," "Drive the Yankees out of Chile, now."

Allende's speech ended on this note: "Tomorrow morning the factories will send up their smoke again to salute our free nation; we must go back to work to make up for the time lost on Thursday; tomorrow everyone will work harder, will produce more, will sacrifice himself more, for Chile and for the people. . . . Comrade workers: we must organize. We must create, and create the People's Power. But it cannot be antagonistic to or independent of the government, which is the fundamental force and platform for the workers to advance in the revolutionary process."

That night groups of workers marched home chanting euphorically: "Soldado, amigo, el pueblo está contigo!" (Soldier, friend, the people are with you!)

A LONG MEETING

The morning after the twenty-ninth, nearly all the generals in the Santiago garrison came to a meeting led by Herman Brady, Mario

Sepúlveda, Guillermo Pickering, Sergio Arellano Stark, Javier Palacios, and Oscar Bonilla. A military intelligence report was read, which said that "between 9 and 11 A.M." in the industrial cordons at Los Cerrillos and Vicuña Mackenna, a contingent of about 10,000 workers had gathered to march into downtown Santiago to fight the "mutinous" armored regiment. A general directive was issued to keep a "constant alert," to "increase the rhythm of arms searches in factories and the headquarters of the Unidad Popular parties and the Central Única, to rid the rebel civilian population of warlike elements." As for the mutiny, the generals attributed it to "the harmful influence of civilian persons on our officers," and announced that "this situation gives a bad image to the Army's cohesion." It was agreed to instruct all unit commanders to "suspend all contact with Fatherland and Liberty" and to keep the General Staff informed of "events in their respective areas of jurisdiction." Furthermore, the generals discussed the need to begin a rapid and systematic "education" of the junior officers and the rank and file, with informal talks and small meetings chaired by senior officers. They were to stress that the nation was in danger, that "the Marxists" were preparing to invade the country "with Peruvian aid," and that the hour was approaching to "lay down their lives for Chile."

(In various Santiago regiments, from July on, different companies would be awakened in the predawn hours, taken to the projection room, and shown movies of the jungle war in Vietnam. The session ended with a short talk on the "worldwide Communist threat to our wives, children, and parents." The troops' nerves were kept constantly on edge by this sort of treatment.)

The generals' meeting on the morning of Saturday, June 30, was only the first step in a procedure decided upon by the officers in the most intimate circle of the conspiracy. That afternoon, Generals Oscar Bonilla and Sergio Arellano Stark were delegated by Herman Brady Roche, Mario Sepúlveda Squella, Javier Palacios, Orlando Urbina Herrera, and Guillermo Pickering to speak to General Augusto Pinochet (who, like General Prats, had not been invited to the Saturday morning meeting), to brief him on their plans and ask him, as "the leader of the Army," to join the conspiracy.

The meetings with Pinochet lasted from Saturday afternoon to the morning of July 2. According to information that filtered out later, it appears that in those three days the most important ideological details of the coup were laid down, including the need to get rid of all political parties in Chilean society, and to "put into practice the patriotic task of cleaning up the Chileans' minds, permeated with the Marxist ideology."[19]

Pinochet's decision to join the conspiracy and accept the offer to become "the leader of the operation" was reported to Air Force General Gustavo Leigh Guzmán and to Vice-Admiral José Toribio Merino, presumably in the first week of July. The U.S. military mission, with its offices in the Defense Ministry, was also informed that the conspirators' circle had now been closed at the highest level.

THE PAWNS

The generals' conversations with Augusto Pinochet had led to an agreement to pressure Frei, Jarpa, and the Supreme Court justices to escalate a campaign to discredit Allende "constitutionally" and create a "public opinion" in the majority of Chileans that the military had to overthrow Allende to *return to legality.*

The military scheme to get the politicians moving worked incredibly well. Frei's and Jarpa's desires to provoke a military coup (after which one of them would naturally emerge as Chile's new President) provided a highly fertile field for the generals to sow the idea of "saving" Chile.

In the first week of July, apparently at the instigation of General Pinochet, who had been very disturbed by the unexpected results of the March election, it was decided to ask "the civilian contacts" to demand an investigation to "prove" that the March elections were "a gigantic fraud." With this the generals hoped to cast much darker shadows on the "legitimacy" of Allende's government. This task fell to the dean of faculty at the Catholic University Law School, Jaime del Valle, a Fatherland and Liberty sympathizer.[20]

This scientific study was prepared in less than two weeks. It reported, based on 29 cases of faulty voter registration out of a total of more than 3 million, that the government had committed fraud in March 1973, "falsifying" at least 400,000 votes. But most important was the way the "document" ended:

> We can affirm, then, that our democracy is today bankrupt. Our elected administration has allowed a gigantic fraud and does not guarantee that in future elections this will not be repeated. . . . It is clear that at a crossroad such as the one we face, the Chilean people have a wide-reaching task before them and they cannot avoid it any longer. *This is the task of rebuilding democracy by creating a new institutionality that will effectively guarantee it.*

This was the idea that the generals had wanted to appear in the "report." This was the idea drummed into the heads of thousands of Chileans by the daily appearance of such "documents" in the newspapers, in magazines, on the radio and TV, driving in that a "new institutionality" had to be created—a task that could be accomplished only by the military, of course.

On July 8 the president of the Senate, Eduardo Frei, released a declaration that had been made known the night before to Generals Oscar Bonilla and Sergio Arellano Stark. The document said, in part: "It is a fact that Chile is passing through one of the most serious crises in its political, economic, social, and moral history." There followed some slanted details on the political situation. "To this may be added an organized process of hate and violence which is dividing the country." Needless to say, they did not mention the right-wing press campaign that daily described President Allende as a "drunkard" and a "faggot," accused General Prats of "selling out for a few more dollars," and asked Chileans to join the cry that "the best Marxist is a dead Marxist." They also did not mention the economic sabotage perpetrated by the U.S. financial organizations, Frei himself, and the Chilean oligarchy, or the waves of fascist dynamitings, shootings, and beatings (the fascist groups had accelerated their activities to 115 in June; in July they would achieve 128 and in August 300 acts of sabotage).

And in a truly brilliant example of cynicism, the declaration affirmed: "The democratic groups which we represent are not armed. They are confident that Chile's internal security is in the hands of the armed forces and the military police, as stipulated by the Founding Charter, a tradition that has never been broken. This situation is made all the more incomprehensible if one considers that the government insists on its being able to count on the loyalty of those institutions, and that the country is at peace and that the government is in control of the situation."

And they added, "It seems to us fundamental" that the government "should promulgate in its totality the constitutional amendment that has been passed by Congress" (this was a reference to the Hamilton-Fuentealba legislation to freeze the Area of Social Property, reduce its range, and ensure the destruction of the Unidad Popular's economic program).

A MURDER

By July 1973 the situation was deteriorating hourly. According to incomplete data, between January and May 1973 speculative capital in the hands of the national oligarchy had reached the enormous sum of $250 million, with which they managed completely to shatter the already delicate balance between the supply and the demand of consumer goods. The drop in capital reinvestment, according to a preliminary study by the Society for Industrial Development, was going to reach more than 50 percent in the first six months of 1973.

At that point, the economic sabotage was aggravated by an intensive campaign to denounce the incompetence displayed by a number of state officials of leftist parties in their administration of the Area of Social Property, the nationalized businesses. These officials, labeled "interveners,"* made an art of corruption and administrative in-

---

*Government-appointed factory managers in those factories expropriated into the Area of Social Property.

competence, provoking disasters in sectors of the economy. The oligopolies and U.S. multinationals took advantage of this situation to present an economic fable about how Marxism had caused the decay of the Chilean productive system. Hence, "socialism" did not work for Chile and would have to be replaced by a corporate fascist state.

Figures showing the cost-of-living rise were the following:

December 1970 to December 1971	22.1 percent
December 1971 to December 1972	163.4 percent
January 1972 to January 1973	180.1 percent
May 1972 to May 1973	238.5 percent

This meant that during the first five months of 1973, inflation had jumped by an average of 14.6 percent per month. After that, it got worse. The figures for July 1973, compared with the same month in the previous year, gave the incredible index of 323.6 percent annual inflation, the highest in the world. This meant the monthly average had risen to 42.55 percent. According to this, the December 1973 forecast was for an annual inflation of 50 percent.

Against this background, the various right-wing conspiratorial circles continued with their work, but with disagreements among themselves.

The Christian Democrats' viewpoint, expressed by Frei, differed from that of the National party, headed by Senator Onofre Jarpa. Frei was debating the problem of using the armed forces as a "dissuader" against Allende, and maneuvering during a military dictatorship to get the generals to hand over the power to civilian leaders (himself) as soon as possible. Jarpa's position was sterner. He estimated publicly that "the only possible way to keep peace for a long time in our society is a military dictatorship." Hence, his efforts were dedicated to pushing the generals and admirals toward a military coup.

This was creating much friction and dissent in the opposition, especially because Frei's group had been carrying on secret conversations with Allende to "come to an understanding" about freezing the

reforms and diverting the revolutionary potential of workers throughout the country, so that the military would not feel tempted to mount
a coup to stay in the government "forever," as had happened in Brazil
in 1964.

This, naturally, was also reflected in the heart of the high command, especially the Army, the fundamental pillar of any military
insurrection, and it was becoming part of the "fluidity" of the conspirators' plans. In mid-July, there was general agreement in the
heart of the high command on the desirability of terminating the
Unidad Popular "experiment." How to do it was still nebulous.
General Prats, the commander in chief, had coined the idea of an
Allende–armed forces government, including a "political peace
treaty" with the Christian Democrats and restricted participation of
the Chilean Communist party and a group of Socialists. Prats argued that "only thus will we prevent the extremist workers from
rebelling." This idea had the support of Generals Joaquín Lagos
Osorio, Herman Brady Roche, Washington Carrasco Fernández,
Héctor Bravo Muñoz, Mario Sepúlveda Squella, Guillermo Pickering, and Orlando Urbina Herrera, but with variations. While Lagos
Osorio and Urbina Herrera did not object to the Prats plan, the
other five generals thought the Allende–armed forces government
ought to be "transitional" and of "short duration," to prepare conditions for a "purely military government including the military police." Generals Oscar Bonilla, Sergio Arellano Stark, and Javier
Palacios formed another group, joined by Augusto Pinochet, which
posited that the Allende–armed forces phase was not necessary.

Alone and struggling to be "the leader of the uprising" was General
Manuel Torres de la Cruz, the only one saying "we have to operate
now, at once."

It was against this background that President Allende's naval aide,
Commodore Arturo Araya Peters, was assassinated on July 26, 1973
(see Chapter 1).

The assassination led Socialist counterintelligence services to a plot
in the National party, in collusion with the CIA through the ex-Cadet

Commandos, to assassinate President Allende. The CIA had estimated, after its fiasco with Fatherland and Liberty's attempt to cause a military insurrection on June 29, that only the assassination of a "big fish" would provoke enough chaos to force the military to take charge. On Friday, July 27, Socialist counterintelligence services discovered movements in the National party relating to a "big operation" for September 4, with the goal of assassinating Allende. The plan was discovered through a legislator closely linked to Fatherland and Liberty who drank too much at a gathering in a private home on the night of July 27 and said that "Araya's murder [which had occurred the night before] may shoot all our plans to hell." The legislator seemed very concerned that the nationwide commotion provoked by the naval aide's assassination (he didn't know it had been planned by naval intelligence) and the investigations to discover the culprits might take the lid off the National party's plans for Allende's death.

On August 1, Allende informed General Carlos Prats about this plot, and the commander in chief informed his corps of generals. The generals agreed that the assassination of Allende was a "hazard" and took measures to have the plot dismantled by the SIM. Once again the events taking place in Chile showed that there was a definite lack of coordination between the coup preparations of the Pentagon and the generals, and the CIA's efforts to overthrow Allende. All the Unidad Popular parties were informed of this incident, as well.

Less than twenty days later, however, the generals changed their minds (see Chapter 1). They would assassinate Allende, and simulate his suicide, after they had taken control of the entire country in a full-scale military occupation.

From the viewpoint of the civilian conspirators, the murder of Allende's naval aide hastened things. They felt that the time had come to unleash a "new October work stoppage." On July 27 truck owners throughout Chile went on strike, alleging that "the demands that had led to the October 1972 strike had not yet been met." Three days later,

León Vilarín, president of the Chilean Truck Owners Association, made a public statement in Osorno that "this strike will end when Allende's government ends." That day Frei met with a group of friends in Santiago and informed them that he had made up his mind: "I believe only the armed forces can save Chile" (and set him up in the presidency, he hoped). He was accused of this by the daily *Última Hora* on July 30, 1973.

On Tuesday, July 31, General Prats met with 250 officers of the Santiago garrison at their request to discuss "the political situation, the serious economic crisis, and the threats from workers' sectors against the armed forces." The 250 officers asked Prats to tell Allende that "the officers of the Army believe that if an agreement is not reached with the Christian Democrats, and if the armed forces are not given complete charge of running the Area of Social Property, and if the industrial cordons are not outlawed, then the military will have to take action."

Allende countered by pulling out documents revealing the complicity of high-ranking naval officers in the assassination of his naval aide. In what he considered a master stroke, he forced the high command of the three branches of the Armed Forces to accept the appointment of four officers to his new Cabinet, which began life on August 9 as "the last chance."

The day before, on August 8, the Chilean College of Lawyers, led by Alejandro Silva Bascuñán, a financier, released a declaration (in the newspaper *El Mercurio,* on TV Channel 13, and over the network of broadcasting stations belonging to Allende's opponents) which urged public opinion to turn its attention "to the accomplishment of the dictates of conscience by mobilizing the broadest sectors of the citizenry against the destruction of the civil rights and the institutional order which have been the pride of Chileans." They were calling for the support of everything that meant the weakening of the constitutional government. This declaration deftly coincided with the generals' position.

PRATS'S RUIN

On Tuesday evening, August 7, twenty-four hours before the College of Lawyers' declaration was released, the conspirators in the naval high command had decided to start moving on an idea conceived by Vice-Admiral José Toribio Merino. This was to present the coup they were preparing as a "response" to a phony "Red coup." Naval intelligence had found out about a meeting to which roughly two hundred junior officers and sailors in Talcahuano had invited the Socialist party secretary Carlos Altamirano. The purpose of the meeting was to let him know that since June, the commanders of the Navy's warships had been haranguing their crews at sea, telling them that "we have to get that Marxist President Salvador Allende out of La Moneda," and "we Navy men have the patriotic duty to overthrow the present government." Altamirano, along with Miguel Henríquez, secretary general of the MIR, and Oscar Garretón, from MAPU, explained the Chilean political situation to the junior officers and sailors, emphasizing the threat represented by fascist officers, who were serving the North American multinational companies, and the national oligarchs. They emphasized the necessity of letting all the sailors know that "they should not obey fascist officers" should they give orders for an uprising against the government. (Details of this meeting were published in August 1973 issues of *Chile Hoy.*)

Toribio Merino and his intelligence advisers decided that this constituted sufficient evidence of a "Red coup" in the Navy. On August 7 they officially announced that "subversion" had been uncovered on the ships *Almirante Latorre* and *Blanco Encalada,* and the ringleaders were Altamirano, Henríquez, and Garretón. They announced the arrest of about fifty sailors and junior officers, headed by a petty officer named Cárdenas.

In the days following, reporters from left-wing newspapers managed to find out how, at the Talcahuano and Valparaíso naval bases, these sailors had been forced to sign absurd confessions after being brutally tortured. In the Valparaíso Naval Hospital they found a sailor whose testicles had been smashed. Wives and relatives of the arrested sailors gave out to the newspapers the names of naval intelligence captains in charge of the tortures.[21] There were three basic types of tortures:

1. An open oil drum filled with urine and excrement was employed to submerge the head of the man being interrogated, to the point of asphyxiation, every time he refused to answer or to confess to any crime he was accused of.

2. The prisoners were hung naked, head downward, from a gymnastics bar and struck repeatedly on the scrotum and at the root of the testicles.

3. The prisoners were forced to drag themselves naked through a "pool" full of hammer-broken rocks over which was hung, at about a height of one foot, a strong steel net to keep them from standing up. They were made to crawl between the net and the rocks several times during the interrogations.

This situation caused a huge stir and made large sectors of the population all the more eager to organize to "prevent a military insurrection." Newspapers such as *Puro Chile* and *Noticias de Última Hora* devoted special attention to investigating the affair. They were able to expose shameful deeds that took place during the June 29 military mutiny, when the soldiers who occupied the federal buildings next to the Palacio de La Moneda ransacked the government office workers' pockets and drawers. In the Treasury building on the west side of La Moneda, the soldiers stole money, watches, and gold rings from the employees—as well as two cheeses and four sandwiches brought by workers for lunch.

The pressure on the civil politicians began to increase. The military group composed of Gustavo Leigh, César Mendoza, and José Toribio Merino had already agreed on August 20, after César Ruiz Danyau's aborted coup (see Chapter 1), that Allende's removal was essential. On August 21 they received this news: Eduardo Frei had arranged that in no more than forty-eight hours the Chamber of Deputies would issue a statement declaring Allende's government "unconstitutional," along the lines dictated by Generals Bonilla and Arellano Stark. The gist of the statement was that the Chamber of Deputies was "serving the President of the Republic and his ministers of state, the armed forces, and the corps of military police with notice that the legal and constitutional order of the Republic has been seriously abrogated," and addressing themselves to those commanders in chief who were ministers, they urged "that, by the same token, by virtue of your duties, your oath of loyalty to the Constitution and the laws, and the nature of the institutions of which you are high-ranking members, and whose name has been used in drawing you into the Cabinet, we call upon you *to put an immediate halt to all of those situations mentioned herein* which infringe upon our Constitution and laws. . . ."

On August 21 the Christian Democrats and National party organized a "women's" demonstration in front of General Prats's house, to ask him to step down and let the other generals "forge the military power." The demonstration had been arranged to "soften General Prats up" for the visit of General Oscar Bonilla, who would ask Prats, "in the name of our corps of generals, to resign . . . because you are a disgrace to our institution, in your excessive loyalty to Allende's government." Bonilla also warned Prats not to oppose the other generals because "we have taken all necessary steps to cleanse the honor of our armed forces, once and for all." Prats repeated Bonilla's words to President Allende the same day.

Joan Garcés, a Spanish political scientist who was Allende's personal adviser, was an eyewitness of these events and related them as follows in a document read to the U.N. General Assembly on October 9, 1973:

On Tuesday, the right wing organized a women's march on the Defense Minister's house. They coarsely insulted General Prats and demanded that he resign from the Army. The Intelligence Service took pictures of the wives of six generals and various senior officers. That day, General Prats, who was sick in bed, was visited by General Bonilla—a Frei man whose wife had been among the demonstrators—who asked him to resign as commander in chief of the Army. A few minutes after General Bonilla's departure President Allende arrived at General Prats's home. The general warned Allende that he had the impression that the Army was planning some kind of treason, and discussed with the President ways that it might be thwarted.

Returning to his private residence, the President was visited by the Minister of the Interior and the second-in-command of the military police, General Urrutía. He had invited several Army generals to dine, most prominently Augusto Pinochet. [Among the guests were Generals Brady, Sepúlveda, Pickering, Urbina, and Torres de la Cruz, all in on the conspiracy.] The subject of the conversations was possible measures to take against the impending coup d'état. After midnight, the President called together the directors of the coalition of parties in the Unidad Popular and the Central Única to tell them that, given the seriousness of the military situation, he had decided to fire the generals implicated in the coup plot. Rather than exercise his constitutional power to fire these untrustworthy generals, he decided that the Army's high command would study details of a plan to defend the government in collaboration with regular forces and union workers. [The generals named by Allende were Oscar Bonilla, Sergio Arellano Stark, Ernesto Baeza Michelsen, Carlos Forestier, Javier Palacios Ruhman, and César Raúl Benavides.] Around 2 A.M. the President was informed of the arrival of the senior officer sent to meet with the government and the Central Única to finalize the defense plans to put down the coup the next day. I saw this general with my own eyes. His name is Augusto Pinochet.

This account by Joan Garcés shows us how the political ingenuousness of the Unidad Popular leadership, including President Allende, allowed "the leader of the military insurrection," as he was designated by the high command, to learn of the entire deployment of the workers' forces in Santiago as a "responsible" member of the defense against the coup.

The next day, on August 22, General Prats called together his corps of generals and asked them to endorse a declaration of "damages" against his person and rank made by the women's march the day before. Of the twenty-two generals present, eighteen refused. To avoid having Prats, and thereby Allende, suspect them, and since they were already sure that the majority of the generals had turned against the Defense Minister, Generals Pinochet, Brady, Sepúlveda, and Pickering voted in favor of Prats's petition. (Joan Garcés's U.N. document and an article in the Santiago daily *La Tribuna,* August 24, 1973, reported on this episode.)

General Prats immediately drove to La Moneda and tendered his resignation to Allende. According to Garcés's U.N. document:

Given the situation, General Pinochet told President Allende that it was expedient to accept Prats's resignation as a measure to defuse the charges against him by the Air Force and the Navy. In exchange for General Prats's retirement, Augusto Pinochet promised to become commander in chief of the Army and that very week fire six generals implicated in the coup d'état. Heading this list was General Bonilla, Pinochet's Minister of the Defense until his death in a helicopter crash March 3, 1975.

On August 23, 1973, General Carlos Prats González ceased to be commander in chief of the Army and Minister of Defense. From retirement, he wrote a public letter of resignation to Allende, warning him that he had resigned because he could no longer restrain the coup's forces. He thereby warned all of Chile that the military corps was on the move. But his letter had almost no repercussions. On September 15, 1973, Prats was sent into exile in Argentina by the military junta, where he lived with his wife until they were both murdered when their car was bombed on September 30, 1974.[22]

On the afternoon of August 23, at a meeting of the conspiring generals, Sepúlveda and Pickering were given instructions for the mobilization of their troops on "D Day" (still not set, but tentatively planned for the beginning of September). At that time the two generals discovered that, according to plans, the coup was to begin by eliminating some 6,000 middle-level union, political, and community leaders in the first few hours, as well as by destroying workers' settlements and other humble communities with tanks and aircraft. They were told that "with some 50,000 casualties in the first three to five days of fighting, we will have cleared the terrain." Although they protested against this strategy of murder and destruction, they somehow also were informed about the plan to assassinate President

Allende. They were instructed to tell no one, because "not even Pinochet knows." Pickering and Sepúlveda tendered their resignations immediately. On August 24 they left the Army's ranks.[23] Brigadier General Herman Brady Roche was named commander of the Santiago garrison and the Second Division, and General Sergio Arellano Stark took over Pickering's job.

Meanwhile, Pinochet somehow managed not to arouse President Allende's suspicions and at the same time not to fire the generals involved in the conspiracy. Joan Garcés narrates:

> In the last days of August, General Pinochet asked the President to postpone the retirement of the subversive generals until the Army's Qualifications Council met in the second half of September. His reason: this would be an internal, "institutional" decision, which he would impose as commander in chief. This would save the President from the criticism of having political motives in firing generals. I personally had occasion often in the last week of August and the first of September to listen to President Allende repeatedly express his thoughts about the military subversives' movement which we could all feel was on the verge of exploding. I took part in his last work session before his murder, on September 10. On that occasion, the President repeated that at the Councils of Qualifications Ordinary that were to take place in the coming weeks, according to the commanders in chief, he would definitely exercise his legal powers to send the leaders of the coup d'état into retirement. President Allende had personally discussed this with the commander in chief of the Navy, Admiral Montero, and with the commander in chief of the Army, General Pinochet.

AND THE NAVY

On August 31, the shape of the coming insurrection became even clearer when the naval high command, led by José Toribio Merino, forced Admiral Raúl Montero Cornejo to tender his resignation as naval commander in chief.

This happened on the morning of August 31, after Montero had taken part in the Annual Council of the National Navy in Valparaíso to qualify the institution's executive officers. At noon the high command met for lunch. When Montero arrived, the admirals said that he had better leave, because they were going to discuss the national political situation and they felt they could not trust him. Montero announced that he would immediately present his letter of resignation to Allende. According to Joan Garcés,

> That afternoon, on his return to Santiago, he related these events to President Allende and handed him his resignation. Dr. Allende refused to accept it and entreated him to remain in his post, for the good of the country, for a few more weeks while he dismantled the coup in the Navy.
>
> On September 11, Admiral Montero was arrested by the rebels and replaced by the rebel Admiral Merino, a member of the present military junta.

On the same day, August 31, the civilian organizations involved in the conspiracy took a step forward. The College of Lawyers, "by request of various members," had prepared a "legal" report on whether it was possible to "ask the National Congress to declare the constitutional unfitness of the President of the Republic." The report said it could be done, adding this assessment: "This illegal and unconstitutional activity on the part of the President may be motivated by one of two possible causes. Either the President willfully and consciously, and for undeclared reasons, has systematically violated the fundamental bases of our institutional system; or the Right Honorable Salvador Allende cannot bring himself to make his conduct conform to these norms imposed upon him by the duties inherent in his office."

THE LAST DAYS

El Mercurio was already reflecting the national situation on August 31. On page one it carried an item datelined Valparaíso, which reported: "Signed by the naval judge, Vice-Admiral José Toribio Merino, commander of the First Naval District, a petition of legal infraction was presented against Carlos Altamirano, a Socialist Senator, and Oscar Garretón, a MAPU Deputy. . . . The petition of legal infraction is based on the support given by the two legislators to sailors who attempted to take control of two Navy ships to start a civil war."[24]

In twenty of the twenty-five provinces of Chile, the truck owners and professional societies manipulated by the Christian Democrats were on strike.

Also on page one, illustrated with a photo of the general in uniform, *El Mercurio* reported: "Next Tuesday General (Ret.) Roberto Viaux Marambio will travel to Paraguay after he is released at midnight Monday. There Viaux will finish out the exile to which he was sentenced by the military tribunal in connection with actions of the Tacna Regiment that ended in the death of General René Schneider, commander in chief of the Army. General (Ret.) Viaux will be exiled for five years."

In the same issue, *El Mercurio* ran a "study" on page two entitled "Constitutional Impediments to the Presidential Performance," prepared by a professor of constitutional law at the Catholic University. Alongside it in the "Comments" column was an item entitled "The Nation and the Military Conscience," which concluded with: "Consequently, and particularly for the military, to obey and collaborate with the government is to betray our nation."

On the inside pages appeared a declaration by the president of the oligopolistic Construction Industry Guild (Cámara de la Construcción de Chile), in which it was stated: "Chile's problem would be solved by a patriotic step which it would benefit Mr. Allende to take and which has been pointed out to him by all manner of institutions and trade associations in Chile: and that is to resign."

The Sunday, September 2, edition of the leftist newspaper *Puro Chile* provoked a national commotion with a long interview with the defendant José Luis Riquelme Bascuñán, arrested by the Navy and military police intelligence and charged with the assassination of Araya Peters, Allende's naval aide. He had been held in solitary confinement, and this interview with the newspaper's director, Miroslav Popic, was the first contact he had had with the press since his arrest. His statements showed that Riquelme had been falsely accused, and that naval and military police captains were implicated in a cover-up of the true murderers.

Part of Riquelme's story, that of his torture in the Defense Ministry basement, was:

"They set up two chairs, one here and the other there, on one your feet and on the other your hands. Suddenly they tie up your feet with some wires, on your ankles, then you're secured like that in the air. You have to realize that in the middle there wasn't anything; you put your hands on the chair and suddenly you straightened right up where they applied the current to you. They would stick the cables on your waist, right here, and wham! One time they sat me down and tucked some cables here under my armpits and kept me like that, they must have tied me up, and all of a sudden I felt a big jolt right here between the collarbones, as if I was going to choke, and since that time I haven't felt good. . . . What can I tell you? . . . I jumped. They made me jump. Suddenly you were over there and then you were over here, on the other side. . . ."

Puro Chile's accusation was dangerously close to revealing that Allende's naval aide had been assassinated by his own comrades-in-arms in complicity with the CIA and the ex-Cadet Commandos.

September 3 was spent waiting to see "what would happen on the fourth," when the third anniversary of Allende's 1970 victory was to be celebrated. Both for the Unidad Popular and for the opposition parties, it was a moment for "measuring one's strengths." For the generals, it was going to be a day of rehearsals.

September 4 was, beginning at noon, a holiday. By 8 P.M. more than 700,000 laborers and peasants, office workers and students, children and women from all the provinces of Chile had paraded past the presidential box on Constitution Square. It was a huge demonstration of support for the government from the principal victims of the economic catastrophe. But their chants included not only "Viva Allende" and "Viva la Unidad Popular" but "Armas para el pueblo!" (Arms for the people), "Hasta cuándo retrocedes Allende?" (How long are you going backward, Allende?), and "Solo el pueblo armado derrotará al momio armado!" (Only the armed people can defeat the armed reactionary). The celebrating in the streets of Santiago lasted until well past midnight.

All day long, Chilean Air Force planes flew over the city, concentrating on the industrial districts in the south and the downtown streets, where they photographed the groups of workers out for the anniversary parade. They also flew over La Moneda; at night they made "practice flights at El Bosque Air Base simulating bombard-ments with rockets on 200-liter gasoline barrels" with Hawker Hunter jets (reported in *Última Hora,* September 6, 1973).

An urgent meeting was called among Air Force personnel to ana-lyze the aerial photographs taken that day. The conclusion was that some six or seven hundred thousand people in Santiago and the outer provinces were prepared to support the constitutional government. Gustavo Leigh reportedly commented, "If this keeps up, those leftist bastards are going to win the '76 elections," and then "we really will have the Communists on our backs."

The civilian conspiracy also was alarmed. For the fifth they had organized a huge parade of women in front of Catholic University in Santiago to demand "Allende's resignation" and "a military govern-ment." But there were pitched battles in the streets between the sympathizers and opponents of the march organized by the Christian Democrats and the National party.

The news from the provinces was appalling. There were ten and fifteen dynamite attacks every day, on factories, leftist political head-quarters, homes of peasants' and workers' leaders. Ground trans-portation had almost reached a complete standstill. Students, mer-chants, and professionals had partially gone on strike, organized by the right-wing parties.

On September 5, General Pinochet told Allende that "this is not last October," the Armed Forces "can't guarantee anything," because the Navy, the Air Force, "and some of our generals want you to leave —or comply with what Congress asks of you." Allende could not decree emergency zones under military control, as he had in 1972. That night, the President called in three Unidad Popular journalists and told them about this situation.

On the seventh, Allende agreed to capitulate. That morning, he called Pinochet and seven generals from the Santiago garrison into his office and told them he had decided to announce "Monday or Tues-day, or maybe Wednesday would be safer," his decision to call a plebiscite to clear up "the conflict of power between the Executive and the Parliament" and "promulgate the whole of the Christian Democrats' constitutional amendment on the Area of Social Property." The generals received this news "with a gesture of astonishment" (this was the phrase Allende used to describe it to Joan Garcés on the night of September 10). Allende told them that "we are going to bring peace to our country," since those were the causes of the present civil conflict. "Nobody," he told them, "will be able to say now that the President of the Republic does not respect the other powers in the state." He explained that, according to his calculations, he was planning to make the announcement on Tuesday or Wednesday, because "this weekend I have to convince the Unidad Popular—and that's going to be hard."

Allende's decision had taken the generals by surprise. They regrouped a block away from La Moneda, in the Defense Minister's office, and came to a simple conclusion: they had to overthrow Allende *before* he announced his decision to end the quarrel with the Christian Democrats headed by Frei. They discussed the time they would need to be able to start off the "blitzkrieg" they had been preparing for months. It is said that "seventy-two hours" was the technical answer given by General Sergio Arellano Stark. Augusto Pinochet set the date: Tuesday, the eleventh, beginning at midnight Monday.[25]

September 7 was a turbulent day. Around 3 P.M. news reached Santiago that the Chilean Fleet, anchored in Valparaíso Bay ready to sail to join the U.S. Pacific Fleet for the annual Operation Unitas maneuvers, had mutinied and refused to weigh anchor until "Admiral Montero resigns and Admiral Merino is appointed our commander in chief."

General Pinochet announced to the new Defense Minister, Orlando Letelier, that he would personally go to Valparaíso to talk to the "rebels." He flew there by helicopter, accompanied by four other generals, to meet with Merino. Presumably he informed him of the situation created by Allende's decision to remove the basis of public support for the military coup, and of the agreement that morning to deliver the coup on September 11.

When Pinochet returned to Santiago and reported to the Defense

Ministry that "all is quiet, the fleet will sail on the tenth as scheduled," what really was happening was that the lists of nearly 20,000 middle-level leaders of people's organizations, scheduled to be assassinated from the morning of the coup on, were already being distributed to the provinces. The list of the high-level directors to be arrested (some 3,000) was traveling the same route, and the officials in charge of preparing announcements for the day of the coup were already composing rough drafts to present to Augusto Pinochet, Gustavo Leigh, and José Toribio Merino.

The lists were very detailed: name, address, age, profession, marital status, and closest personal friends (usually two to five names). It has been alleged that the U.S. military mission in Santiago and the CIA in Washington had some involvement in their preparation.

As an irony of fate, on the night of September 7, the corps of military police generals gave a banquet to which Salvador Allende was invited. General César Mendoza Durán was also present and behaved very obsequiously toward the President (Mendoza had not yet been notified that the coup would take place the following Tuesday). It was probably Mendoza's obsequiousness that made Allende refer to him, in his last speech, broadcast only by Radio Magallanes at 9:40 A.M. on September 11, as the "groveling general."

The morning of Saturday the eighth, Allende summoned to his office the commanders in chief of the Armed Forces, General Gustavo Leigh Guzmán, Admiral Raúl Montero Cornejo, and General Augusto Pinochet Ugarte. In consideration of the difficult times the country was going through, and since he was going to announce his political concession the next week, Allende asked them to temper their application of the gun control law, so as not to "exasperate" the workers. The commanders in chief said they had always tried to avoid "excesses" in those procedures, and they would now give special instructions to that effect. The meeting was short and friendly, according to what Allende told Augusto Olivares, his press adviser.

September 8 was a boring day for the reporters, particularly for the *El Mercurio* reporters who had been holed up since September 2 in an apartment on the thirteenth floor of the Hotel Carrera with photographic equipment outfitted with powerful telescopic lenses. That day, *El Mercurio*'s management, aware that "something juicy is going to happen at La Moneda one of these days," had rented a suite for an indefinite period and installed a team of reporters on a twenty-four-hour watch. *El Mercurio* was not clear whether the "something juicy" would be Allende's assassination or one of the generals', but the reporters were instructed to keep an eye on the door of La Moneda every second of the day through the telephoto lenses. On the eleventh they were to take some spectacular pictures of the aerial bombardment of the palace.

THE OATH

On Sunday, September 9, from 11 P.M. on, after a social dinner at his home, General Pinochet met with General Leigh, Rear Admiral Sergio Huidobro, the director of the Naval Infantry School (which was training the civilian fascist groups), and Vice-Admiral Patricio Carvajal.

The meeting lasted until 2 A.M. Its apparent purpose was to refine and check the operation. According to later reports, it was learned that during the afternoon of the ninth, Generals Pinochet and Leigh had finally talked to General Mendoza of the military police to get him to assemble his forces for the eleventh. Also, Admirals Huidobro and Carvajal had told Admiral Merino to prepare to arrest Admiral Montero at midnight on the tenth. According to a statement made to the Chilean press by General Leigh in November 1973, they also "signed a document which we keep in strict secrecy." Most likely the document listed the conspirators' names, so that none of them would ever betray the Tuesday coup.

But what is most important is that at 4 A.M. on the tenth, that is, two hours after the conspirators' meeting at Pinochet's house had ended, a Chilean Army colonel in civilian clothes arrived at the house of Nathaniel Davis, the U.S. ambassador, where there were also two members of the U.S. military mission in Santiago.

After this meeting there occurred a strange event: the radio counterintelligence services intercepted a coded message originating from the American radio transmitters in the Defense Ministry. It instructed the Operation Unitas task force, composed of three U.S. Navy destroyers and a submarine, to detach itself. Two of the destroyers were to remain more than 200 miles outside Valparaíso on the high seas. One destroyer and the submarine were to stay more than 200 miles outside Talcahuano. Operation Unitas was postponed indefinitely, the transmission said.

This should explain what appeared so mysterious to some U.S. politicians. According to the Inter Press Service (an Italian news agency) news wire: "The destroyers *Tunner, Tatonall,* and *Vesole* and the submarine *Clagamore* were headed toward Chilean territorial waters the night before the coup. They were halted right at the limit and split into two groups, by a timely warning from the U.S. Embassy in Santiago, ten hours before the bloody coup d'état exploded."

It can also explain the following cable from the Spanish news agency EFE, which came out of Washington on September 13:

President Nixon knew beforehand of the preparations for the coup d'état in Chile, but the American government decided not to warn President Allende, the Washington *Post* revealed today. In a front-page article the *Post* confirmed that the United States knew about the coup for at least twelve hours before it took place. According to the *Post,* a Chilean Army officer informed another officer in the American Army in Chile of the plot against the President. The information was then passed on to the highest levels in Washington, where the decision was made not to intervene.

The newspaper reported that these details were revealed yesterday by Jack Kubisch, Adjunct Secretary of State and coordinator for the Alliance for Progress, to a group of U.S. Senators forming the Subcommittee for Foreign Relations for Western Hemisphere Affairs.

Monday the tenth, in La Moneda, a kind of calm reigned. The only political leader who alluded to what was going on was Rafael Tarud, the director of the smallest party in the Unidad Popular, the Acción

Popular Independiente. He met with President Allende and afterward said: "I told him [Allende] that the API will support him in solving the transportation strike immediately, by law; in promulgating the constitutional reforms in the Hamilton-Fuentealba project, and in other acts that would result in social peace."

At 6 P.M., on the tenth floor of the Defense Ministry, Minister Orlando Letelier called in the directors of newspapers and magazines in Santiago to tell them that "the situation has a political solution that will soon be made known by the President himself," who asked of the directors of the news media that "in the news items about the gun control law searches, please do not try to associate the armed forces with that contingent policy." Letelier's feeling was one of optimism, of confidence that the speech Allende would give on Tuesday was going to solve the problem, and that "everything was calm."

Nevertheless, more than one reporter took note of an ominous sign: not one of the three commanders in chief attended the Defense Minister's press conference, a highly irregular occurrence.

The fact was that at that very hour, on the floors below the one where Letelier was speaking to the press, the conspiring generals were preparing the last details of a full-scale military occupation of the country, to begin in six hours.

6 The Inferno

The excesses of the junta are so systematic that they approach genocide.

> LEOPOLDO TORRES, president of the International Movement of Catholic Jurists, in Madrid, quoted in *L'Express,* in late 1973

Shortly after midnight, September 10, the Chilean people were savagely attacked by regiments from the Army, Navy, and Air Force bases, from the military police barracks, and from the homes of fascist group leaders, where civilian operatives, called "independent units" by the rebel high command, headed the military patrols in the murder or arrest of Chilean labor leaders.

In less than twenty hours this blitzkrieg would leave a broad wake of destruction, death, torture, and shame. The untrammeled brutality was brought about by the military high command, who represented themselves to the nation as fulfilling "the normal duty that the Fatherland requires of us."

At 10 P.M. on September 10, the few drunken stragglers in the Valparaíso dockside bars witnessed something quite peculiar: the war fleet, which had weighed anchor ten hours earlier for the ostensible purpose of joining four U.S. warships on Operation Unitas in their annual war maneuvers, had returned to port; the fleet was landing its troops, and the troops were dispersing throughout the city!

Contingents of Navy infantry, under the personal command of Rear Admiral Sergio Huidobro, occupied the Cerro Baron Station fuel depot, the Municipal Building, Arturo Prat Square, the railroad station, and other strategic sites. Military police troops were coming out to join them.

At First District headquarters, the commander in chief of the Navy, Admiral Raúl Montero Cornejo, was personally arrested by Vice-Admiral José Toribio Merino, deprived of his rank, and left in the custody of a commodore armed with a submachine gun. Merino assumed command in the presence of the admirals led by Patricio Carvajal Prado. After the insurrectional ceremony, Carvajal traveled swiftly to Santiago to take charge of his "combat" post at the Defense Ministry, a few yards from La Moneda.

At the same time, an officer in the Valparaíso military police, having no idea of what was happening, informed the Santiago Highway Control that "the Navy is mounting a huge arms search . . . they're in all parts of the city." After that, silence. The telephone lines out of Valparaíso were cut off from the capital.[1]

Thus the Navy carried out the final plan of action agreed upon with General Augusto Pinochet on September 7: the fleet had left port on Monday the tenth and then two hours before midnight had returned to Chile. It had split into two groups: half the fleet remained in Valparaíso, with tentative support from two U.S. Navy destroyers which had sailed to a position just outside Chile's territorial waters, 200 miles away. The other half was sailing at full speed to the port of Talcahuano. And there two more U.S. Navy ships would position themselves.

The military occupation of Valparaíso, using Navy infantry as a vanguard, took place during the last two hours of September 10 so efficiently that no one in the rest of the country was aware of it until well into the early morning of September 11.

But the credit for this cannot go entirely to the Chilean high command. The plans for the military takeover had been discussed, adjusted, and corrected with members of the U.S. military mission in Chile and with the U.S. Army's Southern Command in the Panama Canal Zone during June, July, and August.[2] This gigantic military operation did in fact have one weakness: the lack of a centralized system for radio communications to connect the armed forces scattered throughout twenty-five provinces, on sea, on land, and in the air.

The Southern Command of the American Army, through its air base in the Argentine province of Mendoza, solved the problem. They sent a specially equipped aircraft to serve as a "relay station" and "centralizer" for military radio messages. This help was provided so openly that Argentine reporters exposed the maneuver three days after the coup. The Buenos Aires daily paper *El Mundo* revealed part of the "transmissions support" operation that the Pentagon was conducting:

> The airplane of type WB57S and the reserve pilots M. B. Lemmons and D. C. Baird, commanded by Majors V. Dueñas and T. Shull of the U.S. Air Force, coordinated all operations of the rebel armed forces before and during the coup.
>
> This aircraft, especially equipped with the most up-to-date communications instruments, operated on the day of the coup as a flying radio station. The flight perimeter included the area enclosed by Mendoza, Argentina [between the 32nd and 33rd parallels south], and the Chilean cities of La Serena [30th parallel south] and Puerto Montt [between the 41st and 42nd parallels south]. This indicated a "triangular flight pattern" of 250 miles from Mendoza to La Serena, 770 miles from La Serena to Puerto Montt, and some 620 miles from Puerto Montt back to Mendoza. This covered nineteen provinces of Chile.
>
> The U.S. Air Force plane began to operate in this zone on September 7. That day it flew two missions; on the tenth it flew others. From the eleventh (the date of the coup) to the thirteenth it was assigned as constant support to the rebels' communications system.
>
> The legal cover for the missions coordinating rebel communications was "Mission Airstream." The task accomplished by the U.S. plane was to connect the Chilean Navy stations with sections of their Army and Air Force.[3]

OPERATION PINCERS

Not all the credit for the destruction unleashed on Chile can go to the Pentagon's generals or the Southern Command of the U.S. Army in the Panama Canal Zone. A good part of the insurrection's objectives (including the junta's intentions of regressing to dependency on the United States[4]) had germinated in the minds of the highest-ranking conspirators. One was Vice-Admiral José Toribio Merino Castro, self-promoted admiral and commander in chief of the Navy as of the night of September 10, and destined to become, a few hours later, one of "the four" members of the military junta.

Admiral Merino was fifty-seven years old, a 1936 graduate of the Naval School. Like the other senior officers of Latin America "destined" to be chiefs of their services, he had had a "long apprenticeship" in the U.S. military system.[5] During World War II he served on the U.S. Navy warship *Raleigh,* patrolling the Panama Canal Zone and Guadalcanal. Between 1956 and 1957 he was a naval attaché in London. Afterward he joined the General Staff and became a professor of geopolitics and logistics.

Merino was the first of the rebel senior officers who "rose up" against the idea of having a coalition of leftist parties govern Chile. By 1971, he was frequently heard, at the Playa Ancha (Valparaíso) Naval Academy, saying that "it is a mistake on the part of the Americans to let Allende govern." On the night of September 10, Merino was a proud man: he was carrying out the plan to "exterminate the Marxist ideology" for which he had fought so hard from 1972 onward. The first person wholeheartedly to support this plan had been Air Force General Gustavo Leigh Guzmán. Then Division General Augusto Pinochet Ugarte joined him, and after him came military police General César Mendoza Durán.

When some Navy officers expressed their horror at the dreadful massacres devastating the country in the wake of the coup, Merino's reply ran through the fleet like a cold chill: "We are the nation's surgeons. When a patient has cancer in his leg, it is eradicated and the patient is saved. We are eradicating Marxism. . . . We are conducting a surgical operation. . . . Our work is humanitarian."[6]

In June 1973, even before Augusto Pinochet was "invited" to become "leader" of the military uprising, the plans for the armed occupation of the country were complete as far as war strategy went. What had not been decided upon was how to "politically" maintain the military occupation over a period of years. Of course, there was general agreement to close down the National Congress, militarize unions and factories in the Area of Social Property, as well as the administrative apparatus, and dissolve the workers' Central Única and all political parties, beginning with those of the Unidad Popular. But was that enough?

For Merino and his fellow ideologues, it was not. For him, the problem with Communism was its people, not its organizations. He therefore proposed a plan which he arrogantly christened the "three-thirds" plan: "in the first hours" kill 3,000 middle-level leaders of all the Unidad Popular's organizations, "from radicals to MIRistas,"* arrest, try, and give long prison sentences to 3,000 leaders well known to the public; "exile" 3,000 more politicians, professionals, and "intellectuals," from "Christian Democrats leftward." That, said Merino, would guarantee "social peace" for a decade.

Merino had been talking about the "three-thirds" since March of 1973 in Valparaíso naval circles. When this talk reached the ears of some leftists (myself among them) that same year, the comment was, "The poor man is insane, he's an old-fashioned Nazi, he doesn't realize he's in Chile." Months later, it would be clear that he was no old-fashioned Nazi, but an up-to-date one. The difference was that his ideological center spoke English, not German.

Merino Castro's ideas were opposed only by a group of "reformist" Army generals, who believed that the sort of action he proposed would result in "hatred against the military, which would provoke guerrilla warfare all the time we are in power." But when the events of March, April, May, and June revealed the strength of the people's desire for national liberation, the balance tipped in favor of the "three-thirds" philosophy. The conspiring generals and admirals decided that the Chilean people were infected with revolution, that it was like leprosy. And, as in the Middle Ages, the lepers had to be burned to cleanse the infected area.

From late June on, the plotters began to finalize their lists of "ex-

---

*Members of MIR, Movimiento de Izquierda Revolucionaria, one of the truly revolutionary and very radical political parties (with MAPU in the Unidad Popular).

tremists," "political leaders," "Marxist journalists," "agents of international Communism," and any and all persons participating with any vigor in neighborhood, communal, union, or national organizations. These lists had been in existence since October–November 1972 in the hands of the SIM and Navy and Air Force intelligence. In addition, the Pentagon had been asked to get the CIA to give the Chilean Army its lists of Chileans linked to socialist countries. These names were sorted into two groups: (1) persons not publicly known, or relatively obscure, but who were important in all kinds of leftist organizations; and (2) well-known people in important positions, including high-ranking officials in the Allende administration.

The first group was dubbed "the motors of Marxism" by Merino; the second, "the leaders of Marxism." By early August, the lists were almost complete, and Toribio Merino's "three-thirds" plan was taking on apocalyptic dimensions.

"The motors of Marxism" consisted of some 20,000 Chileans, from university students to old people who had retired but were still very active in community life. These people were to be arrested and executed in the first hours or days of the military coup. Thus, by August 1973, Merino's 3,000 had become 20,000.

The names on the second list, "the leaders of Marxism," were no surprise to Merino and his associates. Their number did not exceed 3,000. These, it was agreed, had to be arrested, tried summarily, and sentenced to long imprisonment. The rebel high command thought this was a good idea because "if we list such well-known leaders as casualties, the whole world is going to accuse us of being dictators." On the other hand, if they exterminated the obscure people who were the real movers among the laborers, peasants, and office workers, "nobody will ask us about them."

When the Navy infantry began to occupy Valparaíso on the night of the tenth as the first phase of Chile's occupation by air, land, and sea, the generals and admirals had specific goals to accomplish in their blitzkrieg:

1. Hunt down and kill 20,000 people whose names were on lists previously distributed to all commands in the twenty-five provinces. The goal for the first hours of the coup was 6,000 of these people. This search-and-destroy mission was named Operation Pincers.

2. Arrest and confine 3,000 other persons in previously designated concentration camps.

3. Occupy militarily and maintain all administrative, economic, and political centers in the country.

4. Prepare for a combat period of five to seven days, with projected casualties of 50,000 people, of which the armed forces should sustain a portion "no greater" than 2,000 men in order to guarantee the operation's success.

(On these points, the military leaders were to contradict each other in public statements after the massacre. For example, General Gustavo Leigh, in the Santiago daily *La Tercera* on September 17, 1973, stated: "We are taking this course of action because 100,000 dead in three days is preferable to 1,000,000 in three years, as happened in Spain." And General Augusto Pinochet, in a national network TV interview in October 1973, said: "The resistance crumbled rapidly. We expected, we were prepared for them to resist for five days—that didn't happen; there could have been 50,000 dead.")

In any case, it is important to realize the following: the four basic goals of the blitzkrieg on September 11 show that the rebel soldiers were acting very confidently—they *knew* that they would be catching by surprise a totally unsuspecting and unarmed or poorly armed populace. The people's resistance would be the resistance of desperation in the face of certain death. For this reason, they were calculating one dead soldier to every twenty-four dead civilians. (This is worth remembering if one has in mind the alleged Plan Zeta, in which the civilian left was going to wipe out all 100,000 soldiers in the Chilean armed forces. This nonexistent plan was given as an excuse for the September coup by the generals and admirals.)

In the months following September 10, the situation became so brutal that even the Archbishop of Santiago, Raúl Cardinal Silva Henríquez, at great personal risk, made this public statement: "It is our belief that peace will not be brought to Chile on the foundation of destroying a large number of Chileans" (in the Chilean magazine *Ercilla,* No. 2,002, December 12–18, 1973; this magazine belongs to Frei's group in the Christian Democrats).[7]

Nevertheless, in spite of these meticulous preparations for murdering 20,000 Chileans, the surprise of the attack, and the unpreparedness of the people's organizations to successfully resist a slaughter of such magnitude, the results of the first twenty-four hours of the operation to exterminate the "motors of Marxism" were a relative failure.

The estimated figures, which I obtained myself and through friends who risked their lives to inform me during the days immediately after the coup, show that on September 11 the attackers assassinated only a little over 3,000 of the list of 20,000, falling far short of their goal of killing 6,000 the first day.

A tentative breakdown, province by province, of these results judged "unsatisfactory" by the rebel general staff, follows:

Tarapacá Province: 80 middle-level leaders assassinated out of an ideal total of 400. The region was invaded by troops under the command of General Carlos Forestier Haensgen and Colonel Odlanier Mena Salinas.

Antofagasta Province: Around 80 assassinations; the victims, part of a total of about 400, were hunted down in their own homes. The occupation forces were commanded by Brigadier General Joaquín Lagos Osorio and Colonel Eugenio Rivera Desgroux.

Atacama Province: Out of approximately 1,000 people on the list, they were able to kill only some 100.

Coquimbo Province: 100 assassinations out of 200. Atacama and Coquimbo provinces were assigned to Lieutenant Colonels Oscar Haag Blaschke and Ariosto Lapostol Orrego.

Aconcagua Province: 100 out of 500. Colonel Héctor Orozco Sepúlveda commanded.

Valparaíso Province: 250 out of 2,000. Rear Admiral Adolfo Walbaum Wieber commanded.

Santiago Province: "Only" 800 members of civilian leftist organizations, out of a list of 6,500. Brigadier General Herman Brady Roche was in charge of the invading troops.

O'Higgins Province: 80 out of 600. Lieutenant Colonel Cristian Ackerknecht commanded.

Colchagua Province: 100 out of 500. Colonel Hernán Brantes Martínez commanded.

Curicó Province: 50 out of 300. Lieutenant Colonel Sergio Angelotti Cádiz commanded.

Talca Province: 80 out of 400. Lieutenant Colonel Efraín Jaña Girón commanded.

Linares Province: 20 out of 100. Colonel Gabriel Del Río Espinosa commanded.

Maule Province: 20 out of 100. Lieutenant Colonel Rubén Castillo Whyte commanded.

Ñuble Province: The list had more than 500 names. At midnight on September 11, the Santiago intelligence center was notified that they could "report only 98 casualties." Colonel Juan Toro Dávila commanded.

Concepción and Arauco provinces were under the joint command of Brigadier General Washington Carrasco Fernández and Rear Admiral Jorge Paredes Wetzer (the latter was chief of the Navy forces at Talcahuano and Tomé). In Concepción, of 2,000 civilians sought, only about 250 were killed. In Arauco Province, 100 were killed out of an ideal total of 500.

Bío-Bío Province: 120 out of 800. Colonel Alfredo Rehren Pulido commanded.

Malleco Province: 80 out of 400. Lieutenant Colonels Elías Bacigalupo Soracco and Alejandro Morel Donoso commanded.

Cautín Province: 150 out of 600. Colonel Hernán Ramírez Ramírez and Lieutenant Colonel Pablo Iturriaga Marchesse commanded.

Valdivia Province: 40 out of 200. Brigadier General Héctor Bravo Muñoz commanded.

Osorno Province: 140 out of 600. Lieutenant Colonel Lizardo Simón Abarca Maggi commanded.

Llanquihue and Chiloé provinces: 115 out of 400. The troops were commanded by Air Force Colonel Sergio Leigh Guzmán, the brother of Gustavo Leigh Guzmán, a member of the junta. Sergio Leigh Guzmán was promoted to the rank of general a few days after the coup.

Aisén Province: 10 out of 200. Colonel Humberto Gordon Rubio commanded.

Magallanes Province: "Only" 100 out of 500. Division General Manuel Torres de la Cruz was the troops' commanding officer.

The rebel generals and admirals determined to deal with the rest of the Marxist cancer by mass arrests and the installation of torture and concentration camps reminiscent of the Nazi era.

In the first eighteen days after September 11, there were nearly 20,000 civilian prisoners in Santiago alone. For the whole country the figure reached 75,000.

From September 12 to 30, among these tens of thousands of prisoners, the rebel generals and admirals could find only 6,300 more of the people on the lists. They were executed inside the concentration camps.

On another front, during the first five days after the military operation, some workers' groups' desperate and unorganized defense against the war machine resulted in 5,500 civilian casualties "killed in battle," as opposed to about 500 military casualties. This figure included those officers and soldiers who opposed the fascists on the morning of September 11 and afterward. Approximately 100 officers and soldiers had been shot by their own comrades-in-arms.

This makes 15,000 civilian victims in the first eighteen days after the coup: 740 casualties a day, 30 victims an hour, a murder every two minutes.[*]

After this initial torrent of death, the killings grew less frequent. The people reorganized, and this gave the commando assassins a harder time.

During October, November, and December 1973 the rebel officers killed an average of 30 to 40 people a week, using such subtle methods as the "law of flight." An article in the November 15 issue of the Mexico daily *Excelsior,* written by their Buenos Aires correspondent, Giangiacomo Foa, sketches a picture of those months:

"In Chile, the law of flight goes on. Every day, every night, the military junta ruling Chile, in the name of the sacred human rights, liberty, democracy, and religion, executes dozens of Chileans whose only crime consists in having supported the Socialist government of the late President Allende. The peace Pinochet is seeking to implant is the peace of the dead." These are the words of Carmen Hertz, a woman lawyer. Her husband, Carlos Berger, who was manager of the Chuquicamata copper mine [and also a reporter for *El Siglo,* a Chilean daily], has just been executed in the Calama jail, along with 26 copper mine workers. The Chilean military junta continues to be implacable with its prisoners of "war."

"I was with him until 4:30 P.M. We talked for a long time. He was calm, thinking he had only twenty more days to finish out the sentence that the council of war had handed down a few days before. I never dreamed he would be shot ninety minutes later." Carmen Hertz's story is not very different from those of hundreds of victims who have watched their homes, families, and lives being destroyed, as Pinochet's government vents its repressive fury on their loved ones. The national odors of Chile have become gunpowder and blood. The law of flight is the macabre daily fare: "When I asked about my husband, they answered curtly that he had been killed trying to escape, along with twenty-five other prisoners. I thought I would go crazy when they confirmed the news; I still couldn't believe it. I was told that all the prisoners in the Calama jail were dragged out of their cells by surprise and taken to a place called Topater, a target practice area for the soldiers stationed there on the Bolivian border. Afterward I was able to get my husband's death certificate from the Calama coroner. It gives the cause of death as 'destruction of the thorax and cardiac region by bullet impact.' "

Executed with Berger that afternoon were David Miranda, the former national director of the Federation of Mines, and two reporters from Radio El Loa; the rest of the victims were workers. But the Calama execution is only one more in a bloody series of unspeakable events.

In the La Serena jail, fifteen citizens were killed. Among them were the director of the Music Conservatory, Jorge Peña, and a pediatrician, Jorge Jordán. On the outskirts of Antofagasta, on October 19, another twenty-two Chileans were shot, among them a cousin of former President Eduardo Frei's wife [engineer Eugenio Ruiz Tagle, who belonged to the MAPU, a workers' and peasants' party]. All those shot had been sentenced a few days earlier to jail terms ranging from two months to forty years. But the junta chose to have them dead. . . .

While the military junta celebrated the passing of two months since the government overthrow, a long convoy of cage trucks, generally used for cattle, transported 900 political prisoners to the saltpeter works at Chacabuco, recently converted into a concentration camp, where the prisoners will have to tolerate the rigors of a desert climate. The saltpeter works had been converted two years ago into a national monument by President Allende.

Another cable, dated September 28, 1973, from Agence France Presse in Montreal, reported:

Three Canadian priests expelled from Chile on their arrival today denounced the campaign of "murders by the thousands" and "widespread denunciations" that followed the military coup of September 11. Father Jean Latulippe, who worked with a popular initiative organization, said that according to unquestionable testimony, when "the occupants of a military truck on September 13 frisked a twenty-year-old pedestrian and discovered a knife on him, an officer pulled out his revolver and shot him on the spot. They threw the body into the truck and told the witness to disappear. It's clear that the soldiers had the freedom to kill anybody they chose," the priest added. "But the repression against popular leaders was perfectly organized."

There were other cases, such as those attested by Chilean Congressman Eduardo Contreras, in Ñuble Province:

Military Police in Ninhue deposited a dying young teacher, Carlos Sepúlveda Palaviccino, in front of his house. For two hours they prevented his wife from going to him. When he finally died, the military police left and allowed his wife, now his widow, to go to him.

But the end of 1973 did not bring the end of torment for the Chilean people. Even in April 1974, nearly seven months after the coup, the situation remained just as ghastly. On April 1 the Associated Press sent this news wire from Santiago:

Catholic, Lutheran, and Jewish religious leaders in Chile presented an appeal to the courts on behalf of 131 persons about whom, they say, nothing is known since their arrest by the forces of order in the last months. The petition was made by Monsignor Fernando Ariztía Ruiz, auxiliary bishop of the Catholic Archdiocese of Santiago; Helmuth Frenz, Evangelical Lutheran bishop; and Ángel Kreitman, the leading rabbi of Chile, as well as other leaders.

The document was presented last Friday as a habeas corpus in the name of a "Committee of Cooperation for Peace" to the Santiago Court of Appeals.

It states that its purpose is to "safeguard the physical and moral integrity of many persons who today find themselves deprived of freedom and secluded in places that are kept secret from their relatives and friends and who are therefore inaccessible to a just and sufficient public defense."

The writ of habeas corpus was presented by the religious leaders on behalf of 131 presumed victims, none of whom are public figures. The document says: "The human drama that so many mothers, wives, children, relatives, and friends are living through has moved the Committee of Cooperation for Peace in Chile to present, on behalf of arrested persons who have not yet been located, the present habeas corpus."

It adds that "we have been moved, as clergymen, by the anguish of so many people, for the most part innocent, poor, and humble, deprived of all social relief, obscure people with no influential friends. The case of each of these people on behalf of whom we are asking aid today has been carefully studied and submitted for approval not only by relatives or friends of the plaintiffs but also by a body of lawyers and social workers."

All of the above is but a pale reflection of what the generals and admirals have done. Execution has transformed itself from a punishment into a relief for the hundreds of thousands of Chilean men, women, old people, and even children who are brutally tortured every day.

THE TORTURES

In early November 1973, some peasants traveling over the Las Tejuelas bridge, which crosses the Ñuble River about a mile and a half from Chillán, noted that, as usual, the water level was beginning to drop with the end of the rainy season. Along with this phenomenon, they noticed another one, new and horrifying: the appearance of dozens of headless cadavers with their arms tied behind their backs. Some of the bodies were half decayed. When the peasants notified the military police post at the city gates, they were told curtly: "You saw nothing. If you say anything, we will arrest you and cut your throats, just like those corpses."

Those bodies were the leftovers from the "extermination" operation in Ñuble Province, resembling the "leftovers" in any other province in Chile after September 11, debris left by bayonets, machine guns, and torture devices of the Chilean Air Force, Navy, and Army.

Shortly before this incident at the Las Tejuelas bridge, the Arauco Fishing Association, which produces canned seafood in the port of Talcahuano, had to halt work for several days. The fish they were receiving were full of bits of human flesh from bodies the Chilean Navy had tossed into the ocean after they came out of the naval base's torture chambers.

One journalist, still in Chile, whose name I must withhold, told me how corpses of people who had been tortured and later shot appeared in the Mapocho River, which runs through Santiago:

During the first weeks of October I had to cross Bulnes bridge to get over the Mapocho very early every morning. The first time I could not believe my eyes. It couldn't be true. From a distance I could see lots of people gathered along the bridge's railing and the riverbanks. They were looking at the half-floating corpses, four men's bodies. I still remember, one was wearing a red shirt. Farther off, there was a fifth body which had been dragged ashore. This scene went on every day, and not just at this bridge. You could see them at Pedro de Valdivia bridge too. Dozens of women would station themselves at the bridges every day, in hopes of seeing the body of a husband or son who had disappeared after being picked up by the soldiers. One day I saw nine corpses, all with bare chests, hands tied behind their backs. The bodies were perforated by bullet holes. And with them was the body of a girl, apparently fifteen or sixteen years old.

Children were not spared. On September 18 a military patrol went to pick up José Soto, a maker of wrought iron furniture, in his sixties, president of the supply and price control junta in his district, Quinta Normal. Soto wasn't home. His fourteen-year old son was alone in the house. The military patrol seized the boy. Afterward they threw the boy's bullet-riddled body on Soto's doorstep—"so the sonofabitch won't be a faggot and will turn himself in," the soldiers shouted to his neighbors. (José Soto and his family are now out of Chile, so I am able to tell his story.)

During September and part of October, in the Santiago communities around the industrial areas, the soldiers would leave bodies in the streets. When their relatives came to pick them up, they were arrested. The bodies generally had fingernails pulled out, or legs broken, or testicles smashed. Several had their eyes burnt out, apparently with cigarette butts.

In January 1974, Chilean Air Force troops deposited the body of a seventeen-year-old boy, an MIR party member, in a town south of Santiago. Part of the boy's abdomen had been subjected to vivisection. Both his legs were broken, and also his left arm. His entire body was covered with holes made by cigarette burns. He had also been castrated. The coroner later cited as cause of death "acute anemia."

Other common forms of torture practiced by the Army's SIM and military police intelligence officers were to extinguish cigarettes in the victim's anus and to apply electric current to the ears, anus, and testicles. For their part, the officers of Navy infantry appeared to have developed other tastes: seven members of the Valparaíso harbor patrol turned up dead, their legs broken and their testicles smashed.

Persons kept prisoner in September on the freighter *Lebu,* anchored in the Valparaíso harbor, have described to me how the boat was turned into a jail for torture. The second hold housed two hundred prisoners. In one corner was an oil barrel cut in half, used by the prisoners to defecate and urinate in. In one wooden cell there were twenty-five prisoners. They all slept on the floor. At night, when the prisoners had at last managed to go to sleep, the Navy infantrymen would come and walk back and forth on top of them. The *Lebu* would set sail at night until it was out of sight of land, and then the prisoners would be shot and thrown into the ocean, after their chests were cut open with bayonets, "so the motherfuckers won't float." Fishermen from Horcones, Quinteros, and other inlets in the area found bodies or parts of bodies when drawing in their nets.

When, early on the morning of September 11, 7,000 Army infantry, 2,000 Air Force infantry, and 4,000 military police under the command of Brigadier General Sergio Arellano Stark launched a general attack on the workers of Santiago, armed forces police had already set up seventeen concentration camps in the city, equipped with torture devices and ready for use. These were: the Air Force's installations at Los Cerros de Chena (San Bernardo), the Chile Stadium, Corridor 5 of the Santiago Jail, a courtyard in the Santiago Penitentiary, Los Cerrillos Air Base, the basements of the Defense Ministry, the eastern enclosure of the Bernardo O'Higgins Military School, the Buin Regiment barracks, the 2nd Armored Regiment barracks, the Navy weather station in Quinta Normal Park, the National Stadium, the Tacna Regiment barracks, the Infantry School, El Bosque Air Base, the Paratrooper and Special Forces School, and Nataniel Stadium.

On the morning of September 11, before the order had been issued to bomb the Government Palace, General Pinochet was concerned (at his command Post Number One, in Peñalolén) to know whether these seventeen concentration camps were ready to begin functioning. He contacted Post Five, Vice-Admiral Patricio Carvajal's command post. According to this recording of his transmissions:

"Post Five to Post One, over . . ."

"Post Five, Post One here. We have to know whether Chile and Nataniel stadiums are ready for prisoners. We want to know who is manning them. And if they're not working yet, when do you expect them to be ready?"

There in those concentration camps, an entire encyclopedia of human brutality was being written. This is the testimony of a prisoner in the National Stadium, Luciano Duque, a worker in the state railroad's printing office:

They buried a rifle point in the scar I have from a hernia operation on my left side. But they didn't hit me very much. I saw Alberto Corvalán, the son of Luis Corvalán, the Communist party's secretary general, in the National Stadium. They had him isolated and you weren't allowed to talk to him. We were something like four hundred prisoners, and they made us line up between two lines of soldiers who had us covered front and rear with their guns. There was young Corvalán, with a blanket over his head. Six soldiers were insulting him, to get him angry and make him talk, I realized. Corvalán wouldn't open up. When the insults exasperated him, he would answer like a man, and then, between the six of them, they kicked and beat him and struck him with their rifle butts unmercifully, as if they really enjoyed it. Then Corvalán screamed for them to stop hitting him. This happened two or three times, and all of us prisoners were desperate because we couldn't do anything and it was clear that if we shouted they would machine-gun the lot of us. Finally Corvalán's screaming stopped. He didn't move anymore. The soldiers ordered some of the prisoners in the line to help move him. I don't know where they took him.

THE WOMEN

The military torture teams, graduates of the Americas School in the Canal Zone, have revealed a degree of human bestiality with Chilean women that puts them way ahead of their American trainers.[9]

A woman professor at the East Santiago campus of the University of Chile, married, with two children, was detained for forty days in the National Stadium. She wrote me this about the "female prisoners of war":

They were obliged to remain all day long face down with their hands on their necks and their legs spread. . . . There were lines of them kneeling or standing against the walls, and at the slightest movement they were struck or kicked—and, in several cases I saw, shot. In rooms fifteen by eighteen feet there were a hundred women. Food came only once a day, at 4 or 5 P.M. There were mainly two groups of women: workers and university professors. Girls and women were harassed, obliged to disrobe, manhandled, and insulted as a preamble to the interrogations. The academics among us had been taken out of our classrooms at gunpoint. One group of schoolteachers had a typically sad experience: at the investigatory commission one of them had her hair cropped off . . . then at Los Cerros de Chena, the eyes were always blindfolded. To go to the bathroom, they had to be accompanied by guards who took the opportunity to manhandle and beat them. They were interrogated naked. Electric current was applied to the mouth, hands, nipples, vagina. Water was poured over their bodies to intensify the pain. The language used with them was completely degenerate; they were forced to repeat, over and over: "I am a cunt, I am a cunt. . . ." A hospital technician was taken to the Quinta Normal naval enclosure. She was kept there for three days without sleep, and subjected to electric tortures every few hours. She also had electricity applied to her vagina. Afterward they brought her to the National Stadium. She was taken for interrogation there too, blindfolded as others were. This time she apparently was taken to the cycle track, where by then the torture chamber had been installed. Besides electric shocks, this time she was forced to take something in her hand. They had given her an injection, which she guessed was Sodium Pentothal, and it had made her dizzy, but she was still conscious. At once she realized the object was a penis which, on contact with her hand, became erect. They thrust it into her mouth, where it ejaculated.[10]

I have other memoranda from women prisoners who were able to write to me afterward. Essentially they tell the same story, although they add that some officials would intimate that there were "hard methods of interrogation" to "soften," "extract information," and "morally intimidate."

Some novelties appear in those memoranda: "They stretched the women out on tables and dripped candle wax on their stomachs." "There were rapes, either in groups or individually. 'Move, you Marxist whore,' they would tell the victims. 'If you don't respond you're going to have to suck cock, even for General Pinochet, you shitty whore.' " "Some officers started by sticking their fingers in my vagina, hoping to excite me. . . ."

There are plenty of examples; the newspapers of the world are filled with them. The cemeteries of Chile are filled with mutilated corpses. I would like to quote, as a kind of summary of the art of torture the military uses in my country, the testimony published by Daniel Samper Pizano, a reliable columnist, in the Bogota daily *El Tiempo,* on March 26 and 27, 1974, on the editorial page. The witness was a university student in Valparaíso.

I was arrested in mid-October right on the university campus where I attended classes. The rector appointed by the military would allow the naval intelligence thugs on campus, and I have the impression that the rector himself was informing against leftist students. They took us with the rest of the prisoners to the Navy Academy of War. This is a four-story steel building located on a promontory over the sea, at Cerro Playa Ancha. When we got there, we were blindfolded and made to climb up to the fourth floor on the iron staircase. The falls and their shoves were the beginning of the torture. As we went up, we heard terrible screams. We thought they were recordings to frighten us, but later we realized they were real cries from people being tortured. They stuck us in a room and forced us to remain standing, with our hands on our necks and without talking. Anyone who moved or talked was thrown on the floor and beaten with rifle butts and kicked. We spent a whole afternoon there waiting for them to call us for interrogation. They caught us talking and punished us brutally, but that was how I found out that in that room there were already people from Customs who were being tortured. One of them was a professor of literature at the University of Chile. There was also a Catholic priest, and another, a man named Juan, well known in the workers' districts of Valparaíso, who later died during a torture session. They gave us reasonably good food, but nobody could eat because of the ghastly screams in the area and the fear we felt. The guards would say sadistically: "You better take advantage of it, it's your last meal." Nobody slept the whole time I was in the building because the screams were really nerve-racking. They were unbelievable howls of pain, and they never stopped, day or night.

The first day they took away a lot of people who had arrived before us: the Customs people, the literature professor, and the Catholic priest. They never came back. Later I caught a guard remarking to his companion: "The priest fell apart on them right away; they're going to make it look like suicide." . . .

I was interrogated the second day for more than three hours. They undressed me and beat me, using their fists and boots all over my body. There seemed to be a lot of them. Then they applied electricity to my testicles. When they turned off the current, they began to hit me again with their hands and feet. They concentrated on my stomach. This was because when the torture began I felt a karate chop and instinctively hardened my muscles. The torturer shouted at me: "So you're trained, eh? Now you're going to get it." During the entire interrogation they kept me blindfolded and my wrists handcuffed. The muscular contractions caused by the electricity made the handcuffs tighter each time, and the flesh of my wrists was cut down to the bone. By that point I didn't feel pain anymore. I only realized that I was being burned by the electricity. After the interrogation, in which they hoped to find out whether there were weapons in the university, they led me to another room where they took off the blindfold so I could walk, but I kept falling down. They made me crawl to another room where there were tortured people lying on the floor. I knew one of them, a university professor, by sight; one whole side of his body was black with bruises; they had punctured his eardrum, which made him howl with pain. The rest of them were all as badly beaten up as I was, or worse. Many had broken ribs and couldn't even breathe. None could walk; their legs were fractured, both from the blows and from the muscular contractions produced by the electricity. There were a lot of women as badly beaten up as the men were. They had also been brutally raped; they had internal ruptures and were bleeding profusely. One kept moaning. The torturers had inserted a sharp object in her vagina, and it had cut through the peritoneum. Some of the people there said they had recognized the interrogators: they were Navy infantrymen trained at the American bases in Panama.

The third day they sent me over to the *Lebu,* which had been turned into a jail. I was put in Hold 3, where there were already 160 people. Going down, I smelled a nauseating stench of excrement. There was no toilet, and we had to relieve ourselves in cans right there in the hold. There were laborers, office workers, physicians, lawyers, students, professors. Among them, I remember, were Patricio Muñoz, president of the University of Chile Student Federation in Valparaíso; Sergio Fischer, a prominent cardiologist; Nelson Osorio, a professor of literature; Félix Laborde, a chemical engineer; Carlos Pabst, a physicist, and many others whom I cannot name. I lived with them for sixty-five days. The food was disgusting. They served us *poroto* beans with grubs, that is, with worms. For a while they tried to be a little more humane and the commandant of the place, a naval officer named Osorio, let us go up on deck, but so they wouldn't be able to see us from the city, we were forced to stay seated without moving in the sun. Our heels and thighs were burned by the heat of the deckboards. Then Osorio realized that we were being photographed from an Italian boat, I think it was the *Verdi,* and after that he forbade going up on deck.

We were made to get up at 6 A.M. and do exercises naked. Offenses—smoking, talking, not saying "sir" when we were interrogated—were punished by blows with rifle butts and having to stand rigidly upright with our hands on our necks without moving for as long as twenty-four hours. The slightest movement was rewarded with rifle blows. Every morning and evening we were forced to sing the national anthem as the flag was struck or lowered. We were forbidden to sing the verse that goes "O la tumba serás de los libres, o el asilo contra la opresión" [Either you (Chile) will be the tomb of free men, or the asylum against oppression], because it seems that at the beginning the prisoners would sing those verses louder and the sailors took it as an innuendo against them.

One day we were very surprised because they made us clean up. They gave us mess kits, and lowered mattresses into the hold for all of us. That day a delegation came from the International Red Cross. As soon as the Red Cross left they took away our mattresses and we never saw them again. In rare cases the Navy was interested in hiding the very serious tortures inflicted on people the international organizations asked after, or whose death might cause a scandal abroad. These people were taken to the Naval Hospital, where some of them committed suicide. This happened, as I know for certain, with a girl who had been repeatedly raped. When she committed suicide, all the fourth-floor personnel were summoned to the hospital to find out who had allowed the suicide to happen.

When the news came that the *Lebu* had been sold for scrap, they released me under the supervision of the military police district commissariat. I had to present myself there every day for checking. Once they had the new concentration camp ready [the torture camp in Colliguay Alto, Valparaíso, where the ships' prisoners were transferred in December], they rearrested the people who had been freed. Before they sent me home under guard, they tried to leave me psychologically conditioned and they took me to the Academy of War for a new torture session. I was there four days. I realized their methods had gotten much crueler and more refined. They beat me more often and they used more electricity. I nearly lost my mind, not so much because of my own suffering but because of that of people weaker than myself. I saw young university women who were unspeakably tortured; one of them, who was pregnant, had been repeatedly struck on the stomach and was showing symptoms of aborting. Men over sixty had been burned all over their bodies with cigarettes and electricity. Men and women had their fingernails pulled out with pliers. Afterward, they took me to the Navy Infantry's Silva Palma barracks. After two days, they inexplicably set me free, demanding that I present myself once a day for checking and not tell what I had seen. I never found out why I was arrested, since I didn't know about any weapons at the university. I wasn't an extremist, and I didn't belong to any leftist party. I had only participated in the volunteer youth work programs, as had all the other university students. I had excellent grades, and my professors thought highly of me. My parents asked the rector to intercede on my behalf, and perhaps that's why they let me go. The fascists are so arbitrary that I'll never know why.

Other information about the present Chilean torture system has revealed that beginning in February 1974, the Peñalolén Military Camp in Santiago's Andean foothills, which had served as general headquarters for the rebel generals and admirals, was turned into a "pilot torture camp" for political prisoners. For three or more months, Brazilian police and army advisers were training Chilean Army, Navy, Air Force, and military police officers in the difficult art of torturing "prisoners of war."[11]

This Brazilian "technical" aid is not surprising, since according to the rebel generals' own statements published in Santiago a week after the coup, they had sent Chilean Army and Navy officials to Brazil, Bolivia, and Paraguay, to "brief" those governments on the uprising to take place on September 11. The day after the coup, the Brazilians, Bolivians, and Paraguayans began to send intelligence experts from their respective armies to "collaborate" in identifying, capturing, and torturing Brazilians, Bolivians, Paraguayans, and Uruguayans who had sought political asylum in Chile during the previous years.

One example is the case of a Brazilian sociologist and university professor, Theotonio Dos Santos, who had taken refuge in Chile seven years earlier, and after September 11 took asylum in the Panamanian Embassy. Refused a safe-conduct out of the country, he had to stay there for five months. In Washington, when a delegation from Hostos Community College of the City University of New York asked at the Chilean Embassy why a safe-conduct was not being granted to Dos Santos, the Chilean Embassy's press attaché, Carmen Puelma, asserted: "An investigation is under way because the Brazilians have 'suggested things' about his background . . . and also because he was the editor of *Chile Hoy (Chile Today),* a political magazine" (*New York Times,* November 24, 1973, page 24).

The Brazilian "advisers" were the ones who introduced the technique of softening morale by the "simulated" firing squad: taking prisoners to the execution wall, putting them through the execution ceremony in a group, but shooting only one out of every four or five people in the row. This technique was frequently used during the first two months after September 11. It is now being used in the various concentration camps, such as Chacabuco, in Antofagasta; Pisagua, near Iquique; Juan Fernández Island, 360 miles out of Valparaíso;

Quiriquina Island, outside of Talcahuano; Dawson Island, in the Beagle Channel; Colliquay Alto, in Valparaíso; and the Peñalolén Camp in Santiago.

CORRUPTION

The military occupation of Chile has developed a new kind of corruption in the ranks of the Air Force, Navy, Army, and military police. Here is a schematic summary of this new life style of Chile's present bosses:

Corruption in the Military Police

1. Teams of three or four officials, dressed in civilian clothes and carrying nonregulation weapons, go out during curfew hours to search homes and steal valuables. First, they extract information from domestic servants or civilian fascists about the neighborhood, and then they attack. They call this *fona* (a slang word meaning something like a legal hold-up). Military policemen Daniel Vargas and Carlos Cáceres of the 13th Commissariat are two of the many soldiers who belong to these teams.

2. When the military policemen are on guard duty, for example at embassies, they hold a blank notebook in their hands, stop cars for alleged traffic violations, and accept bribes of money or valuables. They call this "moonlighting."

3. They collect money from the families of people who have taken asylum in embassies to get permission to talk to them, for a minute or two, through the iron grilles in front of the house. The rates in December 1973 ran from 2,000 escudos to 15,000 escudos, depending on how rich the relative looked.

4. They try to force former Unidad Popular officials who have not been arrested to pay for "protection." In January 1974 the rates ran from 10,000 to 15,000 escudos a month.

5. They take liberties with the wives of prisoners. This happens at the level of ranking officers, who insinuate to the wives that if they

will sleep with them, it might be possible to intervene on their imprisoned husbands' behalf. This happens every day, and there are thousands of cases in Santiago alone.

6. They manhandle the women servants in houses near their guard posts and force them to have sexual relations in their own houses under the threat: "If you don't submit, we'll arrest you for being a Marxist."

Corruption in the Armed Forces

1. Some officers select the best-looking women prisoners to rape personally, as "part of their interrogation." Like the military police, they put psychological pressure on the wives of prisoners to let themselves be raped in exchange for "improvements" for their imprisoned husbands. Officers in administrative positions demand the same favors from female workers and secretaries under the threat of "firing them as Marxist sympathizers."

2. During searches, they manhandle women. It has become customary to have the women disrobe, "in case they are concealing weapons," and remain so while searches are carried out. They drink any liquor in the house. In downtown Santiago, a woman living alone experienced five searches of her apartment in a month, and each time she was raped by the patrol's officer.

3. Searches are carried out in two stages. On the first visit they look for the "fugitive." On the second they remove electrical equipment, household appliances, paintings, antiques, and so on. Books are destroyed.

4. They employ threatening language with women whose houses have been searched several times. I know of at least three cases of threats of "If you don't give us dollars, all of us will rape you."

As time has passed and the military has taken over all positions of responsibility in public administration, the corruption has acquired more refined forms, and so a large percentage of the money circulated in the country, the valuables, and the women have become part of the military's war booty.

Lest we think that because of his late joining of the conspiracy, General Augusto Pinochet was not of the same stripe as his troops, here is the order he transmitted from Peñalolén on the morning of September 11, recorded by a ham radio operator:

"Post One here, General Pinochet speaking. Prepare a bulletin: state that for each member of the armed forces murdered, five Marxist prisoners in the hands of military authorities will be shot immediately . . ."

"Repeat the last part, please."

"I repeat: five Marxist prisoners in the hands of the military authorities will be shot immediately. . . . Prepare a bulletin to that effect."

"I read you."

Here is another of Pinochet's conversations, also recorded by a ham radio operator:

"I would appreciate a report—"

"This is a report on Operation Population Reduction, La Legua, at 10:14. Three hundred military police, three Army companies [300 men], and five companies from El Bosque [300 men] have encircled the town. Once the target is isolated, the softening operation will begin, using tank infiltration, air support from helicopters, and fighter planes if necessary. The essential requirement is to isolate the target. For this, direct cooperation from the military police is necessary."

"Yes, but coordination with military police . . . this also has to do with Army . . . who is in charge of the operation?" [General Pinochet is asking the question.]

"In the Second Division they decided we should do it because we're responsible for the zone. The tank commander, Colonel Calderón, is in charge. The Army is coordinating. We have to deliver the target to the tanks . . ."

"Listen, I want you to explain to me just exactly what the term *reduction* means. Does it say reduction of the population? What exactly does reduction mean?" [Still Pinochet questioning.]

"It means exactly that, if the need arises. If the population surrenders, the reduction is over, General. Until yesterday there were insurgent groups creating problems, but it seems they're on the defensive now . . ."

"So *reduction* means making entry. Here is a basic point that is very important. Anybody caught bearing arms is to be arrested, and if he resists, he is to be eliminated. Is that how you understand it?"

"Yes, General. The tanks soften . . ."
"Good, that's clear."

General Pinochet was very clear; nearly a thousand soldiers equipped with tanks, artilleried helicopters, fighter jets—against a population living in houses of corrugated tin, cardboard, and newspapers. No more than 12,000 inhabitants, including children, women, and old people. But this was the method begun on September 11. That morning Pinochet's soldiers killed more than 200 men, women, and children in the La Legua settlement in Santiago.

Here is another communication recorded by a ham radio operator:

"Post One to Post Three, Post One to Post Three. General Pinochet to General Leigh. Carry out the air attack on the State Bank and the Ministry of Public Works, as soon as possible. Attack the roofs of these buildings. Do this as soon as possible. Tell me when you are going to do it, and coordinate action with land forces."
"Post Three to Post Two, General Leigh speaking. Carry out air attacks as soon as possible."
"Understood. One moment, please. Post Two reporting to General Pinochet. Artilleried helicopter will open fire on the roofs of the State Bank and the Ministry of Public Works in fifteen to twenty minutes."
"Understood. The air attack is to be directed only at the roofs of the buildings . . ."

There were about twenty civilians in the State Bank and the Ministry of Public Works, lightly armed at best. Against them and La Moneda nearby, Pinochet turned an army of five hundred men, tanks, armored cars, cannon, and air support. Meanwhile, at Río Blanco in the Andes, at the Alta Montaña School, General Pinochet's wife was spending the day skiing with their sixteen-year-old son and fourteen-year-old daughter. At seven in the evening, she phoned her husband and he told her, "Everything is quiet." President Allende had already been assassinated, La Moneda had been destroyed, and a carpet of thousands of dead civilians assured the "quiet" of Chile, from north to south, east to west.

But desperation works miracles. Groups of laborers, office workers, students, and women came out of their homes that day to resist the military invasion of their country. The radio communications went on.

"Correct, Post Five. 1000 Las Acacias Avenue. They're handing out arms there. There's a crowd of people being given arms."

"Understood, Post Two."

"Go ahead, Post Two."

"Please report on measures being taken with respect to the situation at Station 6 in Santa Rosa. Our ground forces there are being shot at by a large number of armed persons . . ."

"Post Three to Post One, please report."

"Post Five, Post Three here. The general needs a report."

"Post Five here, for Post Three. What you asked about Santa Rosa Station 6: The command reports that tanks have been sent there with reinforcements from the Infantry School."

"Understood."

"Post Five to Post One. Give me the troop commander. This is a report. There is a clandestine radio transmitting at 29 megacycles. Two, nine, 29 megacycles."

"Understood."

"Inform Post Three that we are waiting for help to arrive."

"Listen, Nicanor, Beta One El Bosque thinks we have to announce the curfew again today, because there are a lot of people gathering in the streets. . . . Beta One thinks it should be repeated every ten or fifteen minutes."

"Okay, we'll repeat the announcement."

"General Benavides here. The Military Police Training Center in Macul is under attack. I've asked for air support. There's sniping going on in Los Jazmines. There's only one officer and two enlisted men in that town . . ."

"We urgently need information about leftist intimidation at Villa Las Acacias in Maipú—that's behind Villa Schneider. Do you read me?"

"I don't read you."

"I repeat. Leftist forces are intimidating inhabitants of Villa Las Acacias in Maipú. Now do you read me?"

"Affirmative."

"No press publication of any kind will be permitted. If any comes out, the place of publication will be destroyed."

"Yes."

"I repeat the first part: From the military junta of government to commanders of garrisons and independent units: beginning immediately, arrest any political or union leader or private person who does not obey orders and observe the curfew. These persons will be tried, and if caught with arms and/or explosives, they will be sentenced by courts martial."

"Understood."

One of Allende's colleagues, who was working with him on the night of September 10 when the President was preparing his submission to the demands of the civilian opposition, told of Allende's astonishing ignorance about the real role his generals were playing. This is the report sent out by Spanish news agency EFE on September 18:

During the course of the work session, President Allende was informed by telephone of troop transport trucks coming from San Felipe (100 kilometers from the capital) in the direction of Santiago. The Defense Minister [Orlando Letelier] telephoned General Herman Brady, head of the Santiago garrison and commander of the Army's Second Division. The latter indicated to Letelier that *he knew nothing about it,* but would find out and phone back in fifteen or twenty minutes.

At 00:30 hours on Tuesday the eleventh, the minister called Brady again and the general told him that he had contacted San Felipe and that "everything was in order" there.

Shortly before 07:00 hours, President Allende was awakened with the news that the officers of some ships had mutinied, specifically the cruiser *Admiral Latorre* and the submarine *Simpson.*

At 07:00 hours, Allende telephoned the commanders in chief. None of them answered. [By that time, they were all at the rebel headquarters in Peñalolén, except for Admiral Montero, who had been deposed and put under arrest by Merino.]

At 07:10 President Allende spoke by telephone with General Brady and ordered him to assess the situation and, if he was not going to assess the situation, to tell him so directly.

At 07:30 President Allende arrived at the Palacio de La Moneda. At 07:45 he telephoned Luis Figueroa (a Communist), the president of the Central Única, the workers' organization. At 07:55 he recorded his first message to the country, which was broadcast by Radio Corporación (Socialist). At 08:00

he telephoned Rolando Calderón (a Socialist), secretary general of the Central Única. He had kept on trying to reach the commanders in chief, without success. He intimated that he feared they might be compromised. He said General Orlando Urbina (inspector general of the Army) and Admiral Montero were not at home either.

At 08:20 the President's Air Force aide, Commander Roberto Sánchez, phoned just as Dr. Allende was recording his second radio speech. Commander Sánchez said that he was at Air Force Group Seven (in Santiago), where he had gone to find out what was happening, and that General Gabriel Van Schowen (chief of the Air Force General Staff) had told him that he had an aircraft ready for President Allende. The answer to this message was: "Tell General Van Schowen that the President of Chile is not going to flee in an airplane, and that he knows how to fulfill his duty as a soldier."

At 08:30 the people in La Moneda heard the first proclamation from the military junta.

At 7:40 that morning, a woman alone, Allende's wife, began to live her nightmare along with the rest of the Chileans.

Tuesday at 7:40 a telephone call woke me. It was Salvador, who said: "I'm calling you from La Moneda. The situation has become serious. The Navy has rebelled. I'm going to stay here. You stay at Tomás Moro." He practically forbade me to go out of the house. I clung to the radio. I heard his last message to the people of Chile. By noon, the phone at La Moneda wasn't answering. Around 11:30 a reconnoitering helicopter appeared over the house. At that time I still didn't know that the military police had deserted us. That was when the air bombardment began. The planes would come and fire their rockets and come back again. Between each attack, an insane burst of gunfire was set off. The house was turned into a mass of smoke, smelling of gunpowder and destruction. I made my last calls to La Moneda from the floor, sometimes kneeling, sometimes lying down. That's when Carlos Tello, my chauffeur, came to get me. He had been able to bring the car into the courtyard in back of the house. We went out through the nuns' school behind our house. I decided to go to Felipe Herrera's, and fortunately no one followed us. I stayed there all day. I couldn't go out because martial law had been declared and a curfew announced. I stayed there, not knowing anything about my husband or my children.

When the Chilean Air Force began to bomb the Tomás Moro Street residence to "reduce" Salvador Allende's wife, the first plane made a very serious mistake. Instead of striking the Allende house, the first four rockets hit the Chilean Air Force Hospital, twenty blocks north of the target. "The windows' glare confused me," the pilot confessed to his companions later in the day. The rockets struck a wing of the hospital: one landed in the basement laundry, the second on the third floor, the third on the terrace, and the fourth in the garden. The only casualty was a nurse who broke both legs.

That evening General Leigh announced to the nation on television: "The Marxists are vicious. They did not hesitate to attack a hospital, the Air Force Hospital in Las Condes," and he went on to declare that now the sun would shine for Chileans, because they would be governed by honest people, because "we military men never lie."

The Tomás Moro house, the residence of the presidents of Chile, suffered the first effects of the rule of these honest people. After it was bombed, it was left open to be looted by crowds of the upper class, who avenged themselves on Allende by stealing his belongings.

General Leigh was not the only soldier who "never lied." There was General Pinochet, who stated by telephone to the Franco-Luxembourg radio RTL: "Pablo Neruda is not dead and is free. We do not kill anybody. If Neruda dies, it will be a natural death."

Pablo Neruda, desperately ill with cancer of the prostate and in need of daily medical attention, had been isolated in his house on Isla Negra for five days (September 11–15) by a cordon of soldiers and military police. They let no one, not even people bringing medicine, into or out of the poet's house. No one has been able to determine whether the rebel generals had actually decided to kill Neruda with a "natural death." But Neruda's death was the result of those five days without medical attention. Finally, dying, he was transferred to the Santa Maria Clinic in Santiago. But while Neruda was still at Isla Negra, the troops sacked his house, smashing the poet's belongings, burning his books, stealing his money. Neruda's house in Santiago, at the foot of San Cristóbal Hill, was also sacked, or rather "searched," which is the same thing in the mouths of the generals who do not lie. Neruda's books were burned, and his possessions stolen.

On September 23, 1973, Pablo Neruda died of a "natural death" caused by Generals Pinochet, Mendoza, and Leigh and Admiral Merino.

On September 24, Agence France Presse sent out this wire:

> The body of Pablo Neruda, who died yesterday, was resting this afternoon in the ruins—open to all the winds—of his lofty dovecote in the heights of Santiago. Today at dawn, the soldiers conducted a search in the house of the great Chilean Communist poet. Now the windows are broken, the bed destroyed, the wardrobes in pieces, and his books and magazines burned. The floor of his house and the dovecote that dominates it are flooded. Neruda's body lies in the midst of broken glass, torn-up photographs, and pre-Colombian pottery shattered into rubbish.

Neruda had died in the clinic but, apparently in a gesture of defiance, his widow transferred the Nobel laureate's body to his house in Santiago, which had already been sacked by the military.

A week later, on October 1, the generals and admirals published Decree No. 54, which doubled officers' salaries, placing them among the highest-paid persons in Chile. The same decree gave a 5,000-escudo bonus to the enlisted men of the armed forces. That is, an additional $600,000 dollars to the military.

This comes to something like $40 per civilian murdered from September 11 to September 30: $40 for José Soto's fourteen-year-old son, shot by soldiers and left on his doorstep, $40 for Salvador Allende, machine-gunned in the Salón Rojo of the Presidential Palace, $40 for Pablo Neruda, Nobel laureate for Literature.[12]

Notes

1. The Artful Staging of a "Suicide"

1. This reconstruction of Operation Alpha One is made possible by information from various sources, including tape recordings of radio transmissions between the rebels and accounts passed on to me when some senior officers, who had been part of Alpha One and were overwhelmed by the magnitude of the atrocity they had participated in, took junior officers and even civilians into their confidence. Many of the details about what happened inside the palace were related to me by eyewitnesses.

2. From the signing of the Mutual Aid Pact with the United States armed services, their influence over the Chilean military institutions began to grow. In the early 1960s, journalists and political parties of the left were already denouncing this trend. In one of the best-known exposés, a campaign against U.S. military influence, beginning in 1968, such magazines as *Causa ML* (vols. 2 and 3, 1968; vols. 7 and 10, 1969) published photostatic copies of the textbooks used in Chile's military schools, which were mere translations of those used by the U.S. Army. During 1970 and 1971 the magazine *Punto Final* exposed "anti-Communist" programs in the Bernardo O'Higgins Military School and the Playa Ancha Naval Academy in Valparaíso. In 1972 the Santiago newspapers *El Pueblo* and *El Rebelde* divulged the presence of members of the U.S. military mission in those military academies as "guest professors" with a year's appointment. But this is hardly inconsistent with the philosophy of the Military Aid Pact (PAM). The same sources added the following details:

"In 1963, the U.S. Department of Defense, in a document sent to Congress explaining the philosophy of the Military Aid Pact with respect to Latin-American armies, stated that the pact contributed to the political aims of the United States through its training programs, which brought many foreign military leaders to the U.S., not only to improve the technical ability of the military, but also to expose them to the requirements of reliable military leadership in contemporary society.

"On June 3, 1969, Melvin R. Laird, U.S. Secretary of Defense, said to Congress: '. . . I am certain that the Military Aid Pact will do everything in its power to guarantee that every dollar invested in aid granted will be most effectively employed in helping the foreign policy and security of the United States.'

"In 1963, Robert McNamara, the then Secretary of Defense, said to Congress: 'Military and economic aid are frequently bound together in support of U.S. objectives, providing the native armed forces with able instructors through the military aid program, with the Agency for International Development contributing the material elements . . . to reduce the vulnerability of the native people to the flattery and threats of Communist agents involved in manufacturing revolutions.'

"In 1964, in the House of Representatives, General Robert J. Wood, at the time director of military aid in the Defense Department, stated: 'A Security Program for the Alliance for Progress is being carried out . . . whose principal objective is a Latin-American military leadership.' "

For further information on this subject, see James Petras, "Estados Unidos y el nuevo equilibrio en América Latina," *Revista de Estudios Internacionales,* Jan.–March 1969, Santiago, Chile, pp. 490–518.

3. These words are an approximate reconstruction of what was said by the American adviser to the conspiracy in September 1973; this is based on what was said in speeches and meetings on Navy ships and in military centers by the conspiring officers from May 1973 on. As was reported during the first ten days of September 1973 in *Puro Chile, Última Hora,* and the magazine *Chile Hoy,* the conspiring officers haranguing mainly sailors and pilots asserted that "the Americans are backing us up," adding further details. These officers included: Colonel Juan Soler Manfredini, director of the Air Forces Technical School; Colonel Carlos Ottone Mestre, director of the Captain Avalos Aviation School; Second Lieutenant Jaime Olavarrieta, from the Sailors (Grumetes) School at Quiriquina Island; Lieutenant Julio Meneses from the Valparaíso Naval Hospital; Commodore Alberto Vázquez, commander of the aeronaval base at El Bolloto; Commodore Martiniano Parra, from the naval base at Talcahuano; Commander César Guevara Fuentes, from the El Bosque Group 7, Air Force, Santiago, and his second-in-command Ivan

Doren as well as his assistants Lieutenant Ernesto González and Corporal Florencio Gálvez. One of the most outspoken officers was Air Force Colonel Ramón Gallegos Alonso, who pointed out that "the Americans give us technical advice and backing in everything." He related details of meetings from November 1972 on with representives of the U.S. Army to plan Allende's overthrow. Gallegos Alonso was the public relations chief of the Chilean armed forces until August 1973 and former Commander in Chief César Ruiz Danyau's right-hand man in the conspiracy of the second half of that month—along with officers Juan Pablo Rojas, Guillermo Navarro Vicencio, Raúl Vargas, and Antonio Quirós—in Santiago itself. In Antofagasta, in the north of Chile, the squadron commander Juan Cvitanic, public relations chief at the Cerro Moreno base, was another who touted the coup to his friends by describing its "American backing." Another commander in the Antofagasta group was Patricio Araya Ugalde, who was referred to as "Ruiz Danyau's alter ego." In Los Cerrillos Group 10, there were Germán Fuchslocher and Carlos Álvarez; and in Quintero Group 2 (near Santiago), Group Commander Pablo Saldías Maripangue.

Most of the information about the meetings between the Chilean and the American officers from November 1972 on came from this type of source, when, it seems, the conspirators were absolutely certain that nothing would stop the coup. There were, of course, numerous other sources well informed about what was happening in the core of the conspirators' group, but I cannot name these sources because it would jeopardize the life of many Chileans, both civilian and military, who are still in Chile now.

4. In this parliamentary election, the 44 percent received by the Unidad Popular is really a victory, given the political system of Chile. Never before had any elected Chilean government increased its percentage of the votes after the presidential elections. A case in point is that of Eduardo Frei: elected in 1964 with 56.09 percent of the vote, his party dropped to 42.3 percent in the 1965 parliamentary elections; three years later, in the municipal elections of 1967, his government received 35.58 percent of the vote; this decline culminated in the parliamentary elections of 1969, when the percentage was 21.8 percent. In the pluralistic system of democracy that existed in Chile until September 11, 1973, this relative minority was not a sign of illegitimacy but rather a measure of backing or rejection of a constitutional action. By the same token, in the 1958 presidential elections the winning candidate, Jorge Alessandri Rodríguez, received only 31.2 percent of the vote, but he defeated

Allende, the runner-up, whose total was 28.5 percent, Frei, with 20.5 percent, and the Radical, Luis Bossay, with 15.4 percent. Nobody questioned the legitimacy of Jorge Alessandri's presidency.

With the Unidad Popular government, the opposite was the case. Winning 36 percent of the vote in 1970, it raised this percentage to 44 percent in 1973, a significant expansion of its plurality. However, the conspirators "proved" the illegitimacy of Allende's government using the fact that he "represented only a minority of 36 percent," a false argument given the context of Chile's political system.

5. What happened in this meeting was related by President Allende himself to a small group of Unidad Popular journalists in La Moneda on the night of the same day, August 8. Some of these journalists are in prison in Chile, and others have gone underground; one of them, Augusto Olivares Becerra, was killed.

6. The existence of this tape, a summary of its contents, and this version of the meeting were revealed by Allende to a small group of Unidad Popular journalists in order to explain his request that they not report any of these events, as the situation was "extremely critical." The events of the following day were more or less public, including harangues in the courtyards of the air bases involved and the comings and goings of easily identifiable military couriers. However, the agreement with Allende was respected, and the leftist newspapers did not inform the public of the event in detail, but rather in a general and indirect way. Of course the newspapers of the right were also silent.

7. During the 1970 presidential campaign, many journalists accompanied Allende day and night as he traveled all around Chile, and at day's end the question of what the armed forces would do if Allende won was often discussed. From that time on, it was known from Allende's own mouth that he thought he had "at least one friend, General Torres de la Cruz." Allende was later to define Torres as an "Allendista." He even said that it was enough guarantee that Torres was fifth in seniority at that time, preceded only by Schneider, Prats, Pinochet, and Urbina, and followed by Bonilla. After the events of October 1970, Torres was again mentioned by Allende's military advisers as "loyal." During March–April 1973, when the arms searches of the factories began, Unidad Popular officials went to Punta Arenas to talk to Torres (Allende had sent him there to "reinforce" the struggle against the fascists' arms smuggling from Argentina) to find out what was going on inside the Army. Naturally, Torres said that the brutalization and punishment of the workers of both sexes were excesses proper to that type of action.

8. The case of Augusto Pinochet in the drama that Chile is living through today is very special. Today, he seems to be an extremely cruel head of a fascist military junta. But until June 1973, the conspiring generals were not at all sure of Pinochet, particularly because he always seemed to agree with his superior, Army Commander in Chief Carlos Prats, in his political line, and because many of the courses of action taken by the General Staff under his direction were carried out under Prats's slogan of "defending the Constitution in case of military insurrection." General Pinochet was the last important link in the coup to close. The principal reason for Generals Leigh, Bonilla, Brady, and Arellano and Admiral Toribio Merino to "invite" him to be chief of the junta was to avoid a rupture in the Army. Perhaps the fact that he was excluded for such a long time from the conspirators' group also kept him outside the plan to assassinate Allende.

9. According to unofficial testimony, there were eight dead and forty-three wounded among the soldiers, in addition to a damaged but not inoperable Sherman tank. The official report, however, announced "two dead and seventeen wounded" and made no mention of damaged matériel.

2. Why Was the General Assassinated?

1. The fifth coup attempt was covered in Chapter 1. The first and second military insurrections are treated in Chapter 3; the fourth, fifth, and sixth in Chapter 5. The coup of September 11, the seventh and successful attempt, is discussed in detail in Chapters 1, 4, 5, and 6.

2. The remaining 4 percent of the work force is taken up by the so-called domestic employees, mainly peasant women who work in the houses of the middle and the upper bourgeoisie. Their salaries are so low that they are not included in the national accounts. (Facts taken from "Antecedentes sobre el desarrollo chileno 1960–1970," ODEPLAN, 1971, 30–32, pp. 43, 45.)

3. The greater part of the papers that indicated payments had been received by Gabriel González Videla from the American consortia were published in the Chilean magazine *Vistazo* in November and December 1962 and July 1964; in my articles "La penetración imperialista en Chile" in *Causa ML,* Nos. 1–9, and in the series "La historia sucia de los políticos demócratas" in *Puro Chile* March 15–April 7, 1973. A similar case was that of Rodolfo Michels, which was so scandalous that he was expelled from the Radical party in 1964, when the leftists gained control of this political group; they were later to support Allende's candidacy in 1970. Michels was thrown out for "carrying on illegal

relations with a foreign company, Anaconda." But the right wing regained control of the party, and relations with Anaconda were reestablished (see *ibid.*).

4. When the copper mines were nationalized in July 1971, Robert Haldeman left Chile. In his offices at the El Teniente mine, documents were found attesting to conversations and agreements involving state property and votes in the Chilean Parliament, in the form of correspondence between Chileans and Haldeman and his superiors in the Kennecott Company. There were 70,000 pages of documents. *Mayoría,* a magazine, published copies of 100 of these documents from December 1971 to January 1972; these reproduced the conversations between Frei and Haldeman in 1963, Haldeman's report on Frei, and documents of money paid to journalists, members of Parliament, and politicians to proselytize for American companies and their tax agreement in Chile. Raúl Morales Adriazola, a rightist Senator, was called into court for this, but the Appellate Court, although it accepted the genuineness of the documents, declared itself incompetent to judge Morales Adriazola owing to his congressional immunity. The court refused to suspend this immunity in order to try him. One of the journalists named as receiving some payment was Carlos Sepúlveda, now president of the Professional College of Chile. About Guillermo Correa Fuenzalida, see "La historia yanqui de un Presidente chileno," a series published in *Puro Chile,* Feb. 17–28, 1973.

5. The story of the $20 million fund for Frei's 1964 presidential campaign was published in the April 6, 1973, issue of the Washington *Post.* The newspaper quotes a witness as saying, "U.S. government intervention in Chile in 1964 was blatant and almost obscene." The *Post* also reported that "the number of 'special personnel' dispatched at various stages of the campaign to Chile from Washington and other posts was calculated by one key Latin American policy maker at the time as being in the range of 100." The leftist political parties PS and MAPU afterward put together "La historia yanqui de un Presidente chileno" in *Puro Chile (op. cit.),* revealing the relations between Frei and the American consortia; other reports appeared in *Causa ML,* No. 5, 1969, and in the June 8, 1973, issue of *Punto Final,* "Acta de acusación contra Eduardo Frei," to bring about action against Frei in the Chilean Congress for providing services to a foreign power during the term of his presidency. The accusation was of course rejected by the reactionary majority in the Senate, but the charges were so well documented that Frei could not enjoin their publication. The denunciations included copies of letters to

Frei from David Rockefeller and his "economic instructions" (published earlier in *Mayoría,* Jan. 1972).

Here are some paragraphs from the texts published in *Mayoría:* "Meeting of November 12, 1963, between Robert Haldeman, vice-president of Braden [the Kennecott mine, El Teniente] and Frei at the home of José Claro Vial [Gabriel González Videla's son-in-law], at the request of Frei. Frei said: 'I am certain that if elected President, we will not have problems in reducing the present high taxes, either by agreement, law, or legal contract. . . . Here in Chile I feel closer to Braden than to the Anaconda people. . . . Mr. Milliken [of Kennecott] is a hard and dry man. I do not doubt his intelligence, but he does not have the human warmth and cordiality that Mr. Roy Glover [world chief of Anaconda] had; I had established a very good friendship with him and he was always grateful to me for voting in favor of the Nuevo Trato law [a 1958 law that scandalized Chile because of its guarantees to the American copper companies].' " (Text found in the El Teniente offices in Santiago after the nationalization, a memorandum of Manuel Illanes, a Chilean journalist and a Kennecott official.)

Another quote: "In August 1968, *Hanson's Latin American Newsletter,* published in the United States, said in a study of the Frei administration: 'No other government of the extreme right has been so generous with the American companies as the Frei administration, through the agreements he has signed. His exceedingly favorable treatment lacked balance and judgment and was so harmful to Chilean interests that it provoked hilarity in Washington.' " (*Hanson's Latin American Newsletter,* mimeographed issues published by a private company in Washington, D.C., regularly sent to Chilean periodicals in 1967–1969.)

6. The relation between Plan Camelot (for details see Gregorio Selser's *Espionaje en América Latina,* Buenos Aires, 1966) and Roy Hansen's study was inferred in the sessions of the Chilean Chamber of Deputies from June to December 1965, which convened as a result of the revelations about that espionage project published in the newspaper *El Siglo* in May, June, and July 1965, and by myself and Miroslav Popic on Radio Portales in Santiago on the Sunday news program "La Gran Encuesta" in June and July of the same year. As shown by the statements of Juan de Dios Carmona, Frei's Defense Minister at the time of the scandal, to the Chamber of Deputies' Investigatory Commission, the Defense Ministry had known about Hansen's study and had authorized it because it "was not considered to be espionage." Hansen himself wrote that "the data was collected during a series of three trips (15

weeks in total) to Chile between 1964 and 1965. Two hundred Chilean civilians were interviewed; there were intensive interviews with 38 generals, and a questionnaire was distributed among active officers of the Academy of War and the Polytechnic School." He adds that his trips took place between December 1964 and June 1965, and that he had access to the documents in the Chilean Army General Staff library (off limits to Chilean civilians). The introduction of Plan Camelot in Chile was under the charge of Hugo Nuttini, a sociologist who contacted Álvaro and Ximena Bunster to begin a team operation.

The Scandinavian sociologist Johan Galtung alerted leftist journalists, and the scandal about Plan Camelot began in May 1965. For details on these events, see my book *Golpe de Estado contra Frei?*, Ediciones Punto Final, Santiago, 1965. Transcripts of the radio program "La Gran Encuesta" were in the files of the Information and Broadcast of the presidency in Santiago until September 11, 1973. On the involvement of American University with Project Camelot, see *The Rise and Fall of Project Camelot: Studies in the Relationship Between Social Science and Practical Politics,* edited by Irving Louis Horowitz, Cambridge, M.I.T. Press, revised edition, 1974, especially pages 23, 24, 25. On Roy Hansen see, also, *The Black Book of American Intervention* by Armando Uribe, Boston, Beacon Press, 1975, pages 26–29.

7.   In 1969 some Chilean journalists gained access to the "classified" copy that existed in Chile, and a summary of its contents was published in the Santiago magazine *Causa ML,* No. 21, Aug. 1971, pp. 20–25. Hansen's work was funded by the Ford Foundation and the Rand Corporation.

8.   The quotes from the text of Plan Camelot come from the Spanish edition published in August 1965 by the Oficina de Informaciones de la Camara de Senadores de Chile as a document appended to the investigation that the Chamber of Deputies was conducting into the alleged "espionage." The introduction to Plan Camelot stated that its purpose was to find a "system" which would "make it possible to predict and politically influence significant aspects of social change in the world's developing countries" (p. 2 of Spanish edition). In late June 1965, UPI released a bulletin from Washington reporting the "suspension" of Plan Camelot: "Responsibility for the operation belonged to the Special Operations Research Office (SORO) of the American University in Washington." A Pentagon spokesman stated on July 8 of that year that the project, launched by the Army's information services, was functioning in various countries: Peru, Colombia, and Chile; that it had already cost some

$300,000; and that already "a great number of specialists in social sciences of international reputation had contributed ideas and information referring to Communist subversive attacks." On July 21, when a group of sociologists at the University of Chile denounced the attitude of Hugo Nuttini, the total funds invested in the project to that time amounted to some $6 million (see Alain Labrousse, *El experimento chileno,* Ediciones Grijalbo, 1973, p. 150).

The quotes from the sociologist Roy Hansen's work on the Chilean high command came from a photographic copy of the mimeographed English version that is kept in the Academy of War's library in Santiago. After September 11, I destroyed the negatives of that photographic copy, while the positive copy in my office at *Puro Chile* was probably burned when the military bombed and set fire to our building on the day of the coup. In my article "Las Fuerzas Armadas chilenas" (*Causa ML,* No. 21, Aug. 1971, pp. 11–25), I published an extensive extract from Hansen's investigations.

9. In August 1968, in *Causa ML,* No. 2, in my article "La Penetración norteamericana en las Fuerzas Armadas chilenas," the first documented denunciations were made of the introduction of anti-Marxist courses in the Bernardo O'Higgins Military School. More were made in *Punto Final* in 1969 and 1970. The expression "Western and Christian" had been in use since the violent presidential campaign of 1964 as an answer to the "Oriental, atheist world" in defining the struggle of capitalism against Communism. From that time on, "Western and Christian" had come to mean the "non-Socialist" world and had lost the religious connotation of "Christian." Speeches, books, college theses, and the armed forces were using this expression in that sense.

   The beginning of the military school's upper classmen going to the Canal Zone in 1968 was made public in an allusive speech by René Schneider, who by that time was director of the military school. For the general anti-Communist orientation in Chilean military education, see Lieutenant Colonel (Ret.) Alberto Polloni, *Las Fuerzas Armadas de Chile en la vida nacional,* Editorial Jurídica de Chile, Santiago, 1972.

10. The quotes from *The Rockefeller Report on the Americas* come from a Spanish translation made by the Oficina de Informaciones de la Cámara del Senado de Chile in December 1969.

11. For a detailed examination of the conspiratorial meetings of civilian politicians and the military in October 1970, see *El Caso Schneider. Operación Alfa,* Section of Special Documents, Editora Nacional Quimantu, Santiago, 1972; Eduardo Labarca, *Chile al Rojo,* Ediciones de

la Universidad Técnica del Estado, Santiago, April, 1971; Sergio Ramos, *Chile: Una economía en transición?*, Casa de las Américas, 1972, pp. 260–286; *Puro Chile* issues throughout November 1970; and the transcript of the trial attorney's report, published in *El Siglo,* June 5, 1971. General Schneider's role in the plot was indirectly denounced, because the political conditions at the time did not permit the destruction of his "constitutionalist image," in *Causa ML,* No. 20, Jan.–Feb. 1971, and in issues of *El Pueblo,* Feb., March, and April 1971 (in these articles, the Pentagon's involvement in the affair was also denounced). Additional documentation of ITT's and the CIA's machinations will be found in *Documentos secretos de la ITT,* Ediciones Quimantu, 1972.

12. The most spectacular proof of Frei's participation in the plot was given by retired General Roberto Viaux Marambio. In *Conversaciones con Viaux* (Santiago, 1972), Florencia Varas, a journalist, published Viaux's confidences made to her while he was in prison. These and the investigations conducted after the scandal provoked by this confession (one of the main charges in the Parliament accusation of Frei in 1973, when he was president of the Senate; see note 5) revealed that Arturo Matte Larrain (of the Matte-Alessandri economic clan) and Guillermo Carey Tagle (a lawyer for Kennecott Copper) were the contacts between Frei and the rest of the conspirators, including the Americans. (See "La historia sucia de los políticos demócratas," a series of articles published in *Puro Chile,* March 7–April 15, 1973.) Viaux explained in detail to Varas how Frei had participated in the conspiracy but asked not to be associated with it publicly. Viaux insisted that Frei's hesitation made the Americans suddenly withdraw their backing from the coup.

13. In hindsight, it is tragic to recall how Allende persisted in his thesis that his government was not socialist but that it was paving the way toward socialism without any prior violence and destruction. On the basis of this thesis, during the three years of his administration he attempted to convince his political enemies that if the Unidad Popular's reforms were not made, social violence would erupt, motivated by the most underprivileged sectors of society. But the curtain of propaganda from the right and the United States painted Allende's government as "socialist" and even "Marxist." Allende's speeches and press conferences are filled with references to his nonsocialist program and his thesis that his reforms were the only way to halt the decay of Chile's social system. One quotation will suffice:

"In the first place, [we need] clarity, clear understanding, to know where we are going, what goal we should achieve at this stage. I have said very honestly: The government of which I am the head is not a socialist government. The Unidad Popular program is not a socialist program. But our government and our program are the beginning of the building of socialism." (Speech of May 1, 1972, made before thousands of laborers; quoted in Salvador Allende's collected speeches, *La revolución chilena,* Ediciones Eudeba, Buenos Aires, 1973.)

The reader will find more such quotes from Allende's speeches in Chapter 5. Regarding the state's "capitalist" nature in its economic reforms, see Sergio Ramos, *Chile, Una economía en transición?,* cited above; Pedro Vuscovic (Allende's Minister of the Economy), "Dos años de política económica," published in *Ute* magazine, Vols. 11 and 12, Jan.–Feb. 1973. A version of Allende's conversation with the generals was given by Luis Hernández Parker on the radio program "Tribuna Política," broadcast by Santiago's Radio Portales, Oct. 20, 1970.

With regard to the terrorist activities, Valenzuela, Schilling, Rodríguez, Huerta, and Viaux confessed organizing them. This was reported in *Última Hora, Clarín, El Siglo, Puro Chile, Le Nación,* etc., in November and December 1970, and afterward. An official summary of these confessions appeard in *The Schneider Case: Operation Alpha,* Editorial Nacional Quimantu, Santiago de Chile, 1972, Series of Special Documents.

14. A version of the talk General Schneider gave in the Academy was known on the night of October 15 in the core of Senator Allende's campaign committee, and it provoked a series of articles on the subject of "The Armed Forces' Constitutionality" in *Última Hora, El Siglo,* and *Puro Chile,* Oct. 17–19, 1970. These articles cited concepts put forth by Schneider to demonstrate that Allende would be elected in the Plenary Congress, because the armed forces were not afraid of the Unidad Popular program. For their part, Kennecott lawyer Guillermo Carey Tagle and Air Force General Joaquín García, both involved in the plot (see Eduardo Labarca, *Chile al Rojo,* cited above), commented on Schneider's talk at a meeting of friends (at the home of Senator Raúl Morales Adriazola, another conspirator; see note 4) on the night of October 18. Colonel Thomas H. Jones, chief of the Army section of the U.S. military mission, was rumored to have influenced the Schneider talk that smashed their plot's hopes of victory. Jones had come to Chile around mid-1968 and was Schneider's constant companion in programing the Bernardo O'Higgins Military School curriculum. *PEC,* a magazine of the extreme right, denounced in an issue in the last week of

October 1970 the "American military" as the cause of Allende's eleva-
tion to the presidency. Later reports showed that Colonel Jones and
Colonel Paul M. Wimert, military attaché to the U.S. Embassy, were
closely attached to Schneider in those weeks and held many meetings
with other officers of the Army and Air Force, chiefly to explain the
lack of opportunity to prevent Allende from becoming President. In
July 1971, in separate actions only three days apart, Colonels Jones
and Wimert were removed from the U.S. Embassy. This followed an
unprecedented series of visits between January 14 and May 25, 1971,
from an admiral and a rear admiral of the U.S. Navy and a U.S. Air
Force general to the Chilean high command, each one spending an
average of four days there. Meanwhile, between December 1970 and
May 1971, Allende held fourteen meetings with the Chilean high command, which he told radio and newspaper reporters were "concerned
with the future of those national institutions." (For details of these
events, see *Causa ML,* No. 21, August 1971, my article "Qué piensan
las Fuerzas Armadas?" the first part of which is translated in Dale
Johnson's book *The Chilean Road to Socialism,* New York, Doubleday Anchor, 1973; in Alain Labrousse's *Reformisme ou revolution,*
Paris, 1972; and in Labrousse's *El experimento chileno,* Grijalbo,
1973.

15.   Admiral Porta Angulo resigned his post because the four admirals who
had spoken to Allende did so without his authorization as commander
in chief of the Navy. That is, they failed to respect the "military hierarchy," which in Chile, particularly in the Navy, has almost the character of a religious myth. Porta Angulo felt that his "hierarchy" had been
abrogated, and so he quit.

16.   Quoted from the documents provided by columnist Jack Anderson to
the Senate Commission investigating ITT in 1972. From NACLA's
(North American Congress on Latin America) *Latin America & Empire
Report,* Vol. 6, No. 4, April 1972, pp. 8–10.

17.   *Ibid.,* p. 13.

18.   *Ibid.,* p. 14.

19.   *Ibid.,* p. 15. This report was dictated by phone from San Juan.

20.   *Ibid.,* p. 17.

21.   *Ibid.,* p. 19.

22.   In November 1970, in his first instructions to the directors of Unidad
Popular newspapers and news media, President Allende said that "General Schneider's tragic murder is of such political sensitiveness that our
responsibility as revolutionaries is to refer to it in the way most conve-

nient to the interests of the political process that we are directing." He went on to declare that the duty of responsible journalists was to confine themselves to the official reports released by the military attorney in charge of the case in referring to anything that had to do with the military personnel allegedly involved. Later, more detailed instructions issued by the President's spokesmen added that the event should be treated as a "personal and isolated adventure" on the part of some generals. Allende had insisted to responsible Unidad Popular journalists that they had to take care to keep the armed forces from collapsing in order to maintain his government's security on that "flank," as he put it. In point of fact, it was an extremely perilous moment, since the Santiago and Concepción garrisons were involved, along with the commanders in chief of the Navy, Air Force, and military police. A notable presence was that of Colonel Washington Carrasco, serving as General Eduardo Arriagada Lasa's chief of staff in the Army Third Division. Carrasco was promoted to Arriagada's position when the latter was fired during the Allende administration; he was to become one of the principal members of the conspiring generals' group, leading the military insurrection of September 11, 1973.

Later, in December 1971, the Santiago daily *La Tribuna* mentioned the Prats–Allende agreement in unsigned articles on pages 2 and 3.

23. *Qué Pasa*, Nov. 2, 1973, p. 7.
24. *The Rockefeller Report on the Americas*, New York Times Edition, Quadrangle Books, 1969, pp. 66, 70.

3. The Bosses Conspire and the Workers Mobilize

1. When Allende became President, Chile was for the most part a developing capitalist country, but dependent on U.S. transnational capital. To get an idea of the nature of Chilean society at that time, let's look at some statistics taken from "National Accounts of Chile 1967–68" *(Cuentas Nacionales)*, ODEPLAN, Santiago, 1970:

Distribution of expenditures in the national economy: agriculture, forestry, and fishing, 10.5 percent; mines, 9.7 percent; manufacturing, 25.7 percent; construction, 4.5 percent; electricity, gas, and water, 1.7 percent; transportation, warehousing, and communications, 4.4 percent; wholesale and retail commerce, 21.6 percent; other services, 21.9 percent.

Percentage distribution of the work force: agriculture, forestry, and fishing, 25.6 percent; mining, 3 percent; manufacturing, 21.6 percent; construction, 6.2 percent; electricity, gas, and water, .8 percent; transportation, warehousing, and communications, 6.3 percent; commerce and services, 36.5 percent.

The same accounts showed that 50 percent of the work force was laborers and 1.4 percent employers. This gives an idea of why the combative strength of the workers in Chile was so great and was able to push such movements as the Unidad Popular forward. Its fighting capacity was tragically set in motion in 1907 when the saltpeter works went on strike, to be suppressed by the government through the Army's slaughter of 3,000 workers in the Santa Maria de Iquique schoolhouse.

The 1.4 percent of the work force comprising the employers and bondholders was organized into guilds in the Sociedad de Fomento Fabril, the Sociedad Nacional de Agricultura, and the Confederación de la Producción y el Comercio, through which they had always controlled the Chilean government. The degree of concentration of economic power in this 1.4 percent is revealed by the following facts, from the same source: 17 percent of the stock companies possessed 78 percent of the total assets of the stock companies. In those dominant companies, the ten biggest shareholders owned more than 90 percent of the stocks in almost 60 percent of those companies. It was there that the eleven oligarchic clans mentioned were concentrated, consisting of no more than 1,000 adults, for whom 1,500,000 laborers worked.

This oligarchy was closely related to major American capital. The facts show this: machinery and equipment, 50 percent American control; iron, steel, and metal products, 60 percent; rubber products, 45 percent; automotive assembly, 100 percent; radio and television, nearly 100 percent; office equipment, nearly 100 percent; copper fabricating, 100 percent; tobacco, 100 percent; advertising, 90 percent. To this data should be added the power of Anaconda, Kennecott, and ITT, in copper and telephones (Dale Johnson, ed., *The Chilean Road to Socialism,* New York, Doubleday Anchor, 1973, p. 13).

Combining this situation with the state's foreign debt and private Chilean companies having North American organization, the outlay for technology, and the dependency of the country's armed forces on the U.S. Army should give an idea of what is meant by calling Chile "a capitalistic country dependent on imperialism."

After 1907, the organization of workers and peasants began actions to obtain legal recognition, which was achieved only in 1953, when the Central Única de Trabajadores was formed. In 1972 the Central Única had a million members, that is, 33 percent of the work force. The agricultural workers' unions began to gather strength after the 1967 peasant unionizing law, forming various "confederations" which by 1972 represented more than 100,000 agricultural workers.

Such political parties as the Communists and Socialists depended on the strength of the urban and rural workers' organizations to be able to participate in the country's political life, finally obtaining the presidency in 1970. It was against this rapidly rising force that the Chilean generals mobilized their troops on September 11, 1973.

The Chilean unions, in addition to serving the workers as a weapon to obtain wage increases, better working conditions, and fringe benefits, traditionally took an active part in politics, being the vanguard in the struggle against the domination of the American multinationals and paralyzing the country whenever political crises threatened to bring in fascism and its derivatives. The owners' guilds (for example, the Sociedad de Fomento Fabril) traditionally took the opposite position.

Lying somewhere between these adversaries were some 1,400,000 employees and self-employed workers, whose inconsistent political position tended to oppose that of the workers. These formed the middle stratum in the city and country, and traditionally they served as a kind of buffer zone to the 1.4 percent of exployers and bondholders. Some 400,000 of these people were government employees during the Allende administration. It was this middle stratum that the fascist military movement depended on for the success of the September 11 coup.

2. Pedro Vuscovic's words are taken from his article "Dos años de Política Económica del Gobierno Popular," *Revista de la Universidad Técnica del Estado,* special issues 11–12, 1972–1973, Santiago, pp. 53–67.

3. In the first week of July 1973, National party Deputy Domingo Godoy Matte (of the extreme right wing), gesticulating menacingly with his right hand toward the seats of the leftist Deputies, cried out: "The Marxists had better not be so happy! Djakarta is coming!" From the first days of 1973, the words "Djakarta is coming!" scrawled in black paint had been appearing all over the walls of Santiago. Shortly afterward, leftist politicians and progressive journalists began to receive anonymous letters that said simply: "Mr. So-and-so: Djakarta is coming: Number X." For example, José Gómez López, director of *Puro Chile* (presently a prisoner of the military, since his arrest on September 15, 1975), received anonymous letter number 31; *Puro Chile*'s assistant director, Eugenio Lira Massi (in exile in France, where he died in June 1975), number 28; I received number 37. In August 1973 the scenario of Plan Djakarta began to be revealed when attacks commenced against the homes of these people. The selective terrorizing of leaders and

journalists of the left was carried out by groups of ex-Cadet and Rolando Matus Commandos, advised by two Americans. The investigation of Plan Djakarta was halted by the September 11 coup. The selection of the name Djakarta for the plan of killing was obvious: it referred to the September 1965 coup in Indonesia, in which approximately 300,000 Indonesian leftists were massacred by the Army, overthrowing President Sukarno. A leading member of Plan Djakarta was Brigadier General Hernán Hiriart Laval (sent into retirement in early 1973 for conspiring with the *latifundistas* and giving orders to kill two peasants in Valdivia Province). Hiriart is currently ambassador of the military junta in Peking. (Reports on Plan Djakarta appeared in *Puro Chile* and *Última Hora* during July and August 1973.)

4. This case is a typical one that demonstrates the contradictions, deceits, and stratagems in the inner circle of the high command. Justiniano denounced Canales because he jeopardized any serious plan for a coup with his frivolity. Prats had to accept his generals' opinion to maintain the precarious cohesion of the Army, in the hopes of proceeding with his thesis of forming an armed forces–Allende government to save the critical situation and avoid a military coup commanded by the "hardliners." After September 11, 1973, General Canales was appointed ambassador to Lebanon.

5. From *Punto Final,* No. 190, Aug. 14, 1973, p. 7.

4. The Pentagon Tells the Generals to Go Ahead

1. The decision of the Pentagon to encourage a coup without the participation of Prats, the commander in chief of the Army, seems to have been a reaction to Prats's behavior from the beginning of Allende's policy of inviting the "participation" of the Chilean high command in some aspects of his government. Before that time, General Prats, like the rest of the Chilean generals, was perfectly aware of the "ideological" influence of American senior officers on the top ranks of the Chilean armed forces. Nevertheless, following the October 1970 suggestion of "wait and see," Prats had dedicated himself to promoting a line of conduct in his generals that would avoid a bloody coup. In that sense, he tried to develop support for a possible armed forces–Allende government. This gradually drew him inside the inner circle of Allende's advisers, which won him the distrust of the Pentagon and the coup's high command. Until November 1972, the coup attempts from the heart of the armed forces had all been "erratic" and incoherent, lacking organization; Prats had disarmed all of them himself, though he yielded to some

internal pressure not to punish the generals most deeply involved. In sum, he tried throughout to be loyal to his generals and at the same time to Allende in a play that would put him in a position to be considered a presidential candidate in 1976. His indecisive character is well expressed by this testimony Joan Garcés gave to *Le Monde,* Oct. 5, 1974, p. 3, after Prats was killed in Buenos Aires: "Last July, Prats said to me: 'I want to tell you something I never told President Allende. In May 1968 certain Christian Democratic ministers in Frei's government wanted to provoke a coup d'état.' He did not believe it to be compatible with his position and duties to reveal something of that political character to the late President." Prats's murder on September 30, 1974, occurred at a time when the CIA's participation in the destabilizing of Chile's Unidad Popular government to pave the way for a coup was being denounced in the United States; this suggests that Prats knew many details of the conspiracy which he did not tell Allende and did not dare to reveal after September 1973, when he was in Argentina in exile. Apparently, his game of being "loyal" to two antagonistic sides at the same time caused his death.

2.   It is very possible that this title, "October in Chile," given to the Pentagon report was a figment of the coup generals' imagination when they mentioned it to some civil politicians in late 1972 and late 1973. Fragmentary knowledge of this text was leaked out through conversations of General Oscar Bonilla with such civilian conspirators as Eduardo Frei and Juan de Dios Carmona, leaders of the right wing of the Christian Democrat party. Later, after the September 1973 coup, my information about this report was more detailed, coming through channels that I cannot reveal at this time. In the same way, I found out that "October in Chile" had two parts, or two sections: the Pentagon's opinion on the necessity of a coup, of preparing a coup against Allende, which was first made known only to the senior officers who met in November 1972 with the Pentagon envoys; and second, the "routine" report shared with the entire General Staff regarding the armies of countries adjoining Chile (Peru and Bolivia). These "routine" intelligence reports from the Pentagon to the Chilean armed forces were not published on a regular basis; their normal number is one or two per year, and they belong inside the framework of "exchange of intelligence" as envisioned by the Mutual Aid Pact. The second section was the one known to Prats at that time.

3.   The Pentagon's meddling in the Chilean oligarchy's efforts to overthrow Allende was exposed in a series of articles by Julio Zapata Bernales in

Puro Chile's Sunday supplement, Dec. 1972 and Jan. 1973, under the titles "Anatomía de un golpe de estado," "Cómo la gran burguesía quiere derrocar a Allende," "El Fascismo como técnica del golpe de estado," "Estados Unidos detrás de Frei y Jarpa," and "La Sociedad de Fomento Fabril y el imperialismo: Golpe." These articles revealed the general orientation of the instructions to isolate Prats, leave the politicians in the background, create the "trade guild power" base of fascism, and induce the senior officers to form a conspiratorial bloc. *Punto Final,* March–April 1973, took up again these denunciations of the Pentagon plans. After July 20, 1973, when General Washington Carrasco traveled from Concepción to Santiago to talk to Air Force Group 7—that is, to its commander César Guevara Fuentes and fifteen other officers—about a scheme to "attack Santiago by air from La Serena, Quintero, and Concepción" (this referred to attacking the industrial sectors and working-class living areas), more information came out about the Pentagon's meddling (see *Chile Hoy,* Aug.–Sept. 1973).

4. The Bolivian chief of state, General Hugo Banzer, had, from the time he took power after the 1971 coup, repeatedly uttered the slogan "We will regain our coastline," as he led campaigns to strengthen the Bolivian Army to recover "our historic territory." He was referring to the 66,000 square kilometers that form part of the present Chilean province of Antofagasta, which Chile snatched from Bolivia after winning the war of 1879 against Bolivia and Peru. (Chile took from Peru the present province of Tarapacá, 55,000 square kilometers in area.) Both provinces contain Chile's richest copper and saltpeter resources. Banzer's campaign to "regain the coastline" at times acquired the character of real war hysteria, naturally for his own internal political purposes.

5. The size of that "campaign fund" may be inferred from the following facts, revealed later: The *New York Times,* Sept. 8, 1974, p. 26, reported: "The CIA director also said that after Dr. Allende's election, $5 million was authorized by the 40 Committee for more 'destabilization' efforts in 1971, 1972, and 1973. An additional $1.5 million was provided to aid anti-Allende candidates in municipal elections last year. Some of these funds, Mr. Colby testified, were provided to an unidentified influential anti-Allende newspaper in Santiago."

The unidentified newspaper was *El Mercurio,* property of the Edwards economic group, whose chief, Agustín Edwards, was living in New York, as vice-president of Pepsi Cola. *Puro Chile* and *Última Hora* in Santiago February 26, 27, 28, 1973, denounced ITT, Anaconda,

Kennecott, Dow Chemical, Grace, Chase Manhattan Bank, and First National City Bank for contributing to the "campaign fund" through the Edwards clan. For their part, the Chilean magnates also opened up their pocketbooks: the Feb. 19–26, 1975, issue of the Chilean magazine *Ercilla* interviewed Orlando Sáenz, president of the Sociedad de Fomento Fabril (SOFOFA, Society for Industrial Development) at that time. He stated: "I never saw the CIA. It was so easy to collect money during the UP that there was no need to use hot money . . ." (p. 14). *Time* magazine (Sept. 30, 1974, p. 21) reported: "Approximately half the CIA funds were funneled to the opposition press, notably the nation's leading daily *El Mercurio*. . . . Additional CIA funds went to opposition politicians, private businesses and trade unions." The *Time* article also said: " 'You buy votes in Boston, you buy votes in Santiago,' commented a former CIA agent assigned to the mission. But not enough votes were bought; Allende had a substantial following."

6. It may seem absurd to affirm that the civilian fascist groups were trying to infiltrate the armed forces, but the situation was that fascism at that moment was operating on two parallel levels: the civilian and the military. The civilian fascist groups were used as political tools by the oligarchs who supported Frei's election as "emergency President" after a military coup, to try to convince the high command to mount a coup "for Eduardo Frei." But events were to show that "military fascism" won the game and retained power on all levels.

7. According to the text later included in his Third Message to Congress, on May 21, 1973.

8. In October 1972, regarding the strategy to be used to destroy the owners' conspiracy, the great crisis between the leaders of the Communist and Socialist parties broke open, as did that between Carlos Altamirano and Salvador Allende, the top leaders of the Socialists. Allende felt that Altamirano was falling over the precipice of the extreme left, as he would tell anyone who would listen to him. This was reflected in violent personal attacks on Altamirano in *Puro Chile* during November–December 1972 by the journalists and editors sympathetic to Allende and the Socialist party leadership. In January 1973, in relation to an argument about the supply and price control juntas (people's organizations to control food distribution and speculation) with Treasury Minister Fernando Flores, the President, in the presence of journalists in La Moneda, shouted that the Unidad Popular parties bored him, that they were "a bag full of cats" (a Chilean expression for very intense, serious disputes), and that they did not know how to lead the people. For

months, ever since the December 1971 crisis created by the Empty Pots March staged by the right, Allende had said the same things semipublicly. These were used by right-wing newspapers, which even ran front-page stories on the subject (e.g., "Allende Fed Up with the UP," in *La Tribuna,* first week of Sept., 1972). It may have been owing to this situation that General Prats stated to his military colleagues that Allende was almost ready to unite with the armed forces in his government. However, later events show that the President never had that intention, although his private and public declarations might seem to lead to the opposite conclusion. About this leadership crisis and fragmentation at the top of the Unidad Popular, see, for more information, Chapter 5.

9.   From April 1973, the newspapers *El Siglo, Última Hora,* and *Puro Chile,* and the magazines *Punto Final, Chile Hoy, De Frente,* and *El Rebelde* were constantly denouncing the conspiratorial activities of Juan de Dios Carmona, Patricio Phillips, Eduardo Frei, Pedro Ibáñez, and Generals Oscar Bonilla and César Ruiz Danyau, not to mention Vice-Admiral Merino. This situation climaxed in August 1973, when Allende accepted Ruiz Danyau's resignation and decided to retire Oscar Bonilla and five other generals, as well as Vice-Admiral Merino, in the second half of September. The coup, however, came first. See Joan Garcés's U.N. document, already cited, and details of this affair in Chapter 5.

5. The General Is Not an Honorable Man

1.   The Allende government's treatment of the armed forces in terms of their share of the budget was truly remarkable. Figures for 1971 and 1972 taken from "The State of the Public Treasury," by Treasury Ministers Américo Zorrilla and Orlando Millas, revealed the following:

In 1971 the armed forces budget in escudos was 8.9 percent of the total government budget in escudos and 13.1 percent of the dollar budget. In 1972 it rose to 10.2 percent in escudos and 14.6 percent of the dollar budget. (The Chilean budget contains two separate entries, one in escudos and the other in dollars, for different expenditures. In both, spending for the military was increased during the Allende administration.)

In 1971 the defense budget was only 17 percent larger than the Department of Health's; by 1972 it was 35 percent larger.

In 1971 the defense budget was equivalent to 49.5 percent of the Department of Education's budget; by 1972 it was 61.3 percent of Education's.

On November 16, 1971, an additional budget of 390,972,000 escudos (some $32 million) was accepted from the Treasury Ministry for a five-year Unidad Popular project to provide housing for the armed forces (some 7,000 houses for officers and junior officers were projected). The January 15, 1972, edition of *La Nación,* a daily, reported a speech by General Oscar Bonilla, the Army director of personnel, when 56 new houses were presented to the officers: "We are only beginning. Our determination to go forward is plain and unbending. . . . The institution has planned this initiative and will fight for it, knowing that it is defending something vital to each one of its members."

In salaries, the period 1970–1972 also represented a great jump ahead. According to figures from the 1972 Senate Commission on the Treasury and the National Planning Office, the following comparisons could be made:

In 1964 the Army commander in chief earned six times the national average for a worker's salary; in 1972, eighteen times the national average. At the lowest end of the senior officers' wage scale, a colonel in 1964 earned almost four times more than the average worker; in 1972, thirteen times more.

2. For more details on these plans created in the Pentagon, see *Causa ML,* No. 8, May 1969, in which is printed the complete text of the *Manual FM 31–15* as it is used by the cadets of the Bernardo O'Higgins Military School in its postgraduate courses at Fort Gulick in the Panama Canal Zone. This publication caused "violent polemics" in Chile (Alain Labrousse, *L'Expérience Chilienne,* Paris, 1972, p. 152; Spanish edition, *El experimento chileno,* Grijalbo, 1973, pp. 152–153): "But even before General Schneider's new regulation went into effect [this refers to postgraduate attendance at Fort Gulick by the Bernardo O'Higgins Military School cadets], between 1950 and 1965, there were already 2,064 Chilean military men who had been trained in the U.S. and 549 who were trained outside the U.S., that is, in the antiguerrilla schools of the Latin American countries." See also Chapter 1, note 2, on what the Mutual Aid Pact means to the U.S., and *Causa ML,* No. 2, Sept.–Oct. 1968. More documentation on the same subject will be found in Alain Joxe, *Las fuerzas armadas en el sistema político de Chile,* Editorial Universitaria, Santiago, Chile, 1972; and Robinson Rojas in *Causa ML,* No. 21, July–Aug. 1971, pp. 20–25.

3. A denunciation of these "six points" was published in the official newspaper of the Santiago industrial cordons, *Tarea Urgente,* in June 1973. It had a circulation of 45,000, primarily workers, and was staffed by MIR people and a group of Socialist party members. The newspaper

had been able to acquire this information through "patriotic military police officers." The paper felt that the "six points" revealed Manuel Torres de la Cruz as a conspirator. Nevertheless, the events of June 29, 1973 (military mutiny), obscured this spectacular denunciation with the storm of news on the uprising, and it was not revived until August–September 1973, in the dailies *Puro Chile* and *Las Noticias de Última Hora.* In these same publications, the military source of the gun control law was denounced; it had come about through Juan de Dios Carmona's connection with General Oscar Bonilla. Emphasis was placed on the antipopular character of this legislation. See *Aurora de Chile,* Aug. 1973 (a Socialist party newspaper with a circulation of 35,000).

4.   These gun search statistics come from the dailies *Última Hora* and *Clarín* and the magazine *Punto Final* at the end of August and early September 1973. The fascist organizations' attacks and acts of sabotage were reported by the agency Prensa Latina, in news wires published in the Lima, Peru, daily *El Expreso,* Sept. 13–30, 1973.

5.   In March 1973, this event was denounced indirectly (without naming Rear Admiral Ismael Huerta Celis) by Eugenio Lira Massi, a journalist whose "La columna impertinente" appeared three times a week in *Puro Chile,* and by Fernando Rivas Sánchez, in the same daily. Both columnists presented the anecdote as proof that there were "senior officers in the Army and Navy" involved in the conspiracy to overthrow the constitutional government, and that these senior officers were protecting saboteurs and dynamiters belonging to the right-wing terrorist groups.

6.   The Central Única de Trabajadores was a national organization of laborers' and office workers' unions founded in 1953; it became the most powerful tool of Chilean union organization. In 1973 the laborers' and office workers' unions were joined by the peasants'. The Central Única had a centralized national organization in Santiago and regional organizations at the provincial level. Its directors were elected by direct ballot. In 1973 it comprised almost one-third of the country's work force, that is, almost half the laborers, office workers, and farm workers. Traditionally it was directed by representatives of the Communist and Socialist parties, and in the last years (1970–1973) the Christian Democrats had a greater participation than before. It was active on two planes: in organizing the workers' struggle for higher salaries and in serving as a support to the leftist parties in their political campaigns.

7.   Generals Herman Brady Roche, Mario Sepúlveda Squella, and Washington Carrasco, in addition to Colonels Augusto Lutz (after the military coup promoted to brigadier general and named secretary general

to the military junta, rising from the position of chief of the SIM, which he held until December 1973) and Sergio Julio Polloni Pérez (in December 1973 promoted to chief of the SIM, from the position of commander of Army Telecommunications) formed the central team of the SIM during the three years of the Unidad Popular government. From its office in the Defense Ministry (9th floor, office No. 85), the SIM group was in charge of coordinating work with U.S. Army intelligence advisers (according to a January 1973 issue of *Tarea Urgente*), headed until June 1971 by Colonel Thomas H. Jones, chief of the U.S. military mission in Chile. (When Colonel Jones left Chile on July 21, 1971, he was decorated with the Chilean Star of Military Merit, pinned on him by General Carlos Prats González in the farewell ceremony.) All of these men, along with Colonel Manuel Contreras Sepúlveda, commander of the Tejas Verdes Regiment (stationed at the Santiago port of San Antonio), and the commander of the Paratrooper and Special Forces School, Lieutenant Colonel Dante Marchesse, are graduates of the United States Armed Forces School, specializing in intelligence, at the Southern Command of the U.S. Armed Forces in the Panama Canal Zone. SIM chiefs who made frequent trips to the Southern Command were Generals Brady and Carrasco and Colonels Lutz and Polloni, using the air bridge that existed between the U.S. Command and the various intelligence corps of Latin America (Chile's air bridge is set up like this: Los Cerrillos Air Base, Santiago; Cerro Moreno Air Base, Antofagasta; Albrook Airfield, Canal Zone). To give the reader an idea of what this direct line between the Pentagon's Southern Command and the Chilean generals means, I quote a brief account by François Schlosser, which appeared in *Le Nouvel Observateur,* No. 467, Oct. 28, 1973: "The Panamanians call it the Wall of Shame. It is the wire-and-bars barrier that separates the world of Latin America from the 'Canal Zone,' under U.S. jurisdiction. Behind the chicken wire, the American way of life reigns. Enormous buildings house the services of an organism that today makes Latin America quail: the Southern Command. Its latest triumph: Chile. . . . The Southern Command is at the same time an information center, a many-disciplined 'military university,' and a base of operations. In the antiguerrilla school, thousands of Latin American senior and junior officers are trained for war against subversives. These officers receive complete technical training in the different military schools scattered throughout the Canal Zone: Communications School, General Staff School, Aviation School, etc. Underground constructions, places excavated in the rocks, house the nerve center of a communications system that covers the entire continent. . . . Here, the U.S. authorities maintain direct contact, by telephone or teletype, with their correspondents installed in all the South American capitals, where their role is more important than that of the 'official' American ambassador. An air network reinforces the communications network. To travel to Rio, Santiago, etc., the Southern Command civilian agents and its military 'students' make use of its own aircraft, its own airports. . . . The center's creation goes back to the early sixties. It represents a strategic option put into effect by Washington. After the Alliance for Progress's failure against 'Castrista' subversion, the U.S. decided to play its military ace. . . . In the Panama Canal Zone military schools, a myth was born: that of the 'solidarity' of the Latin American soldiers. This psychological ploy produced excellent results. Its theme was: 'We have the same concerns, we are patriots, we want reforms, and we have a common enemy, Communism.' For the Catholic officers from the South American armies, generally members of the middle class, these simplistic formulas were enough to cement an elementary political conscience. Thirty-five thousand of them received training from the Southern Command. These officers made up the staffs that took power in Brazil, Bolivia, Chile, etc."

The *New York Times,* Oct. 23, 1973, carried an article signed by Drew Middleton that published other details about the purpose of the Southern Command as an element of control for the U.S. Army over the majority of Latin American generals. "Scattered across South America and the Caribbean are more than 170 graduates of the United States Army School of the Americas who are heads of governments, commanding generals, chiefs of staff, and directors of intelligence. . . . 'We keep in touch with our graduates and they keep in touch with us,' said Col. William W. Nairn, the commandant. The school offers 38 separate courses, all of them conducted in Spanish. Last year about 1,750 officers, cadets, and enlisted men from 17 countries attended courses." "The school's four instructional departments deal with command, combat operations, technical operations and support operations."

Generals Brady, Carrasco, and Sepúlveda are typical of these graduates. The oldest of them, Brady, had the following career: in 1943, he was chief of the military district that included Chuquicamata (a copper mine controlled by Anaconda); in 1946 he was graduated from the Southern Command; from 1947 to 1953 he was the military delegate to the Production Development Corporation; in 1959 he traveled to Fort

Benning, Georgia, for a military course; after that, he was made commander of the 6th Armored Division in the north of Chile; he became chief of staff of the 2nd Division, then commander of the 2nd Division. Afterward, in 1974, he was appointed head of the Joint Chiefs of Staff of National Defense, and in March 1975, Defense Minister, replacing General Oscar Bonilla, who died on March 3 in a helicopter crash 300 kilometers south of Santiago. General Carrasco, having the same U.S. military diplomas, was appointed chief of the Chilean military mission in Washington in January 1974, and later, in December of the same year, commander of the Army's Fifth Division, replacing General Lutz, who died suddenly on November 28, 1974.

8. Carrasco was replaced in the Third Division by Agustín Toro Dávila, who was hastily promoted to brigadier general in October 1973, when he was still military attaché in the Chilean Embassy in Mexico City. Toro, whose career is obscure, was a close personal friend of Augusto Pinochet.

In July 1974, Agustín Toro Dávila was appointed the junta's Minister of Mines and was replaced in the Third Division by Brigadier General Nilo Floody Buxton. While Carrasco was chief of the military mission in Washington, the U.S. sold $68 million worth of arms to the junta. On October 25, 1974, General Pinochet's aide Colonel Enrique Morel Donoso was promoted to brigadier general and sent to Washington to replace Carrasco.

When Carrasco was commander in chief of the Third Division in Concepción, Senator Bulnes Sanfuentes, who represented Concepción Province, made frequent trips there, making no attempt to conceal his long visits to Carrasco at his headquarters (the implications of these visits were denounced in *Punto Final, El Rebelde,* and *Puro Chile* from August to September 1973).

9. "The Chilean military has had a long and close relationship with the United States, and the Pentagon regards the 90,000 Chilean soldiers, sailors, airmen and carabineros (the national police force) as among the best armed forces on the continent. Between 1950 and 1970, Chile received more military aid ($175.8 million) than any other Latin American country except Brazil. This amounted to about 10 percent of Chile's total defense budget in the same period. The largest amounts of aid were supplied prior to the elections of 1964 and 1970 to placate discontent in the military that might otherwise have been exploited by the strong Leftist parties. This high level has been maintained throughout the last three years which, including projected grants for 1974, total $45.5 mil-

lion. This is double the corresponding total for the previous four years. At a time when economic aid has shrunk to less than $4 million, this signifies a liberalization of military aid to Chile.

"The U.S. Air Force has a particularly close relationship with their Chilean counterparts, built up by the U.S. Air Force Mission in Santiago over the last 20 years. More than 70 percent of the Chilean Air Force planes and helicopters are manufactured by the United States. At the present time, the Chilean military is awaiting a shipment of 20 ex-U.S. Navy A-4B Skyhawk fighter jets, previously used in Vietnam, which are sitting on an airstrip at the Davis-Monthan AFB in Arizona. The State Department saw no problem in selling these jets to a Marxist government. In fact, last Spring the United States offered to give credit to Chile and four other Latin American countries to purchase F-5E Freedom Fighter jets. The offer is particularly significant in that President Nixon had to sign a special statement waiving the restrictions placed on selling sophisticated weaponry to underdeveloped countries. This can only be done if the President determines that such financing is important to 'U.S. national security,' which he obviously did in this case.

"This proposed sale (Chile has not yet bought the jets) was greeted with disbelief by Congressman Wayne Hays (D-Ohio) in recent hearings on foreign assistance, who wondered what Chile would do with these aircraft. The events of recent weeks seem to have answered that question.

"During the Senate hearings on foreign assistance, Senator Inouye (D-Hawaii) also questioned the logic of granting military credits to a country which had expropriated U.S. interests. (The possibility of a cutback in these military credits due to the UP's 'intransigence' on the issue of compensation, must have worried the Chilean military.) Admiral Raymond Peet justified this policy toward Chile before the Senate committee. He explained that the United States prefers that underdeveloped countries 'buy American' rather than have them look elsewhere for military equipment (Chile was considering the purchase of jets from the Soviet Union and France). Furthermore, according to Peet, 'one of the big advantages that accrues to the United States from such a foreign sales program is the considerable influence we derive from providing the support for these aircraft.' Providing the F-5E jets or the Skyhawks, would preserve a certain pro-American orientation in the Chilean military at a time of strain between the governments of the two countries.

"The Chilean Navy has also continued to receive military credits and to carry out joint maneuvers with the U.S. Navy. In fact, on the day of the coup, U.S. ships were en route to Valparaíso to conduct routine maneuvers, but turned back after a brief meeting with a Chilean vessel.

"Providing hardware is only one tactic the United States uses to influence the Chilean military. In the past 20 years, over 4000 Chilean officers have been trained in the United States and U.S. schools in the Panama Canal Zone. General Pinochet, the head of the military junta, served as military attaché to the Chilean embassy in Washington D.C. and went to the U.S. Southern Command in the Canal Zone several times. Pinochet is known to be a hard-liner and in 1971 he warned, 'I hope the army will not have to come out, because if it does, it will be to kill.' In addition, according to *Newsweek* magazine of Sept. 24, 1973, the other members of the Chilean junta, Gustavo Leigh of the Air Force, Admiral Toribio Merino of the Navy and General César Mendoza Frank of the Carabineros, have all spent some time in the United States. And in 1971, a high-level military mission from the United States visited with Chilean military leaders. [See above, Chapter 2, note 14.]

"The Carabineros have also received U.S. aid through the Office of Public Safety of the Agency for International Development. The program funneled nearly $2.5 million to the Chilean police forces since 1961, but was ended in 1971 by the UP government. In 1970, according to a *Washington Post* article of October 1, 1970, the OPS advisor stationed in Chile, Joseph Vasile, was expelled for his involvement in a right-wing terrorist plot to discredit President Allende. Vasile was then transferred to Vietnam where he worked with the pacification program. The Carabineros are playing an important role in the junta and will most likely come increasingly under the influence of the military. As in other countries throughout the world, the Chilean police have emerged as a strong paramilitary force engaging in counterinsurgency activities for the new regime." Extract from "Chile: The Story Behind the Coup," NACLA's *Latin America and Empire Report*, Vol. VII, No. 8, October 1973, pp. 8–9.

For more on this see *Senate Hearings before the Committee on Appropriations* concerning Foreign Assistance and Related Programs Appropriations, FY 1974, and *Hearings before the House Committee on Foreign Affairs* on the Mutual Development and Cooperation Act of 1973.

More information on U.S. military aid to Chile and its influence on the Chilean military will be found in Alain Labrousse, *El experimento chileno*, Grijalbo, 1973, pp. 150–154.

10. The battle for economic power between the Unidad Popular on the one hand and the Chilean oligopolies and American multinationals on the other was a battle between the state's capitalistic economic power, managed by the Unidad Popular, and private capitalistic economic power, managed by the national and foreign oligopolies. In this struggle, the Unidad Popular was hampered from operating freely by the entire capitalistic legal structure of the state system that it governed, and it therefore was doomed to lose the game against the national and foreign oligopolies.

11. As indicated above, Chapter 4, note 2, the existence and reconstruction of the Pentagon's "October Report" was deduced by some leftist groups through the speeches, harangues, and semipublic meetings of middle-level officers with their troops. But, of course, there was also additional, and very exact, information from some officers sympathetic to the aims of Chilean democracy, whose names I cannot cite because they are still in Chile. This Pentagon report had represented a radical change from the earlier attitude of "wait and see," maintained until October 1972, and it reflected the thinking of an important sector of U.S. multinational consortia whose influence carries much weight in Washington. This sector, led by the Rockefellers, was opposed to the hard-line attitude advocating immediate destruction of the Allende government, urged by groups like ITT, Anaconda, and Kennecott. This duality of opinion explains what was happening during 1970, 1971, and 1972 in Chile, when the armed forces, manipulated by the Pentagon, kept on the fringes of the developing political situation. For a detailed study of the duality of opinion among the groups of U.S. consortia and their attitude to Chile and the Allende government, see Dale Johnson's *The Chilean Road to Socialism*, New York; Doubleday Anchor, 1973, section 2 of Part I, "U.S. Policy in the Making: Chile, to Accommodate or Crush," and Section 3 of Part I, "The Coincidence of Internal and External Counterrevolutionary Forces." See also Robinson Rojas, *El Imperialismo Yanqui en Chile*, Ediciones ML, Santiago, 1971, pp. 102–110, Addenda I and II. An illustration of the causes of "wait and see" may be given by these paragraphs extracted from the NACLA account of the Council on Foreign Relations of the United States' sessions: at the December 14, 1970, meeting, Jerome I. Levinson of the IDB (Inter-American Development Bank) says: "Experimentation with different political systems in Latin America is inevitable. The process of change in Latin American societies will provoke variations in the status quo of U.S. property in the hemisphere. But U.S. interests are not incompatible

with the social development of Latin America. We can reach compromises with change, as has happened in Mexico." Covey T. Oliver, of the State Department, said: "Chile should be given all the opportunities to achieve success with its new government. Just as Cuba cannot be considered a failure because of the effects of American policy after Castro rose to power, Chile must be given a chance." And Walter Sedwitz, of the OAS, said at the same session: "If the government fails, there will be a radicalization in Chile and a security problem for the U.S."

Naturally, this attitude changed when a popular revolutionary movement began to develop that was not controllable by the leftist political parties and, by the same token, was outside the reach of being controlled by the classic bourgeois democratic game that was so solid in Chile.

12. Allende's "incapacity" to get out of the crisis was due to the alliance among the Christian Democrats, the National party, and the Radical Democrats. This alliance blocked in Parliament any legislation to tax the oligarchy, which would reduce the budget deficit and control the runaway speculation in which the great industrial and commercial magnates were indulging, or to make certain economic activities a crime, which would stop the scandalous way in which the industrialists, merchants, and *latifundistas* were sabotaging the national economy. In the Parliament elected in 1969 (before Allende took office) the party distribution was as follows: Unidad Popular parties: 80 Deputies and Senators; Christian Democrats: 75 Deputies and Senators; National party and Radical Democrats: 45 Deputies and Senators.

Thus, the opposition majority was 120 to 80, which permitted foiling government legislative initiatives and allowed "constitutional challenges" to the Cabinet Ministers: in Allende's 33 months of government, he had to change the composition of his Cabinet 22 times on account of these maneuvers. This was a long way away from October 24, 1970, when the Parliament had voted: 153 Senators and Deputies for Allende as President; 35 for Alessandri, and 7 abstentions.

This kind of deadlock between the Parliament and the President continued even after March 1973, when the government's Senators and Deputies increased to 84 and the oppositions' dropped to 111. It was because of this that on July 18, 1973, the Socialist party's secretary general, Carlos Altamirano, said: "The political forces of Chile find themselves temporarily at an impasse. In the face of this impasse, our strategy is oriented to breaking it up and using this break to promote a strong process of mobilization of the masses . . . and to radicalize the revolutionary process." This strategy was firmly rejected by Salvador

Allende and the majority of the Chilean Communist party's Central Committee, who were always playing on the thesis of "don't radicalize" and "consolidate what we have won." This brought Allende and the Chilean Communist party to the idea of holding conversations with the Christian Democrats, which the Socialist party and the MAPU refused to do. The MAPU magazine, *De Frente,* No. 12, June 29, 1973, denounced "the bourgeoisie, led by Frei and Jarpa," for attacking "by double entry, meaning to overthrow the government or oblige it to compromise. . . . They are putting seditious generals into the cockpit. . . . They are warming the climate for the moment of the fascist insurrection. . . . What the Christian Democrats hope is that the Unidad Popular will commit hara-kiri by freezing the process of change and repressing those who are demanding to move ahead, and thus cut themselves off from their most genuine social base. . . . In case the government holds firm, the Christian Democrats are counting on their allies, who they know are preparing another way out" [the fascist insurrection]. For its part, *Chile Hoy,* another Socialist magazine, explained in the same month that the dialogue with the Christian Democrats was only a pretext on the part of the conspiring generals to "exploit the unacceptable demands that had been made to strengthen their final assault against the revolutionary process." And that was indeed the case: when Allende announced his political concession for September 11, give or take a day, the generals settled on that date for the coup, precisely to prevent Allende from conceding.

13. The laws in force at that time in Chile with respect to television were so ambiguous that the government could not order the pirate station to close because it would violate articles in the Political Constitution regarding freedom of the press. But at the same time, since the pirate station did not have a legal permit to operate, the government could obstruct its broadcast while the situation was being discussed in the courts.

14. In May 1973 the civilian police, at that time commanded by the militant Socialist Alfredo Joignant, managed to arrest Rafael Undurraga Cruzat, one of the members of the commando team, and through his confessions the CIA's connections with this incident became known. *Puro Chile* and *Última Hora* published the facts at that time, but the law courts sabotaged the civilian police investigation by refusing to provide search warrants for the homes of the people implicated and forcing the civil authorities to suspend the investigation for the time being.

15. For a detailed study of the IPES, see my book *Estados Unidos en Brasil,* Ediciónes Prensa Latinoamericana, Santiago, 1965.

16. A denunciation about this was made by Fernando Rivas Sanchez in *Puro Chile* during January and February 1973, and by Marlise Simons in the Washington *Post* during January 1974, page B-3.

17. This summary of Rodríguez Grez's interview with Viaux in the Santiago Penitentiary was published in July 1973 in a mimeographed report by the MIR.

18. On August 25, 1973, after a spectacular hunt, the Santiago civilian police arrested the second national chief of Fatherland and Liberty, the industrialist Roberto Thieme, who, in order to be able to operate more succcessfully in the underground smuggling arms from Mendoza, Argentina, for his group, had passed himself off as "dead in an airplane crash" in January 1973. Roberto Thieme's confession provided the Socialist party (the civilian police chief was a Socialist) with proof that Manuel Fuentes Wedling was the "contact" between the CIA and the fascist organization, that Fuentes and the CIA had prepared the incident against Prats, and also that the CIA had approved the June 29 coup plan. Roberto Thieme's confessions uncovered such a huge net of "contacts" between the CIA and Chilean politicians that the police had to continue the investigation in strict secrecy. The investigation was terminated, of course, on September 11, 1973.

19. For the surgical approach to cleaning up the Chileans' minds, see p. 193 and p. 258, note 6. On March 11, 1974, the military junta published a "Declaration of Principles of the Government of Chile," in which they stated that "it is of the utmost importance to change the mind of the Chileans," and that for this they "will exercise with energy the principle of authority, dealing drastically with every breach of discipline or act of anarchy" (AP news wire, dated Santiago, Chile, March 11, 1974, carried in *La Estrella de Panamá,* March 13, 1974). On June 18, 1974, *La Estrella de Panamá* published on the first page of its second edition an AP news wire from Santiago under the headline "Education to Be Reorganized with Anti-Marxist Focus" which began: "About 600,000 professors and schoolteachers yesterday began a two-day national conference to study an education reorganization with an anti-Marxist focus." It added that the military junta's document had one stipulation for this reorganization: that "the educational system will not permit the participation of professors who promote the teaching of national or foreign doctrines such as Marxism." Professors had to personally indicate to the military authorities whether they were in agreement with this document. In Chile a "state of war" exists, it said, "martial law" is in effect, and "civil rights are suspended."

20. The generals' request was doubly cynical because on March 6, 1973, the

acting commander in chief of the Army, Division General Augusto Pinochet, head of all the armed forces in the country, which "guaranteed a democratic, clean election without incidents and with absolute impartiality," made a statement using that exact phrase. The same thing was done by the director of the Electoral Register, Andrés Rillon, a Christian Democrat, thirty days later, after the College of Examiners (composed in the main of Christian Democrats and National party members) checked the votes *one by one*. Rillon said that it had been "one of the cleanest elections in the history of Chile." His words appeared in all the national newspapers at the time.

21.   The torturers were the chief of Navy intelligence, Captain Gajardo; Navy Infantry Captain Koller; Navy intelligence Captain Acuña; Lieutenants Jaeger, Letelier, Luna, Alarcón, Tapia, and Maldonado; and a Navy Infantry second lieutenant, Boetsch. The tortures took place in Fort Borgoño at Talcahuano and at the Valparaíso Naval Academy (denounced in *Última Hora, Puro Chile, Clarín, Punto Final,* and *Chile Hoy,* Aug.–Sept. 1973).

22.   One paragraph of Prats's letter said: "In realizing, during these last days, that those who wished to denigrate me had managed to disrupt the judgment of a segment of Army officers, I deemed it a duty of a soldier of solid principles not to allow myself to become a factor of *fragmentation* in institutional discipline and in the State of Right [civil rights], nor serve as a pretext for those who are seeking the downfall of the constitutional government" (from *Chile Hoy,* No. 64).

23.   After this incident and the coup of September 11, there has been no word about Generals Pickering and Sepúlveda. Nevertheless, since they were very closely connected to the conspiracy and had the confidence of the rest of the coup's generals, it is likely that they are now leading anonymous civilian lives.

24.   The second paragraph of the news item revealed the extent of the duplicity of Merino's maneuver in accusing Carlos Altamirano, Garretón, and Enríquez of "subversion" in the Navy, to give the "Red coup" pretext. It happens that now Merino was not requesting censure of these legislators on the basis of "subversion" (obviously, because he could not present any proof to the Senate or the Chamber of Deputies), but rather on the basis of "the backing both legislators gave to the sailors," which apparently was his interpretation of their *having publicly and repeatedly defended the sailors who had been falsely accused of subversion.* The truth was that at this point in the military conspiracy, its leaders did not even take care to maintain the intellectual decorum

of making their statements, accusations, and sentences coherent.

25. The *coincidences* between the movements of the rebel Chilean generals and the U.S. diplomatic and military missions in Santiago are worth noting. On the morning of September 7, the generals agreed to overthrow Allende on the 11th, four days later: "U.S. Ambassador to Chile Nathaniel Davis traveled to the United States on Friday, Sept. 7, 1973 (four days before the coup), met with Kissinger on the 8th, and returned to Chile on the 9th" (NACLA's Latin America and Empire Report, Vol. VII, No. 8, Oct. 1973, p. 10). Davis was the director of the Peace Corps in Chile in 1962, and in 1968 was sent to Guatemala, where he directed a "pacification program" resembling the ones carried out in Vietnam. "In 1971 this program had left 20,000 people dead" *(ibid.)*. Jack Anderson, in the Washington *Post,* Dec. 10, 1972, quoted a cable sent by Davis to Nixon from Santiago "long before the political crisis erupted, which said: 'Perhaps what is significant now is growing conviction in opposition parties, private sector and others that opposition is possible. . . . [Allende's] objectives are increasingly seen as incompatible and as going beyond what can be accepted. If opposition interests are to be protected, confrontation may not be avoidable.' "

6. The Inferno

1. Admiral José Toribio Merino, in *La Tercera,* Sept. 19, 1973, said: "I mobilized the Valparaíso garrison on the pretext of searching for arms. At a quarter to six, the 'silence' plan began. The ships had come back. We cut off all the telephone lines except one, and all of the radios, except the Navy's. The one telephone line was left for a person to call Allende in Santiago. . . . At the moment we had planned, they found out in Santiago. But by then the entire country was controlled by the armed forces and the military police." For his part, Augusto Pinochet, very proud of his blitzkrieg against the Chilean people, announced in the Buenos Aires daily *La Opinión,* Oct. 5, 1973: "Only some officers knew what we were to do. I sent them to Antofagasta, Iquique, Concepción, and Valdivia with the final details, to avoid useless deaths and disorder. I kept it secret until fourteen hours before the arrival of the military junta of government. Everything came out according to the elementary principles of the strategy. Allende was worrying about Valparaíso, when the center of gravity was the capital."

2. For the way in which these contacts between Santiago and the Southern Command in the Panama Canal Zone were carried out, see Chapter 5, note 7. Additional information on the meticulous advice and support

given by the Southern Command to the Chilean armed forces for their insurrection and subsequent domination of the whole country will be found in various publications. "The Chilean soldiers receive daily four rations of food, canned and sealed in the U.S. . . . More than 200 soldiers from the latest graduating class of Chile's Military School recently arrived in Fort Gulick (Canal Zone) to undergo intensive training in urban guerrilla warfare." (*Boletín del Comité de Solidaridad de Panamá con Chile,* Jan. 1974, p. 6).

"From the Canal Zone, specifically from Howard Air Base, planes leave for the air base at Antofagasta in the north of Chile. Two types of 'American solidarity' come here. On the one hand, ITT, which instigated and financed the coup, has made an agreement with the junta to send large quantities of necessary products for the Chilean Army, Navy, and Air Force. The American products are flown from California to Howard Air Base in the Zone. From there they leave for Antofagasta. On the other hand, since October 11, 1973, U.S. Air Force Circular No. 17.277, emanating from the Pentagon, is in effect, whereby all kinds of logistic support are allocated for the junta. From the Post Exchange at Corozal in the Canal Zone, according to the exit permits for products from that military post, there are large consignments shipped to Chile: ammunition (bullets for M-1 rifles, 45-caliber bullets for automatics, tear gas, etc.), as well as pharmaceutical products and plasma. Especially noteworthy are the large amounts of drugs and, particularly, a kind of food given to soldiers just before they enter combat" (*ibid.,* p. 5).

3. *El Mundo* added that the plane's identifying number was USAF 63103289. *Crawdaddy* magazine, May 1974, p. 40, said: "A reporter from the Boston *Phoenix,* a weekly newspaper, checked with the Pentagon last month and an Air Force spokesman confirmed that a plane with that license number and crew had indeed left Argentina on the day of the coup. The spokesman, however, insisted that the plane was on a 'weather mission,' and that it did not penetrate Chile's air space.

"Meanwhile, Tim Butz, a former U.S. Air Force reconnaissance expert who now works for the Committee for Action/Research on the Intelligence Community, has examined a series of aerial photographs of the bombed Presidential palace. Butz reports that the photos show that the surrounding area was virtually untouched while the Allende palace was totally demolished, and alleges that that type of precision could only have been accomplished by the use of the advanced American weapons, 'smart bombs and rockets.' "

(In fact, only the façade of the Palacio de la Moneda was demolished; the rest of it caught fire.)

4. Preliminary proof of the junta's intentions of regressing to dependency on the U.S. is provided by this news:

Buenos Aires, Sept. 12, 1973 (Prensa Latina): "Juan Domingo Perón today condemned the fascist coup in Chile. . . . Asked if there could have been U.S. intervention in this coup, Perón answered: 'I could not prove it, but I believe so, I deeply believe there was. As I have experience in these processes, how am I not going to know! Only yesterday, the rumors were that they were going to have a party in the State Department' " (published in *El Expreso,* Lima, Sept. 13).

Washington, Sept. 12, 1973 (EFE). "An independent organization today asked the Senate to investigate the possible participation of the CIA in the coup d'état that yesterday overthrew President Allende in Chile. The Committee for an Open Society, whose offices are in Washington, asked Senator William Fulbright, chairman of the Senate Foreign Relations Committee, to conduct an investigation to decide whether there was any direct U.S. intervention in the events in Chile. 'We believe that the U.S. government was deeply involved in the overthrow of Allende's government,' said its director, William Higgs" (published in *El Expreso,* Lima, Sept. 13).

"In round numbers, up to September 11, 1973, 170 businesses were requisitioned, 155 had interveners, and a significant percentage of the stocks of 90 others [of these monopolies] was bought, which gives a total of 415 businesses" (statement of General Sergio Nuño, vice-president of the Production Development Corporation, CORFO, made to the Chilean magazine *Qué Pasa,* Nov. 2, 1973, p. 8).

"On January 23, 1975, the CORFO announced officially that 220 companies had already been returned, 59 had been sold to private persons, 26 were ready to be returned, and at a later time, another 80 would be put up for sale" (*La Opinión,* Buenos Aires, Jan. 24, 1975).

Santiago, Chile, Nov. 15, 1973 (Agence France Presse): "About 50 U.S. companies which were nationalized by the overthrown Allende government will be returned to their former foreign owners, military junta sources confirmed today" (published in *El Día,* Buenos Aires).

"In New York, *Business Week* magazine estimated yesterday, November 14, that 50 North American businesses nationalized by Allende would be returned to their former owners. . . . The magazine adds that it is 'unlikely' that ITT will regain control of the Chilean Telephone Company, but it emphasizes that in exchange, 'it will have a much greater possibility of receiving better compensation' " (*El Día,* Buenos Aires, Nov. 16, 1973).

"During the past week, experts from the missions of the International Monetary Fund, the World Bank, the Inter-American Committee for the Alliance for Progress, and OAS observers arrived in Chile. . . . They are working at the Banco Central de Chile [in conjunction with General Eduardo Cano], from where they get in touch with all the organizations that interest them" (reported in the Chilean magazine *Ercilla,* Nov. 14–20, 1973).

"A mission to acquire oxygen, led by Chancellor Admiral Ismael Huerta, was sent to the U.S. and Canada, and its purpose was accomplished. They made contact with international agencies, with the government, and with private North American corporations, with whom there is much business pending" (*ibid.,* p. 23).

In Washington, on November 5, 1973, UPI reported that Chile promised to repair alleged injustices in the expropriations of the North American copper companies, and announced that compensation would be negotiated. The new Chilean Ambassador to the U.S., General Walter Heitman, declared that it was unfair to deny compensation unilaterally to the expropriated enterprises, under the pretext that they had not paid taxes in previous years.

The Buenos Aires daily *El Día,* quoting the Bank of America's report on the Chilean coup, Dec. 14, 1973: "The report says that 'the national banks will, in the future, as was the case before being nationalized by the overthrown government, act independently and directly in their foreign operations, but under the supervision of the Banco Central and the Superintendent of Banks.' "

Washington, Dec. 22, 1973 (Prensa Latina): "Chile agreed with the U.S. to pay $124 million as the first installment of its foreign debt and to grant 'fair compensation to U.S. interests.' The decision was made known in a joint communiqué from the State Department and Chile's National Treasury. The U.S. government's document says that 'the new military junta of Chile has promised to pay the compensations corresponding to American enterprises and assures a climate propitious to investments' " (*El Expreso,* Lima, Dec. 23, p. 15).

New York, Jan. 4, 1974 (Reuter Latin): "Dow Chemical today announced the signing of a contract with the Chilean government to reassume administration of two companies. . . . Fernando Leniz, Minister of the Economy, said that the government has a plan ready to return the banks federalized during the regime of the late President Salvador Allende to their former owners."

El Mercurio, Santiago, Jan. 19, 1974: "Robert Haldeman, a top executive in Braden Copper, which owned the El Teniente mine until 1971, has arrived in Chile." He met with Eduardo Simián, a junta adviser. "After his Santiago talks, Haldeman began a tour of the large copper mines, in particular Chuquicamata."

New York Times, Jan. 28, 1974 (datelined Santiago, Jan. 23): "The austere economic program that the junta has put into effect to overcome the economic chaos inherited from the three-year Marxist Government has earned the praise of conservative economists and has reaped a number of modest successes, including loans from abroad and sharp production increases.

"However, virtually all Chileans have been hit hard by a sharp decrease in their purchasing power as prices have been allowed to reach realistic market values without corresponding increases in wages.

"The economic burden has proved devastating for the poorest Chileans, who in four months have faced such increases as 250 per cent for bread, 600 per cent for cooking oil, 1,400 per cent for sugar and 800 per cent for chicken.

"In the shantytowns where a fourth of greater Santiago's 3.5 million people live, concern over repression and civil liberties now places a distant second to concern over food prices."

In Washington, on January 29, 1974, the AP reported that according to the RUNDT Economic Intelligence Service the businessmen felt greatly relieved by the change of government, and that feeling was affirmed when the properties that President Allende had confiscated were returned.

Washington, Feb. 8, 1974 (EFE): "The Chilean government today paid more than $1.5 million to the U.S. in compensation for the nationalization of copper companies and paper manufacturers that had American interests."

Mendoza, Argentina, March 28, 1974 (Prensa Latina): "Regarding the payment of compensation [to Anaconda and Kennecott], the junta's economic adviser, Raúl Sáez, announced that the amount would be 'between 300 and 600 million dollars.'"

Miami *Herald,* April 14, 1974, datelined Santiago, April 13: "General Motors has formally agreed to return to Chile after having suspended operations under the Allende regime."

Santiago, Chile (a plant by the Chilean Embassy in Panama, in *La Estrella de Panamá,* May 30, 1974): "They have now passed 'the phase of standardizing some 3,000 agricultural properties which had been illegally expropriated by the former Marxist regime' " (this meant returning nearly 50 percent of the land expropriated in agrarian reforms carried out by the Frei and Allende administrations).

In Santiago, Chile, on June 13, 1974, the AP reported that on the previous day the government had put up for sale 107 companies that were expropriated during the three-year administration of President Salvador Allende. The CORFO published a list of a total of 150 firms to be returned to the private sector. The list contained seven companies that once operated on American capital, two on British, and one on Italian. Nine months earlier, the military junta had returned about ninety companies to their former proprietors. A CORFO spokesman said that the state would sell all companies presently under its control, with the exception of public or strategic services (*La Estrella de Panamá,* June 14, 1974).

5. As examples, let us look at the Army commanders in chief: General Luis Miqueles Caridi, commander in chief in 1967: courses at Fort Belvoir and Fort Monmouth in 1941 and 1942; in 1952, military mission at the Chilean Embassy in Washington. General Sergio Castillo Aranguiz, commander in chief in 1968: Fort Knox in 1969. General René Schneider Chereau, commander in chief in 1969–1970: Fort Benning in 1953. General Carlos Prats González, commander in chief in 1970–1973: Fort Leavenworth in 1954. General Augusto Pinochet, commander in chief from 1973: Fort Leavenworth, 1955; Southern Command, 1956; military mission in Washington, 1956. See also p. 221, note 2, and p. 242, note 7.

6. The first official reference that the Chileans had to the rebel generals' surgical idea (earlier, the leftist dailies had reported on this primitive notion, especially in August and September) was on the night of September 11, 1973, when General Gustavo Leigh explained over nationwide TV that the coup was intended "to extirpate the Marxist cancer in Chile." On September 19, *El Mercurio* reported that General Augusto Pinochet had declared that "when we have extirpated the malignant tumor of Marxism . . . the country will have all its liberties restored, since it is for these that we have fought." There are some phrases approaching this idea which will probably pass into history, such as General Pinochet's statement quoted in the Caracas weekly *Punto en Domingo,* Sept. 30, 1973: "Democracy carries in its core the seed of its own destruction. Democracy every so often has to bathe itself in blood for it to go on being democracy." For his part, General Sergio Arellano Stark, head of the Santiago garrison, interviewed on "A Esta Hora se Improvisa," Channel 13 TV, Sept. 23, 1973, at 11 P.M., said: "There

really haven't been that many casualties. . . . If there had truly been 700,000 dead, we wouldn't have any security problems at all." These ideas have their civilian antecedents, such as a statement by Patricio Phillips, the National party Senator, who on the same TV program, Feb. 1973, had said: "We have to keep it clearly in mind that the best Marxist is a dead Marxist." See also p. 235, note 3, for "Plan Djakarta."

7. Beginning in April 1974, a violent conflict developed between the generals and the Catholic Church, because Raúl Cardinal Silva Henríquez began to publicly protest the murders, arbitrary arrests, and tortures, as well as the misery the Chilean people were being condemned to. On April 14 the Cardinal said in a sermon delivered in Santiago Cathedral: "We have said it to our people, to our authorities, that we cannot offend against the principles of respect for humanity. Human rights are sacred, and no man can violate them. For this reason, today we cry out in the pain of a father who watches his family being torn apart, the quarrels between his sons, the death of some of them, the imprisonment and the pain of others. . . . We have said that violence generates nothing but more violence and that this is not the way." On April 24 the majority of the Chilean bishops published a dramatic document deploring "the denunciations, false rumors, the increased unemployment, firings for arbitrary or ideological reasons"; the fact that "the unsalaried are being made to bear an excessive share of sacrifice"; the "lack of effective judiciary guarantees for personal security"; "arrests for arbitrary reasons or prolonged imprisonment"; "interrogations with physical and psychological pressure." "There are rights which touch upon the human being's dignity, and these are absolute and inviolable."

This provoked a very irate reaction from the junta, and General Gustavo Leigh, speaking for the junta, said: "The bishops are the tools of international Marxism" (*El Mercurio,* Santiago, April 30, 1974).

8. When the military coup was unleashed on September 11, there were two political groups reasonably prepared to withstand the attack: the MIR (Revolutionary Left Movement) and the PCR (Revolutionary Communist party), who had had a clandestine information network since the beginning of the Unidad Popular government (even the membership of the overwhelming majority of their active members was secret). These two information networks, plus the remnants of the Socialist and Communist parties, allowed me to make a very rough reconstruction of the September battles' casualties. In early 1974 the French representative to the International Congress in Strasbourg released very similar figures, which were: 15,000 dead; 30,000 political prisoners; 200,000 workers

expelled from their work centers for having belonged to the Unidad Popular or sympathized with it; and 25,000 students expelled from the universities. On December 5, 1973, Martin Reynolds of UPI, in an annual news report published in Lima's *El Comercio,* said: "On October 5, it is revealed that according to the CIA's calculations, some 3,000 persons died in the process of consolidating the military coup in Chile." He added that 250 members of Fatherland and Liberty had been trained by military men in Paraguay, Bolivia, and Brazil, who had received prior training in the Panama Canal Zone.

For their part, the Chilean military was more conservative: on October 4, 1973, they reported that the casualties had been 476 civilians and 17 soldiers. But in March 1974, *Ercilla* magazine published a different statement, from General Pinochet: "We have had 1,600 dead, of which 200 were on our side" (taken from a version of that interview published in the March 1974 edition of *Le Monde Diplomatique*).

9.   Among the torturers, the following men have been identified: Special Forces Captain Bender Hoffer (in Chillán); Colonel Manuel Contreras Sepúlveda (Tejas Verdes Regiment, in San Antonio); Army Lieutenant Medina, in Rancagua Jail; Colonel Horacio Oteiza; General Orlando Gutiérrez; Captain Nelson Arturo Duffey (who has a platinum plaque in the back of his skull, owing to the explosion of a North American training plane at Los Condores–Iquique Base); Captain Víctor Matic; Captains Florencio Dublé and Alvaro Gutiérrez; Lieutenant José García Huidobro; Captain Alberto Bastendorf; War Auditor Christian Rodríguez; Squad Commander Jaime Lavín Parina; Group Commanders Gonzalo Pérez Canto and Erick Barrientos Cartagena; Squad Commander Engineer Edgardo Ceballos (all of the above from Santiago Air Bases 7 and 10); and military police Colonel Daniel Ivaceta, in Santiago.

10. There are hundreds of testimonies about these horrifying tortures. One of them was presented to the International Commission in Helsinki, which was in operation beginning March 21, 1974. The denunciation was written in the form of an affidavit letter sent to Chile to the military. Here are excerpts:

"We know, Mr. Daniel Ivaceta, how you interrogated and tortured Ana Alicia Flores, a Chilean woman, age twenty-five, physical education teacher in Santiago, wife of Manuel Matamoros, a bank manager during the government of President Allende." The affidavit states that the tortures were intended to find out where Matamoros was. There were blows, insults, and "you waited a few seconds and when you did not receive an answer, you ripped off an article of her clothing . . . you beat her head and breasts; you grabbed her hair in your hands and yanked her head back and struck her face." It goes on to say that they left her alone for a time, and then they took her, in her blouse and stockings, down two flights of stairs in the military police's Zañartu barracks in Santiago. "There you, Mr. Daniel Ivaceta, were waiting with five officers. They were older men, with white hair, approximately the same age as yourself. Before beginning the interrogation, you and your henchmen obliged her to undress completely, and then you ordered her to walk stark naked back and forth in front of you, repulsive old men. Afterward you forced her to run and dance. Naturally Ana Alicia Flores could not dance. Then you forced her to roll over on the floor; afterward you threw her on the table in front of you, and you, Mr. Ivaceta, began to disrobe first. . . . The unfortunate woman found the strength to jump off the table and run to a corner of the room, where she shouted everything she thought about you into your filthy, sweaty faces. When she fainted, you threw her on the table and three of you raped her." The affidavit states that she fainted again and they locked her up until the following day, when she was interrogated again. "You again beat her up in a group and raped her, and she lost consciousness again." But Alicia Flores didn't talk (she didn't know where her husband was, in any case). "The next day you threw her out of the Commissariat, realizing you weren't going to get anywhere with her. You put her in a car, half naked and covered with blood, and drove her several blocks away from the Commissariat—and left her in the street. Strangers helped her home" (from *Unidad Internacional,* April 4, 1974, p. 8).

11. This situation was denounced on March 23, 1974, before the International Commission in Helsinki, with documentation that was accepted as valid by the president of the Organizing Committee, Finland's Minister of Public Instruction, Ulf Sundqvist, and the members of the Committee. These advisers have produced highly sophisticated tortures of a psychological nature, such as the ones perpetrated on Clodomiro Almeyda, Allende's Minister of Foreign Relations, who was kept blindfolded for fifteen days, day and night, in the Air Academy of War in Santiago, according to his statements to the director of Mexico City's *Excelsior* (May 18, 1974, p. 16A). The same newspaper printed a detailed report on the tortures carried out by these "technical experts," denounced by Catholic bishops, Protestant leaders, and Jewish rabbis in Chile (AP news wire, datelined Mexico City, May 17).

12. In September 1973 a Chicago priests' group, Pro Justice and Peace,

wrote a report entitled "Chile: Zero Hour," in which they stated: "The U.S. policy in Chile was not 'Let's leave them alone' but rather 'Let's aim for the jugular vein, let's cut off their food and water, let's force them to die economically, and afterward let's watch them fall.' While they stopped all economic aid, the U.S. continued sending military aid to the country, and as it happens, Nixon's military aid to Chile in 1974 was the largest they ever received. Nixon is as innocent in Chile as he was in the last election. Chile is Watergate with a passport" (taken from Panama's *Diálogo Social,* No. 50, Oct. 9, 1973, p. 25).

The figure of $40 per death is based on the escudo/dollar rate of exchange for the period. In October 1973 the military junta raised this rate 1,000 percent—that is, from 25 escudos to the dollar on September 11, 1973, to 280 escudos in October. At the same time, it fixed the rate of exchange for brokers at 850 escudos to the dollar. It is this figure that I used for my calculations. The $40 spent by the Chilean generals had impressive results, according to information gleaned from AP, UPI, EFE, and Agence France Presse news wires:

October 24, 1973: The U.S. Department of Agriculture issues a $24 million credit to Chile to buy grain. It had been requested by the generals on September 26, and it is the largest credit in the history of Chile for this purpose. During Allende's three-year administration, only $3.2 million were received for this purpose; between 1962 and 1965, $6.5 million.

November 8, 1973: $20 million for rural electrification from the International Development Bank.

November 9, 1973: $24 million for manufactured goods, granted by Manufacturers Hanover Trust, and $20 million for the Banco Central; eight U.S. and two Canadian banks offer the junta $150 million in credits. James Green, president of the New York Bankers' Association, in signing the agreement, says, "We are lending a hand to the new Chilean government, in psychological help and in good faith."

November 14, 1973: $28 million credit to buy feed corn, granted by the U.S. Department of Agriculture, breaking another Chilean record (naturally, payable over a three-year period and at 9.5 percent and 10.5 percent annual interest).

December 12, 1973: $80 million from the International Monetary Fund, on standby, breaking another Chilean record.

January 18, 1974: Inter-American Development Bank grants the junta $128 million in credit. In the last fourteen years, prior to September 11, 1973, Chile had received a total of $314.1 million from IDB.

That is, in four months, the generals received, in cash or credit, $454 million from the U.S. government and international organizations it controls: quite a return for their investment of $40 for every dead Chilean. But this was not all. On February 9, 1974 (AP news wire from Washington), the Inter-American Committee of the Alliance for Progress recommended that a credit of $785 million ought to be extended to the generals.

Index